Reading for Information in Elementary School

Content Literacy Strategies to Build Comprehension

Nancy Frey
San Diego State University

Douglas Fisher
San Diego State University

PEARSON
Merrill
Prentice Hall

Upper Saddle River, New Jersey
Columbus, Ohio

Library of Congress Cataloging in Publication Data

Frey, Nancy
  Reading for information in elementary school: content literacy strategies to build comprehension / Nancy Frey and Douglas Fisher.
     p. cm.
  Includes bibliographical references and index.
  ISBN 0-13-170749-3
  1. Reading (Elementary) 2. Reading comprehension. I. Fisher, Douglas II. Title.
  LB1573.F67 2007
  372.21—dc22
                                                                2005027625

Vice President and Executive Publisher: Jeffery W. Johnston
Senior Editor: Linda Ashe Montgomery
Senior Development Editor: Hope Madden
Senior Production Editor: Mary M. Irvin
Design Coordinator: Diane C. Lorenzo
Senior Editorial Assistant: Laura Weaver
Production Coordination and Text Design: Amy Gehl, Carlisle Editorial Services
Cover Designer: Jeff Vanik
Cover Image: Sally Smallwood © Dorling Kindersley
Production Manager: Pamela D. Bennett
Director of Marketing: David Gesell
Marketing Manager: Darcy Betts Prybella
Marketing Coordinator: Brian Mounts

This book was set in ITC Century Book by Carlisle Publishing Services. It was printed and bound by R. R. Donnelley & Sons Company. The cover was printed by R. R. Donnelley & Sons Company.

Photo Credits: Courtesy of Nancy Frey.

Pearson Prentice Hall™ is a trademark of Pearson Education, Inc.
Pearson® is a registered trademark of Pearson plc
Prentice Hall® is a registered trademark of Pearson Education, Inc.
Merrill® is a registered trademark of Pearson Education, Inc.

Pearson Education Ltd.
Pearson Education Singapore Pte. Ltd.
Pearson Education Canada, Ltd.
Pearson Education—Japan

Pearson Education Australia Pty. Limited
Pearson Education North Asia Ltd.
Pearson Educación de Mexico, S.A. de C. V.
Pearson Education Malaysia Pte. Ltd.

10 9 8 7 6 5
ISBN: 0-13-170749-3

Most of the time that a student spends reading in school is with informational texts. From textbooks to reference materials to nonfiction trade books, students spend their school days immersed in information. But what happens if these students never developed skills in their early reading instruction to read effectively for information? These students face a struggle, particularly as they enter the intermediate grades, when their reading attention is focused so much more completely on textbooks.

Without a strong foundation in reading informational text—whether in textbooks, reference materials, or nonfiction trade books—primary and elementary school students will not be prepared for the demands of intermediate grades or life beyond the classroom. We wrote *Reading for Information in Elementary School* to give you the background and the tools to lay a solid foundation with elementary schoolchildren, developing in them the skills they need to be successful with informational text. We have filled these pages with research-based and classroom-proven strategies that focus on the processes required to develop content literacy.

Because we believe that teachers learn from one another, in this text you'll meet the teachers, sit in on their lessons, and witness their students' responses. Our goal is to move you beyond a cursory understanding of a strategy and prepare you for the implementation phase by sharing these models of exemplary classroom teaching. You will come away from the reading with a model for teaching students to read successfully for information, and you will have a handbook of proven strategies to implement.

In this book we use a traditional approach in education writing: define a practice, discuss its origins, and cite evidence of the strategy's effectiveness. As we do this, we introduce a number of instructional strategies with examples across traditional content areas, always grounding these strategies in the classroom with teacher dialog and student samples. The strategies include:

- Anticipatory activities
- Vocabulary instruction
- Read-alouds and shared reading
- Questioning

- Graphic organizers
- Note taking and note making
- Writing to learn

Each of these instructional strategies will enhance your students' comprehension of the content—the ultimate goal of all good educators. Together we can help students better understand the world and their role in it.

abc Organization

Our book follows a before-, during-, and after-reading format that models the most effective approach to teaching reading for information. After describing the need for content literacy instruction and covering the classroom structures that best support that instruction in Chapters 1 and 2, we begin our exploration of the most effective approach to reading for information, focusing on the processes required to develop content literacy.

Before Reading: Anticipatory Activities, Vocabulary Development, Read-Alouds, and Shared Reading

The instruction that takes place to prepare students to read for information is critical because it lays the foundation for what is to come. One of the best ways to activate background knowledge, build interest, and establish a schema for new knowledge is through *anticipatory activities*. These activities seek to gain student attention through demonstration, thought-provoking questions, and visual displays of information. Some well-known anticipatory activities discussed in Chapter 3 include K-W-L charts (Ogle, 1985) and anticipation guides.

Chapter 4 focuses on *vocabulary development* through conceptual understanding and self-awareness. The demands of vocabulary rise throughout the elementary years, and students who do not acquire methods to sustain acquisition of new vocabulary quickly fall behind. The instructional strategies in this chapter focus on active involvement and immersion in vocabulary, especially as it applies to making connections and consolidating meaning through multiple information sources (Blachowicz & Fisher, 2000). Instructional approaches highlighted in this chapter include word sorts, Semantic Feature Analysis (Pittleman, Heimlich, Berglund, & French, 1991), and word lists.

Chapter 5 prepares the reader for the section on processes used during reading with a discussion of *interactive read-alouds and shared reading*. We model the processes used by effective readers as they monitor understanding and apply fix-up strategies when meaning is lost. This chapter includes a discussion of the benefits of this method for students, including English language learners, and helpful rubrics for planning and delivering meaningful read-alouds and shared readings.

During Reading: Questioning, Graphic Organizers, Note Taking, and Note Making

Part 3 covers what occurs during reading. The material is predicated on a gradual release-of-responsibility model of instruction (Pearson & Fielding, 1991). As you read these chapters, consider how the instructional strategies move from modeling through read-alouds and shared reading, then allow students to assume more responsibility for their comprehension through the use of questioning (Flood, Lapp, & Fisher, 2003). Finally, learners begin to transform information in their minds and on paper by using graphic organizers and note-taking methods.

Questioning is the next instructional approach for supporting reading for information. Although questioning takes place throughout the reading process, we have chosen to situate it in the "during" phase because it is a linchpin process for comprehension. We have observed many young readers who have incorrectly viewed self-questioning as either a step to complete before reading ("What do I predict this chapter will be about?") or an assignment to be fulfilled after the reading is done ("Do we answer the end-of-chapter questions in complete sentences?"). When teachers use the instructional approaches described in Chapter 6, such as Question the Author (Beck, McKeown, Sandora, Kucan, & Worthy, 1996) and Directed Reading-Thinking Activities (Stauffer, 1969), students begin to understand that questioning is an active process that occurs continually throughout the reading.

Chapters 7 and 8 contain information about using *graphic organizers and note taking and note making* to support student understanding of informational texts. Learners' ability to capture essential information from a reading is an important step in transforming knowledge by making it their own. We view graphic organizers and note taking as intermediate steps in that transformation process, steps that lead into what occurs after reading.

After Reading: Writing to Learn and Assessments

Part 4 covers what occurs after reading, emphasizing how learners transform the information they have read into new applications. Chapter 9 examines many methods of fostering understanding through *writing*. This chapter is not devoted to process writing, but rather to how learners can apply new knowledge to create original ideas. Techniques discussed include RAFT writing (Santa & Havens, 1995) and other brief writing activities that tap into students' declarative, procedural, and conditional knowledge (Paris, Cross, & Lipson, 1984).

Of course, these instructional strategies do not occur in a vacuum. In Chapter 10 we discuss the necessary school and classroom structures that support reading for information, including grouping strategies, school-wide approaches, and professional development. We address the importance of *assessment* and the role of testing as it applies to reading for information.

As you move through these chapters, you will come to know the teachers who have shared their classrooms with us, and you'll develop a solid understanding of why reading for information can be such a challenge and such an important skill for your students. You'll also find that you have a text that will become a valuable tool for you in your classrooms as you cover all the content areas.

Acknowledgments

We have had the opportunity to learn alongside a number of skilled teachers as they delivered their content in ways that have increased their students' literacy learning. We thank all of the teachers who invited us in to their classrooms and provided us with detailed information about their practice.

This book could not have been completed without the support, assistance, and encouragement of several key individuals in the City Heights Educational Collaborative. Rita ElWardi, Christine Johnson, and Lee Mongrue originally pushed our thinking about reading for information at the secondary level. Their contributions have been invaluable. Dr. Ian Pumpian's vision of schools in which all students are respected and valued learners has been a constant force in our writing. And finally, our editors Linda Montgomery and Hope Madden's belief in this project and skill in guiding us from concept through production has resulted in this book that you are reading.

We would also like to acknowledge the reviewers who offered their thoughtful comments as this work progressed. Their feedback made this a better book and we thank them: Bonnie Armbruster, University of Illinois, Urbana-Champaign; Deanna Birdyshaw, University of Michigan; and Danny Brassell, California State University, Dominquez Hills.

Nancy Frey & Douglas Fisher

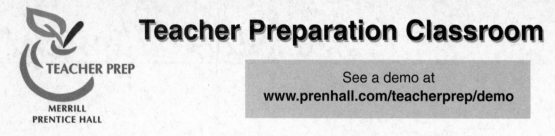

Teacher Preparation Classroom

TEACHER PREP

MERRILL
PRENTICE HALL

See a demo at
www.prenhall.com/teacherprep/demo

Your Class. Their Careers. Our Future. Will your students be prepared?

We invite you to explore our new, innovative and engaging website and all that it has to offer you, your course, and tomorrow's educators! Organized around the major courses pre-service teachers take, the Teacher Preparation site provides media, student/teacher artifacts, strategies, research articles, and other resources to equip your students with the quality tools needed to excel in their courses and prepare them for their first classroom.

This ultimate on-line education resource is available at no cost, when packaged with a Merrill text, and will provide you and your students access to:

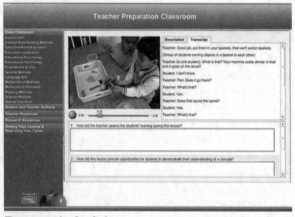

Online Video Library. More than 150 video clips—each tied to a course topic and framed by learning goals and Praxis-type questions—capture real teachers and students working in real classrooms, as well as in-depth interviews with both students and educators.

Student and Teacher Artifacts. More than 200 student and teacher classroom artifacts—each tied to a course topic and framed by learning goals and application questions—provide a wealth of materials and experiences to help make your study to become a professional teacher more concrete and hands-on.

Research Articles. Over 500 articles from ASCD's renowned journal *Educational Leadership*. The site also includes Research Navigator, a searchable database of additional educational journals.

Teaching Strategies. Over 500 strategies and lesson plans for you to use when you become a practicing professional.

Licensure and Career Tools. Resources devoted to helping you pass your licensure exam; learn standards, law, and public policies; plan a teaching portfolio; and succeed in your first year of teaching.

How to ORDER *Teacher Prep* for you and your students:

For students to receive a *Teacher Prep* Access Code with this text, instructors **must** provide a special value pack ISBN number on their textbook order form. To receive this special ISBN, please email **Merrill.marketing@pearsoned.com** and provide the following information:

- Name and Affiliation
- Author/Title/Edition of Merrill text

Upon ordering *Teacher Prep* for their students, instructors will be given a lifetime *Teacher Prep* Access Code.

Meet the Authors

Nancy Frey

Nancy Frey, Ph.D., is Associate Professor of Language and Literacy Education in the School of Teacher Education at San Diego State University and the Coordinator of Professional Development Schools for the City Heights Educational Collaborative. A former classroom teacher in Florida, Dr. Frey now teaches preservice and graduate courses and is the President of the Greater San Diego Reading Association. She is the author of numerous books and articles, including *Language Arts Workshop: Purposeful Reading and Writing Instruction.*

Douglas Fisher

Douglas Fisher, Ph.D., is a Professor in the Department of Teacher Education at San Diego State University and the Director of Professional Development for the City Heights Educational Collaborative. He is the recipient the an International Reading Association Celebrate Literacy Award as well as the Christa McAuliffe award for excellence in teacher education. He has published numerous articles on reading and literacy, differentiated instruction, and curriculum design and has authored books such as *Improving Adolescent Literacy: Strategies at Work.* He has taught a variety of courses in SDSU's teacher-credentialing program as well as graduate-level courses on English language development and literacy. He has also taught English, writing, and literacy development to public school students.

Meet the Contributors

Maureen Begley

Maureen Begley is a Literacy Resource Teacher and University Supervisor for the City Heights Educational Collaborative in San Diego, California. After 26 years in the classroom, she currently works with teachers through staff development, classroom assistance, and the BTSA new teacher induction program. In addition, she teaches graduate classes through San Diego State University and supervises candidates earning their graduate degrees as reading specialists. Mrs. Begley has been active in the California Reading Association, the International Reading Association, and local reading councils for the past 15 years, participating in local, statewide, and national conferences. She is the 2005–2006 President of the California Reading Association.

Kelly Moore

Kelly Moore, Ph.D., is a literacy resource teacher in the San Diego Unified School District. She teaches at a large urban school, Rosa Parks Elementary, that is part of a Professional Development School. She is a former classroom teacher, having spent several years teaching in the primary grades. At her current school site, Dr. Moore collaborates with teachers from all grade levels on literacy staff development, beginning teaching support, and student teacher supervision. Additionally, Dr. Moore teaches undergraduate and masters courses at San Diego State University in the areas of literacy and curriculum and instruction. She is the co-author of *Teaching Literacy in First Grade* and *Designing Responsive Curriculum: Planning Lessons That Work.*

Sheryl Segal

Sheryl Segal is a literacy resource teacher, peer coach, and staff developer in the San Diego Unified School District, where she teaches at a large urban elementary school. Ms. Segal, a former classroom teacher, collaborates with teachers from all grade levels on literacy staff development, with an emphasis on writing instruction for English language learners. Additionally, Ms. Segal teaches masters courses at San Diego State University in the areas of literacy and curriculum and instruction.

Elizabeth Soriano

Elizabeth Soriano, M.A., is a bilingual resource teacher for the City Heights Educational Collaborative working at Rosa Parks Elementary. In addition, she teaches classes in the preservice credential program as well as for the City Heights Masters. Mrs. Soriano provides support for new teachers as a BTSA mentor teacher, as well as university supervision for student teachers. A former elementary bilingual classroom teacher, she has presented at IRA, CRA, and ACT. Mrs. Soriano is also a member of the Rosa Parks professional development committee and the City Heights Literacy Leadership team.

Meet the Teachers

Dani Cole

Dani Cole teaches a full-day Mainstream English Cluster kindergarten class. Her class is composed of 20 students—11 boys and 9 girls. The class is 70% Hispanic, 15% Asian, 10% African American, and 5% African.

Although parent involvement is limited, there are many people who assist in Ms. Cole's class. In a year's time, four student teachers, three college students, and one reading intervention teacher have worked in her classroom.

Ms. Cole's students sit at tables in groups of four. Throughout the day they work independently, as well as in homogeneous, heterogeneous, and flexible groups. Three times a week her class integrates with a bilingual class for language experience.

Ramon Espinal

Ramon Espinal teaches first grade. His class consists of 20 students, all of whom speak Spanish as their primary language. Fifteen of the students attended the school during the previous year and speak a limited amount of English. He has two students who are in their first year of formal schooling and are new to the United States. The other three students have come from other schools within the district and speak no English. Sr. Espinal partners with two other first-grade teachers. These three teachers teach specialized courses in the afternoons and rotate and integrate their students for language experience.

Pam Pham-Barron

Pam Pham-Barron teaches 20 second-graders. Eleven girls and nine boys make up her class, 16 of whom speak a language other than English at home. Ms. Pham-Barron uses many second-language strategies in her classroom, as she must communicate with her Spanish, Vietnamese, Amharic, Laotian, and Hmong speakers. Fourteen of her students have been at the school since kindergarten, two came to the school in first grade, three came in second grade, and one student arrived in the United States one month before school began in September. The students' proficiencies in literacy range from significantly below grade level to significantly above grade level. By February of the school year, three students were still reading at a kindergarten or first-grade level, 11 students were reading at second-grade level, and five students were reading at a third-grade level.

Ms. Pham-Barron believes in a student-centered classroom. Student work is displayed around the room on brightly colored bulletin boards. Print is everywhere you look. Books, charts, labeled objects, student work, and word walls make this second-grade classroom a very attractive place to learn. Student desks are configured in clusters in order to promote a community of learners. Cooperative group activities and peer discussions dominate this classroom and set the tone that this is a safe and comfortable place to take risks and share ideas as the students learn the English language.

Roberta Dawson

Roberta Dawson has been teaching in culturally diverse inner-city schools for 15 years. During this time she has been a Basic Skills reading teacher and a school-site ESL Coordinator. She has taught grades 2, 3, and 4, and is currently teaching a third-grade Mainstream English/GATE cluster class. Her class consists of 20 third-graders, including 12 boys and 8 girls. All of her students speak a language in addition to English. Her nine years of experience as a Guide Teacher and three years of experience as a Lead Teacher have had a great influence on the many preservice teachers in the school's program.

Colleen Crandall

Colleen Crandall teaches fourth grade. She loops with her class from fourth to fifth grade. Her class of 32 students consists of 21 students who are classified as English language learners. Five of her students have qualified for the Gifted and Talented (GATE) program and nine have been redesignated as proficient in English, having learned English and Spanish. Mrs. Crandall has taught for nine years, seven of which have been at Rosa Parks Elementary. She was the school's Teacher of the Year for 2003–2004. Mrs. Crandall is GATE certified and has also been awarded National Board Certification.

Aida Allen

Aida Allen teaches fifth grade and is the lead teacher for a group of four teachers and their students who have been together since kindergarten. The cohort model is designed to promote differentiated, small-group instruction, and students spend a major portion of their day in project-based learning. Ms. Allen's class consists of 30 students who received biliterate instruction in K–3, and now receive instruction in English with Spanish support. Nine class members have been designated as gifted; four have IEPs and have been included in regular classes since kindergarten. Twenty-two students have been redesignated as fully English proficient.

Contents

Chapter 4: WORD FOR WORD: VOCABULARY DEVELOPMENT FOR INFORMATIONAL TEXTS

Chapter 5: READ-ALOUDS AND SHARED READINGS: BUILDING VOCABULARY AND BACKGROUND KNOWLEDGE DURING READING

PART 3: During Reading Activities   135

Chapter 6: QUESTIONS, QUESTIONS, EVERYWHERE   136

PART 4: After Reading Activities   217

Note: Every effort has been made to provide accurate and current Internet information in this book. However, the Internet and information posted on it are constatly changing, so it is inevitable that some of the Internet addresses listed in this textbook will change.

Organizing Texts, Students,
and Classrooms for Students to
Learn to Read for Information

Part 1

Chapter 1

Reading for Information in the Elementary School

*P*erhaps the most significant change in elementary reading instruction in the last few years has been the emphasis on reading for information. Now more than ever, teachers are seeking well-written and engaging informational texts to use with their students (Moss & Newton, 2002; Yopp & Yopp, 2004). Publishers have recognized the need for such materials and have responded to a growing market with guided reading titles focused on science, mathematics, and social studies topics. Popular news magazines have developed products that offer short informational articles rewritten for young readers. Textbook publishers highlight features like graphic organizers and discuss readability formulas. Professional developers and consultants regularly offer workshops on integrating informational texts into literacy programs.

Findings such as these suggest that teaching students to read for information must begin in the primary grades. Although classrooms today have a better selection of well-written and brightly illustrated informational texts, the task of teaching students *how* to read them remains daunting. Students need to learn that they do not read for information in the same way that they read narrative text. The strategies needed when reading for information differ from those used for reading stories. The research evidence suggests that

- Children's attitudes toward, and motivation for, academic reading is generally positive in first grade and steadily declines to a negative attitude by sixth grade (McKenna, Kear, & Ellsworth, 1995).
- Instructional practices for textbook reading used in fourth grade classrooms commonly focus on round-robin reading, and virtually no independent reading takes place (Armbruster, Anderson, Armstrong, Wise, Janisch, & Meyer, 1991).
- Fifth graders' ability to locate information in a textbook is virtually nonexistent (Dreher & Sammons, 1994).
- Students who experienced a "fourth grade slump" on measures of achievement continued to decline and scored in the 25th percentile by eleventh grade. Notably, these same students were achieving similarly to their peers in second and third grade, suggesting that the shift to reading for information creates a new task demand that students are not prepared for (Chall, Jacobs, & Baldwin, 1996).

In response, Duke (2004) suggests that "we should not wait to address this problem until students reach late elementary, middle, and high school" (p. 40). She identifies four approaches to address this problem:

1. Increase students' access to informational text.
2. Increase the time students spend working with informational text in instructional activities.
3. Explicitly teach comprehension strategies.
4. Create opportunities for students to use informational text for authentic purposes. (p. 40)

Several questions remain as we attempt to address the needs identified earlier. For example, how then can we effectively teach reading for information? In what ways can we help our students accomplish that goal? This book aims to provide elementary teachers with tools for teaching students how to read for information.

What was the last informational book you read? What motivated you to read that particular book?

Why Do Many Students Have Difficulty Reading for Information?

As students begin to use more complex reading materials, their need for additional strategies increases as well. While students are more comfortable using narrative texts, especially stories and chapter books, they are often less adept at using informational reading materials like textbooks, reference materials, and nonfiction books. Informational text contains "ideas, facts, and principles related to the physical, biological, or social world" (Fountas & Pinnell, 2005, p. 399). This unfamiliarity may be due in part to the relative lack of exposure to informational texts in elementary school. A study of basal readers revealed that no more than 20% of the selections were informational texts. This means that students had few opportunities in their reading program to receive instruction in how to understand informational texts (Moss & Newton, 2002). Another study found little use of informational texts in first-grade classrooms—as low as 3.6 minutes per day (Duke, 2000). Lack of instruction using informational texts may explain why even on-grade-level readers in middle school score a full-year-level lower on comprehension of informational texts when compared with their narrative reading levels (Langer, 1985). Let's continue our thinking about reading for information by examining the types of informational texts students can, and should, read.

> A basal is a collection of leveled readings published as a textbook for use in public schools.

> For more information on text leveling, see Leveled books (K–8): Matching texts to readers for effective teaching by Irene Fountas and Gay Su Pinnell.

What Are Common Types of Informational Texts?

Textbooks are arguably the most common source of informational texts in the elementary school. Textbooks, by design, use common and predictable styles to help scaffold information for readers. In addition to textbooks, teachers use trade books, music and videos, web sites, poetry, newspapers and magazines, graphic novels, biographies and autobiographies, and authentic sources such as diaries and letters to engage students in topics of study. These materials contain information that can be used to build background knowledge, develop interest, and extend learning beyond the textbook. Examples of some of these appear in the Appendix at the end of this chapter.

> Carol Hurst's children's literature web site offers information and lesson ideas on award-winning books at www.carolhurst.com.

Textbooks

We use this term to refer to a large group of materials purchased by schools for teachers to use in their classrooms. Textbooks are produced by commercial publishers exclusively for the school market and are designed to provide teachers with material that is gauged to the students' reading and interest levels. Textbooks come with a number of support materials for teachers. The primary support material is the teacher's edition, which contains all of the material in the student edition, as well as suggestions for teaching the content, assessing student learning, and making accommodations for English language learners, struggling readers, or students with disabilities. Additional support materials for teachers may include assessment guides, blackline masters to be reproduced as worksheets, and multimedia components such as CD-ROMs and audiotapes. Supplementary materials are produced for students as well, including student workbooks to practice skills, and additional readings related to the stories in the main textbook. Taken together, these materials are designed to ensure that students have increased access to informational texts.

Trade Books

Books produced for the public market are called trade books. These titles are typically found in bookstores and libraries around the country and are often used in the classroom during independent reading or group studies. Trade books are available to schools in text sets—multiple copies that can be read simultaneously by a group of students and their teacher for discussion as part of a shared, guided, partner, or independent reading activity. There are many types of trade books, including chapter books, biographies, picture books, poetry collections, and graphic novels.

> Information on classroom structures and student grouping will be presented in Chapter 2.

An exciting development in informational trade books is series books. Books in a series have specific characteristics as well as unique information. As Kurkjian and Livingston (2005) note, "As children progress through a series, the predictability of the external and the internal characteristics allows readers to learn to negotiate various aspects of nonfiction while delighting in the content and deepening conceptual understanding" (p. 592). A sample of informational series books can be found in Table 1.1.

Chapter Books

As their name implies, these books are divided into chapters and are designed to be read over multiple sittings. They are typically for upper elementary school students who can read longer pieces of text. In a unit of study on the skeletal system, a teacher might provide students an opportunity to read from *The Head Bone's Connected to the Neck Bone: The Weird, Wacky, and Wonderful X-Ray* (McClafferty, 2001). It is important to note that chapter books can be from different genres, from biographies to reports of information.

Picture Books

In addition to these traditional classroom texts, it is common to find picture books in classrooms. In picture books, a majority of the page

Table 1.1 Informational Series Books (and Three Sample Titles)

Series	Publisher	Age Group	Sample Titles
Animal Close-Ups	Charlesbridge	Grades K–2	*The Cheetah* *The Dolphin* *The Penguin*
Animal Predators	Carolrhoda	Grades 3–5	*Great White Shark* *Polar Bears* *Wolves*
Biography: A Photographic Story of a Life	DK Publishing	Grades 4–6	*Anne Frank* *Dr. Martin Luther King, Jr.* *John F. Kennedy*
How Artists View	Heinemann	Grades 1–5	*Animals* *Families* *Weather*
It's Not Catching	Heinemann	Grades K–2	*Allergies* *Asthma* *Stings & Bites*
Meet the Dinosaurs	Lerner	Grades 2–4	*Duck-Billed Dinosaurs* *Giant Man-Eating Dinosaurs* *The Smallest Dinosaurs*
Rites of Passage	Heinemann	Grades 2–4	*Birthdays* *Funerals* *Weddings*
Words Are CATegorical	Carolrhoda	Grades 4–6	*Dearly, Nearly, Insincerely: What Is an Adverb?* *To Root, to Toot, to Parachute: What Is a Verb?* *Under, Over, by the Clover: What Is a Preposition?*

Adapted from Kurkjian, C., & Livingston, N. (2005). Learning to read and reading to learn: Informational series books. *The Reading Teacher, 58,* 592–600. Used with permission. Copyright © 2005 by the International Reading Association.

contains an illustration, and the text is more limited in length. The finest picture books combine "two distinct forms of creative expression, words and pictures . . . [to] create conditions of dependence and interdependence" (Cullinan & Person, 2001, p. 624). Working together, they tell a story that uses both visual and textual elements to engage readers.

As with chapter books, there exists a wide variety of genres in picture books. *The Boy on Fairfield Street: How Ted Geisel Grew Up to Become Dr. Seuss* (Krull, 2004) is an example of a biography, *The Story of Money* (Maestro, 1993) is a reference book, and *How to Talk to Your Dog* (George, 2000) is a "how to" book.

Photo-essays

A photo-essay is often defined as a unified collection of photographs that explore some aspect of the human experience. The idea is that this collection of photographs, and the words that go with them, translate into a complete discussion of the topic. For example, in his book *Lincoln: A Photobiography*, Freedman (1987) explores the life of President Lincoln through words, photographs, newspaper clippings, and Lincoln's original writing. He starts the book with a photograph and a quote that reads:

> As I would not be a slave, so I would not be a master. This expresses my idea of democracy—Whatever differs from this, to the extent of the difference, is no democracy.

Source: From *The Boy on Fairfield Street: How Ted Geisel Grew Up to Become Dr. Seuss* by Kathleen Krull. Steve Johnson and Louise Fancher, illustrators. Copyright © 2004 by Kathleen Krull. Illustrations copyright © 2004 by Steve Johnson and Louise Fancher. Used by permission of Random House Children's Books, a division of Random House, Inc.

Newspapers

Newspapers in the classroom offer current local, national, and international information at a relatively low cost. Because multiple copies can be easily obtained, the newspaper can be useful for collaborative small group work among students. The contents of the newspaper offer a wealth of materials for teaching reading and writing. For example, editorial cartoons can be analyzed, and maps that accompany news articles can be used to teach about geography. Even the youngest readers can cut apart comic strips and reassemble them to practice sequencing in stories. Many local papers participate in the Newspapers in Education program, a partnership of newspapers that distribute classroom sets of newspapers at no cost. Related web sites contain lesson plans and teaching ideas for using the newspaper to teach reading and content skills.

See www.nieonline. com for more information.

Digital Sources

To say that technology is changing rapidly is certainly an understatement. Consider the circumstances of students graduating from high school in 2004:

> Many graduates started their school career with literacies of paper, pencil, and book technologies but will have finished having encountered the literacies demanded by a wide variety of information and communication technologies (ICT): Web logs (blogs) . . . World Wide Web browsers, Web editors, e-mail . . . instant messaging . . . listservs, bulletin boards, avatars, virtual worlds, and many others. These students experienced new literacies at the end of their schooling unimagined at the beginning. (Leu, Kinzer, Coiro, & Cammack, 2004, p. 1571)

The challenge in classrooms is to offer students access to technology at an ever-increasing rate, even as the technology evolves at an ever-increasing pace. This challenge is not new—teachers have faced it throughout the history of education. A more recent phenomenon is that of student knowledge of technology outpacing that of the teacher. How many of us have seen a teacher appeal to a student for help with a truculent piece of technology? While the pace of technology development shows no signs of slowing, we as teachers must consider how students will use technology-based texts in our classrooms.

In particular, the standard on using technology research tools is meaningful in our discussion about informational texts. This refers to a student's ability to locate and evaluate information located on the Internet and in other digital forms, including CD-ROM and DVD-R. Teachers can facilitate development of these skills by ensuring that some reading material is always available in digital form. For example, web sites can be bookmarked on the classroom computer, and digital source software can be installed to provide students with up-to-date information on a variety of topics.

National standards of technology developed for use in K–12 classrooms can be viewed in their entirety at http://cnets.iste.org/students/s_stands.html.

Graphic Novels and Anime

Wade and Moje describe a category of readings as "unacknowledged and unsanctioned texts" because they are rarely used by the teacher in the classroom (2000, p. 621). However, these texts play an important role in the lives of students, because they are the texts chosen by them to read outside of school. This is particularly true for older and reluctant readers. Comic books, professional wrestling magazines, even some kinds of trade novels are often deemed unworthy of attention by the teacher. (Dav Pilkey's *Captain Underpants* series is criticized by some teachers for its mildly naughty humor.)

Graphic novels and anime have recently drawn the attention of researchers interested in engaging reluctant readers (Chandler-Olcott & Mahar, 2003; Frey & Fisher, 2004). Graphic novels look much like comic books but are usually longer and contain a single story, rather than employing the serial format common to comic books. These books are derived from a Japanese literary form called *manga* and have seen a surge in popularity among adolescent readers in the last decade. The art most commonly used in graphic novels is *anime,* a style associated with Japanese animation featuring characters with large heads and oversized eyes. Although many graphic novels focus on superheroes, a growing number examine broader topics. Indeed, the adult graphic novel *Maus: A Survivor's Tale* (Speigelman, 1990) won a Pulitzer Prize in 1992, and the movie *Road to Perdition* was developed from a graphic novel by the same name (Collins, 2002).

Like any text, graphic novels should be carefully screened before placing them in the classroom. Pairing a graphic novel with another type of informational text is one effective way of facilitating student understanding and knowledge. For example, using the graphic novel *Alia's Mission: Saving the Books of Iraq* (Stamaty, 2004) with the picture book *The Librarian of Basra: A True Story from Iraq* (Winter, 2005) and a *New York Times* article about this series of events is a powerful way to engage students in the topics of people who make a difference, the importance of books, and the impact of the war in Iraq.

With so many kinds of informational texts available for the elementary classroom, the challenge to support reading for information can appear daunting. However, the challenge can be addressed by knowing the characteristics of common text structures and evidence-based comprehension strategies required to read for information.

Source: From *Alia's Mission: Saving the Books of Iraq* by Mark Alan Stamaty, copyright © 2004 by Mark Alan Stamaty. Used by permission of Random House Children's Books, a division of Random House, Inc.

What Are the Characteristics of Informational Texts?

Informational texts differ from narrative texts in their tone, style, structure, features, and authority. It is perhaps this last attribute that is most distinguishing. Informational texts, first and foremost, possess a level of authenticity and accuracy related to various topics. The author is an authority on the subject and seeks to convey information, often by speaking directly to the reader. Informational texts are sometimes called expository, meaning that they explain through definition, example, classification, analysis, and persuasion (Burke, 2000). These texts can be further described by their structures, features, and styles.

Common Expository Text Structures

The most common types of text structures include the following:

- exemplification (concept/definition)
- compare/contrast
- cause/effect
- problem/solution
- sequential

Exemplification text describes people, places, or phenomena. Nearly all informational texts have passages that are descriptive. Signal words for exemplification text structures include descriptive adjectives, adverbs, and phrases. For instance, the mummy is not merely old, it is

> wrapped in <u>discolored linen</u> bandages wound <u>tightly</u> around the <u>entire</u> body, lying <u>undisturbed for thousands of years</u> deep in the cool, <u>dark mudbrick</u> pyramid.

Compare/contrast text structures also rely on descriptive text, but instead explain how two or more people, places, or phenomena are similar or different. Like exemplification, most textbooks contain some compare/contrast passages as well. Signal words like *although, yet, while, however, same/different, like/unlike* and other words that show opposites are likely to appear.

> <u>Although</u> the first mummies were probably accidental, mummification became an art in ancient Egypt. <u>While</u> members of the noble classes were mummified, poor people usually <u>were not</u>.

Cause and effect text structures, which show the causal relationships between phenomena, can be deceptively similar to compare/contrast, but their signal words give them away. Words like *since, because, as a result*, and *if . . . then* statements are frequently seen in these passages.

> <u>Because</u> the Incas lived in the high Andes, they created ice mummies that were preserved in the thin, frigid mountain air.

Another text structure is *problem/solution*. Seen frequently in mathematics textbooks, they contain signal words like *question, answer, thus, accordingly*, and *decide*. A challenge of problem/solution text is that it is subtler than some of the others, and may develop over the course of several sentences or paragraphs.

> <u>Theft and the desert climate have taken their toll</u> on Egyptian mummies. <u>Accordingly</u>, the government has taken steps to preserve the remaining mummies by installing <u>climate-controlled displays</u> and sophisticated <u>security devices</u>.

More easy to detect are *sequential* or *temporal* (time-based) structures. These passages use chronology or a sequence of events to inform the reader. Common signal words related to sequential or temporal text jump

Signal words are also helpful to students who are taking standardized tests. See Chapter 10 for a discussion about assessment and testing.

out for most readers and include words like *first,*
next, last, before, afterwards, another, and *finally.*

> The <u>first</u> step in the mummification process was to remove
> all the internal organs. <u>Next</u>, the embalmer drained the
> body of fluids. <u>Finally</u>, the body was wrapped in linens.

Text Features

Another distinguishing characteristic of informational
text is the use of text features. These are the structural
items used by the author to organize the content. They
serve as markers for the reader to better understand
the text. For instance, in this book you are using a number of text features to understand this chapter, including the table of contents, headings and subheadings,
margin notes, bulleted items, diagrams, photographs,
and index. These structures support and expand a
reader's comprehension of the concepts in the reading.
A sample page from a children's information text can
be found in Figure 1.1. Note that on this page from *We*
Were There, Too! Young People in U. S. History (Hoose,
2001), there are headings, quotes from a primary
source, captions for a graphic, and a footer.

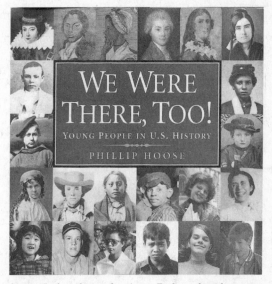

Source: Jacket design by Anne Redmond and excerpt
from "Manjiro: Bringing America to Japan" from *We
Were There, Too!* by Phillip Hoose. Copyright © 2001 by
Phillip Hoose. Reprinted by permission of Farrar, Straus
and Giroux, LLC.

Common Text Styles

In addition to these text structures, each content area uses some common
styles that students should understand. In reading and language arts, for
example, fiction is the most frequent text students encounter. Teachers can
help students understand fiction by providing them with ideas about how
this genre is structured. For example, students should understand plot,
character development, setting, problem, solution, and resolution.

> Chapter 4 contains
> an extensive
> discussion about
> vocabulary
> instruction.

As you can imagine, this categorization system does not work for a
science book. Science textbooks are often organized using introductory
thesis paragraphs, followed by supporting details in subsequent paragraphs. Vocabulary is essential to the field of science and is frequently introduced through a bolded word and an example.

However, students may find this format frustrating because an explicit definition may not be found in the body of the text. Pictures and
charts, not surprisingly, are used to illustrate phenomena and offer more
details about the topic. Although many text structures may be used
throughout the science book, cause and effect is the most common.

> Journalistic style is
> common in
> newspapers—the
> main ideas are
> presented first and
> then explained or
> explored in
> subsequent
> paragraphs.

On the other hand, social studies textbooks use a more journalistic style.
Narrative text may be embedded, particularly in sidebar features about interesting people or events. Readers can expect that the chapters and headings
will be organized by concepts, which may prove confusing at times. For

Figure 1.1 Sample text feature page.

The Cherokees were herded into camps and then driven on foot or in wagons eight hundred miles to what is now Oklahoma. Many died before they got there. The journey was called the Trail of Tears. One elder who was five years old on the leaving day recalled that he had been playing in his front yard when the wagon came and the soldiers told him to get in. He gathered up his toys, but the soldiers made him leave them in the dirt. By the time the wagon pulled out, he could see that a white boy had already moved in and was playing with them.

WHAT HAPPENED TO ANYOKAH?

Little is known of her after she helped her father demonstrate the syllables to the elders. It is not known if she married. If she did, and married a white man, she might have been allowed to remain in the Southeast. If she married an Indian, she would have probably been forced west on the Trail of Tears.

> **A PLAIN-SPOKEN QUESTION**
>
> "What good man would prefer a country covered with forests and ranged by a few thousand savages to our extensive Republic, studded with cities, towns and prosperous farms . . . occupied by more than twelve million happy people, and filled with all the blessings of liberty, civilization, and religion?"
> —President Andrew Jackson, explaining to Congress why Indians should be removed from their land, 1830

"Anyone who secretly enters into a ship and is later detected will be put to death."—Sign posted on the Japanese coast, 1851

Manjiro: Bringing America to Japan

Japan and Massachusetts, 1840s

In the nineteenth century, Japan was a feudal society closed to the other nations of the world. Her leaders drew up the Decree of Exclusion, which said, "So long as the sun shall warm the earth, let no Christian dare to come to Japan . . . If he violates this command [he] shall pay for it with his head." Japanese citizens were forbidden from travel and contact with outsiders. Most obeyed without question, and a boy named Manjiro would have, too, if a gust of wind and a whaling ship hadn't delivered him into another world.

On January 5, 1841, the year of the cow, five Japanese fishermen put out from a port named Usa at the southwest corner of their island. The youngest, Manjiro, a boy of fourteen. As a peasant child, Manjiro rated only one name and had no hope of

Manjiro at age twenty-seven

Source: Jacket design by Anne Redmond and excerpt from "Manjiro: Bringing America to Japan" from *We Were There, Too!* by Phillip Hoose. Copyright © 2001 by Phillip Hoose. Reprinted by permission of Farrar, Straus and Giroux, LLC.

instance, a chapter titled "Setting Sail for New Lands" is more ambiguous than one that reads "How European Exploration Changed the Americas." Prior knowledge is critical—and often assumed—for many social studies textbooks. Gaps in students' experiences or prior knowledge may derail their ability to comprehend the passage. Consider the prior knowledge required to understand the following example from a social studies book:

> About 1,000 years after Hammurabi, a new empire arose in Mesopotamia. It was founded by a people called the Assyrians, who lived in the north near the Tigris River. Assyria had fertile valleys that attracted outside invaders. To defend their land, the Assyrians built a large army. Around 900 B.C., they began taking over the rest of Mesopotamia. (Spielvogel, 2006, p. 143)

Unlike diagrams in science books that are usually conceptual in nature, photographs are used more frequently in social studies materials to illustrate important people, places, and events. Like all textbooks, social studies books rely on a variety of text structures, although cause and effect is dominant within a chronologically arranged format.

Mathematics textbooks are distinctly different from those encountered in other content areas. Each chapter follows a predictable pattern, usually an introduction of a concept or algorithm followed by an explanation, an example, and then a problem. The main idea appears in the chapter title or headings. There are comparatively few extended text passages. Instead, extensive use of symbols and numbers communicate complex concepts. In addition, unique technical vocabulary like *rhombus* and *integers* is used. Students, particularly those who are English language learners, are likely to be confused by mathematical words with multiple meanings such as *set*, *prime*, and *operation*. The text structure is almost always sequential and structured to explain a procedure.

Although physical education, art, and music classes rely less on traditional textbooks as a source of information, they do exist. Students' use of these texts may be complicated by the amount of prior knowledge necessary, as well as the amount of content-specific vocabulary needed. A positive is that these texts tend to use a great deal of primary source information, including newspaper and magazine articles, film, slides, and CD-ROMs and other electronic media. Using these materials requires a great deal of visual literacy, which is the ability to think critically about information presented in graphic forms. This type of literacy mirrors the changing modes of information retrieval and interpretation in our society (Bruce, 1997) and is increasingly common in informational texts.

> Vocabulary instruction is featured in Chapter 4.

What Is Critical Literacy and How Does It Relate to Reading for Information?

Before we explore the types of informational texts available for the elementary school classroom, we would like to raise a caution. Informational books are often called "the literature of fact—or the product of an author's inquiry, research, and writing" (Kristo & Bamford, 2004, p. 12). These informational books attempt to be as accurate as possible. However, lessons learned from them focus on critical literacy (e.g., Alvermann, Moon, & Hagood, 1999; Vasquez, 2004) indicate that every source contains bias, specific points of view, and divergent perspectives. Therefore, teachers must ensure that their students not only learn how to read for information, but how to read *critically* for information.

McLaughlin and DeVoogd (2004) noted that "critical literacy disrupts the commonplace by examining it from multiple perspectives" (p. 16). In their review of 30 years worth of research and professional literature, Lewison, Flint, and Van Sluys (2002) identified four dimensions of critical literacy: "(1) disrupting the commonplace, (2) interrogating multiple viewpoints, (3) focusing on sociopolitical issues, and (4) taking action and promoting social justice" (p. 382).

Disrupting the Commonplace. This aspect of critical literacy invites students to explore their everyday world in a different way. This may mean that we challenge holiday traditions and examine how people around the world celebrate by learning about Kwanza, Ramadan, Christmas, and Hanukkah. It could also mean that we consider the world from the perspective of people who are homeless, people with disabilities, senior citizens, or others. While students need to be able to read books about these topics to find out information, they also need exposure to information that challenges their assumptions about the way the world works. The book *Faithful Elephants: A True Story of Animals, People and War* (Tsuchiya, 1951) describes the killing of the animals in the Ueno zoo during World War II. It disrupts students' thinking about the glory of wars and explores the hidden victims of human conflicts.

Interrogating Multiple Viewpoints. This aspect of critical literacy provides students with an opportunity to notice the voice and perspective of people represented in the books they read as well as to notice those that are missing or silent. Students may wonder why the scientists in their books are often men or what the children's perspective of the Orphan Trains might have been. Reading different informational texts about the same events allows students to develop an understanding of perspective and viewpoints. Imagine the different perspective on World War II students see when they learn about kids in the books *Remember World War II: Kids Who Survived Tell Their Stories* (Nicholson, 2005) and *The Children We Remember* (Abells, 1983). Or consider reading *Encounter* (Yolen, 1996) for the first time and realizing that America was not "discovered" by Columbus.

FAITHFUL ELEPHANTS
A True Story of Animals, People and War
Yukio Tsuchiya

Translated by Tomoko Tsuchiya Dykes   Illustrated by Ted Lewin

Source: Jacket illustration from *Faithful Elephants* by Yukio Tsuchiya. Jacket illustration copyright © 1988 by Ted Lewin. Reprinted by permission of Houghton Mifflin Company. All rights reserved.

Focusing on Sociopolitical Issues. Lewison, Flint, and Van Sluys (2002) remind us that "teaching is not a neutral form of social practice" (p. 383). As teachers, we can explore the different power relationships that exist between and among people and invite students to question the legitimacy of these power relationships. For example, the book *Christmas in the Big House, Christmas in the Quarters* (McKissack, 1994) compares a holiday experience from the perspective of slave owners and their slaves. *Richard*

Wright and the Library Card (Miller, 1997) explores the life of an African-American who was not allowed inside libraries because he was black.

Taking Action and Promoting Social Justice. This final component of critical literacy is often the only definition of critical literacy. However, as Lewison, Flint, and Van Sluys (2002) note "one cannot take informed action against oppression or promote social justice without expanded understandings and perspectives gained from the other three dimensions" (pp. 383–384). Our goal in providing students access to informational books—through good sources and teaching—is to encourage them to take action to create a better world. Students can explore the actions taken by others by reading informational books such as *Harvesting Hope: The Story of Cesar Chavez* (Krull, 2004), *The Harvey Milk Story* (Krakow, 2001), or *Somewhere Today: A Book of Peace* (Thomas, 1998).

In their discussion of the four components of critical literacy, McLaughlin and DeVoogd (2004) note "we don't need to follow the dimensions of critical literacy in sequential order or use them collectively. Whenever we engage in any one of these dimensions, we are engaged in critical literacy" (p. 18). This is an important note. As we share informational texts with our students and teach them how to read for information, we can simultaneously engage in critical literacy, develop their understanding of the world, and teach them how to question it. Therefore, the key lies in the text selection *and* our instruction.

How Do We Support Reading for Information?

The answer to this question also has two parts. The first part focuses on content-area texts as they are used in many classrooms. Each content area uses common text structures and styles to convey information. Therefore, *instruction* of the text structures and styles is critical. We believe that students should be explicitly taught the structures and styles used in texts. We have seen students approach an expository (informational) text as if it is narrative, looking for the familiar story structure of characters, setting, plot, and the like. This may be due, in part, to the lack of access students in the elementary school have to informational texts (e.g., Duke, 2000). Unfortunately, knowledge of narrative structures is unlikely to be of much help in a science textbook. However, explicit instruction in the types of structures found in their textbooks and the signal words associated with the text will sustain and improve their comprehension of the course readings. The second part of this answer lies in instruction of comprehension strategies.

Comprehension Strategies. Comprehension strategies are taught to students of all developmental levels to be used as tools to support their own understanding of the text (e.g., Harvey & Goudvis, 2000; Keene & Zimmermann, 1997). Indeed, comprehension instruction has been identified as an essential teaching practice by the National Reading Panel (National Institute of Child Health and Human Development, 2000). Like tools in a toolbox, the key to the usefulness of these strategies is the proper application of a strategy to suit a purpose. These include

- *Questioning strategies* to predict and anticipate what might occur next in the text, to solve problems, and to clarify their understanding.
- *Summarizing strategies* to identify important information and provide an accurate recount.
- *Inferencing strategies* to "read between the lines" in order to identify clues in the text.
- *Self-monitoring strategies* to determine when readers understand what they have read and to notice when they do not.
- *Connection strategies* to integrate what a reader has experienced and learned with the information being read.
- *Predicting* to use what you know to make an educated guess about what might happen next.
- *Analysis strategies* to identify literary devices, determine author's purpose, and evaluate texts.

Cueing strategies include graphophonics, syntax, and semantics—the systems we use to understand print.

As with cueing strategies, we believe there is a danger in teaching comprehension strategies in isolation of one another. Pinnell and Fountas remind us that

> [t]hese strategies are not linear in that first you engage one then another. In fact, reducing complex systems to a list . . . probably oversimplifies reading. *Teaching* strategies one at a time and telling students to consciously employ them, *one at a time*, may actually interfere with deep comprehension and make reading a meaningless exercise. (2003, pp. 7–8)

Comprehension strategies are a key element in the effort to develop students' ability to attend to their own learning. This awareness of how one learns is referred to as metacognition.

How Is Reading Comprehension Developed?

While reading comprehension is not necessarily "taught" in the sense that it occurs in the mind of the reader, purposeful instruction still plays a key role. As we stated earlier, reading comprehension does not simply happen through lots of reading; it is developed through activities designed to teach students about what good readers do. In particular, good readers are purposeful in reading, and they use strategies to extend their understanding (Paris, Wasik, & Turner, 1991). Three approaches are essential in developing reading comprehension:

- building metacognitive awareness by teaching students what to do before, during, and after the reading
- developing their ability to formulate questions as they read
- providing intentional instruction in using strategies to support their comprehension

Building Metacognition to Develop Reading Comprehension. Metacognition is often described as thinking about one's thinking; it is also being aware of what one knows and does not know. For instance, readers use metacognitive skills in reading when they:

- develop a plan of action
- maintain/monitor the plan
- evaluate the plan (Kujawa & Huske, 1995)

As described earlier, reading comprehension is an active process undertaken by the reader. Therefore, the reader approaches text with a plan, uses the plan, and then checks to see if the plan worked. This metacognitive awareness can be modeled through instruction using questions before, during, and after the reading.

- *Before the reading—developing the plan.* Before beginning any reading, discuss questions like the following:
    - What is my purpose for reading?
    - What do I already know about this topic?
    - How long do I think it will take for me to read it?
- *During the reading—monitoring the plan.* While reading, pause occasionally to ask these questions:
    - Do I understand what I'm reading?
    - If not, what can I do to help myself?
    - What do I already know that I can connect this information to?
    - Do I need to change my pace?
    - What are the important ideas?
- *After the reading—evaluating the plan.* Once the reading is finished, revisit the plan by asking questions such as the following:
    - How did I do?
    - Did the reading meet my expectations?
    - Did I understand?
    - Do I need to revisit any part of the text? (Kujawa & Huske, 1995)

"Modeling" is the practice of demonstrating how a skill or strategy is used for the purpose of teaching and reinforcing information.

"Scaffolding" involves bridging the gap between what students can do and what they need to do through a series of prompts, questions, and tasks.

Kujawa and Huske's (1995) model is based in the mind of the reader and emphasizes what good readers do to prepare to read, to monitor understanding while reading, and to reflect and extend their knowledge after they have completed the reading. However, students need modeling and scaffolding in order to achieve this level of independent and effective reading. This is accomplished by using research-based instructional strategies that mirror the cognition of effective readers.

The model of before, during, and after in reading instruction is useful because it provides a template for the instructional intentions of the teacher and for the cognitive ones of the learner. We will extend this useful model throughout the text, describing specific instructional strategies that support children as they read for information. Learning to use the before, during, and after reading model will serve as a cognitive guide for the teaching and learning that occurs in classrooms committed to instruction in reading for information.

Conclusion

To be successful in middle school, high school, college, and their adult life, students must learn to read for information. There are a number of types of informational texts—as well as common text structures and features—that should be used in the elementary classroom. Guiding readers through informational texts, modeling how to read informational texts, and ensuring that students become successful with informational texts is one of the key responsibilities of elementary school teachers today.

References

Alvermann, D. E., Moon, J. S., & Hagood, M. C. (1999). *Popular culture in the classroom: Teaching and researching critical media literacy.* Newark, DE: International Reading Association.

Armbruster, B. B., Anderson, T. H., Armstrong, J. O., Wise, M. A., Janisch, C., & Meyer, L. A. (1991). Reading and questioning in content-area lessons. *Journal of Reading Behavior, 23,* 35–60.

Bruce, B. C. (1997). Current issues and future directions. In J. Flood, S. B. Heath, & D. Lapp (Eds.), *Research on teaching literacy through the communicative and visual arts* (pp. 875–884). Newark, DE: International Reading Association.

Burke, J. (2000). *Reading reminders: Tools, tips, and techniques.* Portsmouth, NH: Boynton/Cook.

Chall, J. S., Jacobs, V. A., & Baldwin, L. (1996). Reading, writing, and language connection. In J. Shimron (Ed.), *Literacy and education: Essays in memory of Dina Feitelson* (pp. 33–48). Cresskill, NJ: Hampton.

Chandler-Olcott, K., & Mahar, D. (2003). Adolescents' "anime"-inspired "fanfictions": An exploration of multiliteracies. *Journal of Adolescent & Adult Literacy, 46,* 556–566.

Collins, M. A. (2002). *Road to perdition.* New York: Pocket.

Cullinan, B. E., & Person, D. G. (2001). *The continuum encyclopedia of children's literature.* New York: Continuum.

Dreher, M. J., & Sammons, R. B. (1994). Fifth graders' search for information in a textbook. *Journal of Reading Behavior, 26,* 301–314.

Duke, N. K. (2000). 3.6 minutes per day: The scarcity of informational texts in first grade. *Reading Research Quarterly, 35,* 202–224.

Duke, N. K. (2004). The case for informational text. *Educational Leadership, 61*(6), 40–44.

Fountas, I. C., Pinnell, G. S. (2005). *Leveled books (K-8): Matching texts to readers for effective teaching.* Portsmouth, NH: Heinemann.

Frey, N., & Fisher, D. (2004). Using graphic novels, anime, and the Internet in an urban high school. *The English Journal, 93*(3), 19–25.

Harvey, S., & Goudvis, A. (2000). *Strategies at work: Teaching comprehension to enhance understanding.* York, ME: Stenhouse.

Joyce, B. R., & Showers, B. (1995). *Student achievement through staff development: Fundamentals of school renewal* (2nd ed.). New York: Longman.

Keene, E. O., & Zimmermann, S. (1997). *Mosaic of thought: Teaching comprehension in a readers' workshop.* Portsmouth, NH: Heinemann.

Kristo, J. V., & Bamford, R. A. (2004). *Nonfiction in focus: A comprehensive framework for helping students become independent readers and writers of nonfiction, K–6.* New York: Scholastic.

Kujawa, S., & Huske, L. (1995). *The strategic teaching and reading project guidebook* (Rev. ed.). Oakbrook, IL: North Central Regional Education Laboratory.

Kurkjian, C., & Livingston, N. (2005). Learning to read and reading to learn: Informational series books. *The Reading Teacher, 58,* 592–600.

Langer, J. A. (1985). Children's sense of genre: A study of performance on parallel reading and writing tasks. *Written Communication, 2,* 157–188.

Leu, D. J., Jr., Kinzer, C. K., Coiro, J. L., & Cammack, D. W. (2004). Toward a theory of new literacies emerging from the Internet and other information and communication technologies. In R. B. Ruddell & N. J. Unrau (Eds.), *Theoretical models and processes of reading* (5th ed., pp. 1570–1613). Newark, DE: International Reading Association.

Lewison, M., Flint, A. S., Van Sluys, K. (2002). Taking on critical literacy: The journey of newcomers and novices. *Language Arts, 79,* 382–392.

McKenna, M. C., Kear, D. J., & Ellsworth, R. A. (1995). Children's attitudes toward reading: A national survey. *Reading Research Quarterly, 30,* 934–956.

McLaughlin, M., & DeVoogd, G. L. (2004). *Critical literacy: Enhancing students' comprehension of text.* New York: Scholastic.

Moss, B., & Newton, E. (2002). An examination of the informational text genre in basal readers. *Reading Psychology, 23,* 1–13.

National Institute of Child Health and Human Development. (2000). *Report of the National Reading Panel. Teaching children to read: An evidence-based assessment of the scientific literature on reading and its implications for reading instruction.* Washington, DC: U. S. Government Printing Office.

Paris, S. G., Wasik, B. A., & Turner, J. C. (1991). The development of strategic readers. In R. Barr, M. L. Kamil, P. Mosenthal, & P. D. Pearson (Eds.), *Handbook of reading research* (Vol. II, pp. 609–640). Mahwah, NJ: Lawrence Erlbaum Associates.

Pinnell, G. S., & Fountas, I. C. (2003). Teaching comprehension. *The California Reader, 36*(4), 7–14.

Spielvogel, J. (2006). *Discovering our past: Ancient civilizations*. New York: Glencoe McGraw-Hill.

Stauffer, R. G. (1969). *Teaching reading as a thinking process*. New York: HarperCollins.

Vasquez, V. M. (2004). *Negotiating critical literacies with young children*. Mahwah, NJ: Lawrence Erlbaum Associates.

Wade, S. E., & Moje, E. B. (2000). The role of text in classroom learning. In M. L. Kamil, P. B. Mosenthal, P. D. Pearson, & R. Barr (Eds.), *Handbook of reading research* (Vol. III, pp. 609–628). Mahwah, NJ: Lawrence Erlbaum Associates.

Yopp, R. H., & Yopp, H. K. (2004). Preview-predict-confirm: Thinking aloud about the language and content of informational text. *The Reading Teacher, 58,* 79–83.

Children's Literature Cited

Abells, C. B. (1983). *The children we remember*. New York: Greenwillow.

Freedman, R. (1987). *Lincoln: A photobiography*. New York: Clarion.

George, J. C. (2000). *How to talk to your dog*. New York: HarperTrophy.

Hoose, P. (2001). *We were there, too! Young people in U. S. history*. New York: Farrar Straus Giroux.

Krakow, K. (2001). *The Harvey Milk story*. Ridley Park, PA: Two Lives Publishing.

Krull, K. (2004). *Harvesting hope: The story of Cesar Chavez*. San Diego: Harcourt.

Krull, K. (2004). *The boy on Fairfield Street: How Ted Geisel grew up to become Dr. Seuss*. New York: Random House.

Maestro, B. (1993). *The story of money*. New York: Clarion Books.

McClafferty, C. K. (2001). *The head bone's connected to the neck bone: The weird, wacky, and wonderful x-ray*. New York: Farrar, Straus, and Giroux.

McKissack, P. (1994). *Christmas in the big house, Christmas in the quarters*. Boston: Houghton Mifflin.

Miller, W. (1997). *Richard Wright and the library card*. New York: Lee and Low.

Nicholson, D. M. (2005). *Remember World War II: Kids who survived tell their stories*. Washington, DC: National Geographic.

Pilkey, D. (1997). *The adventures of Captain Underpants: An epic novel*. New York: Blue Sky.

Spiegelman, A. (1990). *Maus: A survivor's tale*. New York: Pantheon.

Stamaty, M. A. (2004). *Alia's mission: Saving the books of Iraq*. New York: Alfred & Knopf.

Thomas, S. M. (1998). *Somewhere today: A book of peace*. Morton Grove, IL: Albert Whitman & Company.

Tsuchiya, Y. (1951). *Faithful elephants: A true story of animals, people and war*. New York: Houghton Mifflin.

Winter, J. (2005). *The librarian of Basra: A true story from Iraq*. San Diego: Harcourt.

Yolen, J. (1996). *Encounter*. New York: Yoyager.

Appendix Children's Informational Texts by Genre

Picture Books

Primary
Andrews-Goebel, N. (2002). *The pot that Juan built.* New York: Lee & Low.
Cowley, J. (1999). *Red-eyed tree frog.* New York: Scholastic.
Gibbons, G. (1994). *The planets.* New York: Holiday House.
Micucci, C. (1997). *Life and times of the peanut.* Boston: Houghton Mifflin.
Weitzman, J. P., & Glasser, R. P. (1998). *You can't take a balloon into the Metropolitan museum.* New York: Dial.
Weitzman, J. P., & Glasser, R. P. (2000). *You can't take a balloon into the National Gallery.* New York: Dial.

Picture Books

Intermediate
Aliki. (1986). *Corn is maize: The gift of the Indians.* New York: HarperCollins.
Ancona, G. (1993). *Pablo remembers: The day of the dead.* New York: Lothrop, Lee, & Shepard.
Christelow, E. (1999). *What do illustrators do?* New York: Clarion.
Curlee, L. (2005). *Ballpark: The story of America's baseball fields.* New York: Atheneum.
Deem, J. (1998). *Bodies from the bog.* Boston: Houghton Mifflin.
Jenkins, S. (1999). *Top of the world: Climbing Mount Everest.* Boston: Houghton Mifflin.
Knight, M. B. (1999). *Talking walls.* Gardiner, ME: Tilbury House.
Simon, S. (1998). *Muscles: Our muscular system.* New York: William Morrow.
Yin. (2001). *Coolies.* New York: Philomel.

Biographies and Autobiographies

Primary
DePaola, T. (1999). *26 Fairmount Avenue.* New York: Putnam.
Gerstein, M. (2003). *The man who walked between the towers.* Brookfield,   CN: Roaring Brook.
Jordan, D. (2000). *Salt in his shoes: Michael Jordan in pursuit of a dream.* New York: Aladdin.
Krull, K. (2000). *Wilma unlimited: How Wilma Rudolph became the world's fastest woman.* Orlando, FL: Voyager.
Krull, K. (2003). *Harvesting hope: The story of Cesar Chavez.* San Diego: Harcourt.
Lasky, K. (2000). *A vision of beauty: The story of Sarah Breedlove Walker.* Cambridge, MA: Candlewick.
St. George, J. (2000*). So you want to be president.* New York: Philomel.
Troupe, Q. (2005). *Little Stevie Wonder.* Boston: Houghton Mifflin.
Wilder, L. I. (1973). *Little house on the prairie.* New York: Harper Trophy.

Biographies and Autobiographies

Intermediate
Bridges, R. (1999). *Through my eyes.* New York: Scholastic.
Coerr, E. (1993). *Sadako and the thousand paper cranes.* New York: Puffin.
Harness, C. (2001). *Remember the ladies: 100 great American women.* New York: HarperCollins.
Krull, K. (1995). *Lives of the artists: Masterpieces, messes (and what the neighbors thought).* San Diego: Harcourt.

Appendix Children's Informational Texts by Genre *(continued)*

	Mochizuki, K. (1997). *Passage to freedom: The Sugihara story.* New York: Lee & Low.
	Paulsen, G. (1998). *My life in dog years.* New York: Bantam Doubleday Dell.
	Sis, P. (1996). *Starry messenger: A book depicting the life of a famous scientist, mathematician, astronomer, philosopher, physicist, Galileo Galilei.* New York: Farrar Straus Giroux.
	Winter, J. (2005). *The librarian of Basra: A true story from Iraq.* San Diego: Harcourt.
Poetry	Fleischman, P. (1992). *Joyful noise: Poems for two voices.* New York: HarperCollins.
	Florian, D. (1999). *Insectlopedia.* San Diego: Harcourt Brace.
	Florian, D. (2000). *Mammalia.* San Diego: Harcourt Brace.
	Franco, B. (2003). *Mathatickles!* New York: Simon & Schuster.
	Goldish, M. (1999). *101 science poems and songs for young learners: Grades 1–3.* New York: Scholastic.
	Pappas, T. (1991). *Math talk: Mathematical ideas in poems for two voices.* San Carlos, CA: Tetra/Worldwide.
Graphic Novels	Burleigh, R. (2002). *Into the air: The story of the Wright brothers' first flight.* New York: Harcourt/Silver Whistle.
	Burleigh, R. (2003). *Amelia Earhart free in the skies.* New York: Harcourt/Silver Whistle.
	Delgado, R. (1996). *Age of reptiles: Tribal warfare.* New York: Dark Horse.
	Golnick, L. (2002). *The cartoon history of the universe.* New York: Doubleday.
	Golnick, L. (1996). *The cartoon history of the environment.* New York: HarperResource.
	Stamaty, M. A. (2004). *Alia's mission: Saving the books of Iraq.* New York: Knopf.
Digital Resources	*Bill Nye the Science Guy Complete Video Collection.* (2000). Buena Vista, CA: Disney Educational Products.
	Schoolhouse Rock! Special 30th Anniversary edition. (2002). Buena Vista, CA: Walt Disney Home Video.
	Thirty years of National Geographic Specials. (2001). Washington, DC: National Geographic Society.

Nancy Frey

Douglas Fisher

Kelly Moore

Chapter 2

Conversations for Learning:

Classroom and School Structures That Support Reading for Information

*T*he influence of the classroom and school environment on instruction is significant. A number of meta-analyses and research reviews have confirmed that when teachers and students have opportunities to collaborate with their peers, learning occurs (e.g., Calweti, 2004; Marzano, Pickering, & Pollock, 2001). Learning is a community function, not an isolated one, and the conversations that occur between learners foster growth for all involved (Vygotsky, 1978).

Remember, not all professional development is created equal. The National Staff Development Council has developed standards for professional development that can be found at www.nsdc.org.

As elementary teachers, we focus our efforts on improving literacy achievement at all grade levels. We must ensure that students learn to read and read to learn. We have to provide our students with the ability to read informational texts and to think deeply about these texts. But we also know that reading achievement is profoundly influenced by quality instruction. In fact, several researchers (e.g., Allington & Johnston, 2000; Darling-Hammond, 1999; Joyce & Showers, 1995) suggest that the professional development of teachers is critically linked to student achievement and literacy levels of students.

This chapter focuses on the opportunities for conversations that must occur between learners for real learning to take place. We define learners as both our students and ourselves. In the first part of this chapter, we will discuss grouping strategies to promote peer learning. In the second half, we will turn our attention to school-wide approaches and professional development.

Grouping Strategies to Promote Peer Learning

We could begin with a review of the literature on grouping, but instead we would like to introduce you to three students we know:

- Adrianna has read every book you can name. She is known as a very bright kid. However, she gets bored easily in class, especially when she does not find the task challenging.

- Rangina is a recent immigrant from Pakistan. She is learning English as a third language and wants to get an education in the United States. She struggles with the English language and the social aspects of schooling.

- Charles reads several grade levels below his peers. He has been progressing through school without strong reading or writing skills. As a defense, he often tells the teacher that he was too busy playing soccer or video games to do his homework.

What should be the criteria for grouping students? Should reading skill be the determinant? What about English language learners and students with reading disabilities—how should they be grouped? Are the students most "at risk" always together? These questions are gripping schools all over the country. We support the practice of heterogeneous grouping in which students of diverse abilities and skills are educated together. This contrasts with past practices of ability grouping and tracking, and responds to the research evidence that tracking is harmful to students' emotional well-being (Oakes, 1985). It is interesting to look at the success of schools that have detracked and that do not

use permanent ability groups. Typically, when the low-level and reme-
dial permanent ability groups are eliminated, achievement increases
(Oakes & Wells, 1998).

Placing students in fixed and static groups for the purpose of instruction, with little likelihood of working with a wide range of peers,
constitutes tracking. Instead, we advocate the use of flexible grouping
arrangements in mixed-ability classrooms. Many instructional strategies are available to today's teachers to help them teach academic skills
in heterogeneous groups. However, as the use of cooperative learning
groups increases in elementary school classrooms, we must state some
cautions about grouping. First, we believe that students should be
grouped and regrouped for different activities and for different purposes. Fixed groups, especially based on ability, run counter to all the
wise practices that our best teachers are implementing (Lapp, Fisher, &
Flood, 1999).

Think about someone like Charles. Can you imagine his confusion
when he participates in lessons designed to increase community and the
appreciation of diversity, but then never gets to interact with some of his
peers because they are always in another group? This is not to say that a
teacher would never group students together who are struggling to understand a particular concept. When organizing instruction, teachers often
bring specific students together to provide explicit instruction based on
their needs. After receiving instruction from the teacher, they return to
their heterogeneous groups. The important point here is that class groups
are not permanent; teachers should group students in such combinations
that everyone has a chance to demonstrate their best skills in a particular
setting.

Flexible grouping arrangements mean that the teacher must have a
repertoire of instructional strategies to ensure that students have many
opportunities to work with one another. These strategies include think-
pair-share (Lyman, 1981), learning centers (Opitz, 1999), jigsaw (Aronson,
1978), Collaborative Strategic Learning (Klinger & Vaughn, 1998), and reciprocal teaching (Palincsar & Brown, 1986).

Think–Pair–Share

One of the most transportable teaching strategies is *think-pair-share*
(Lyman, 1981). Think-pair-share introduces an intermediate stage between when the question is asked and when the answered is delivered
and serves as an important strategy for developing accountable talk
(Resnick, 1995). After asking the question, the teacher invites students
to think about the possible answers. When a short amount of time has
elapsed (30 seconds or so), the teacher instructs students to turn to a
partner and discuss their answers. After allowing a few moments to

> Transportable
> teaching strategies
> are effective across
> content areas and
> grade levels.

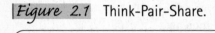

Figure 2.1 Think-Pair-Share.

? **Think** about the question:
What do you know?
What experiences have you had?
What connections can you make?

?!?! **Pair** with your partner:
Listen to ideas.
Share your ideas.
Create new ideas together.

Share your ideas with others:
Listen to ideas.
Share your ideas.
Share your partner's ideas.
Create new ideas together.

For information on instruction for small groups, see Frey and Fisher, <u>The Language Arts Workshop: Purposeful Reading and Writing Instruction</u> (2006).

There is research evidence that reading across texts helps students learn.

discuss, the teacher invites students to offer answers. Invariably, more hands go up because students have had some time to consider their answer, listen to someone else, and refine their response. In addition, the answers are likely to be rich and detailed because of this intermediate step. A classroom poster for think-pair-share can be found in Figure 2.1.

Learning Centers

An optimal time for students to work collaboratively is during *learning centers*. Students work in small heterogeneous groups (three or four children) on tasks designed to reinforce previously taught concepts and skills. These centers are usually related to one another in theme or content. For example, mathematics centers in a first-grade classroom might include one on patterns, another on measurement, and a third on geometry. Each center contains a short informational reading and directions for completing the center tasks. Meanwhile, the teacher is providing direct instruction to small, homogeneous groups of students who have been chosen according to their similar instructional needs. Students move in and out of learning centers using the Center Activity Rotation System (CARS) (Lapp, Flood, & Goss, 2000).

The success of these learning centers depends on the ability of each child to work with others. As you can see from the graphic in Figure 2.2, the majority of students are engaged in heterogeneous small-group learning centers while the teacher meets with a specifically selected group of students for teacher-directed instruction. These lessons can last from 15 to 25 minutes, depending on the developmental levels of the students, so the teacher can meet with several groups per day.

Jigsaw

Whole-class instruction for informational reading often involves a single text, as when the teacher models a think-aloud while reading an article about the skeletal system during a shared reading. However, there are occasions when students need to analyze multiple texts at the same time. When a group of readers is presented with information from several texts, they are more likely to make connections among those readings, called intertextuality (Bloome & Egan-Robertson, 1993). However, it can be difficult to organize multiple readings for use in a

Figure 2.2   Center activity rotation system.

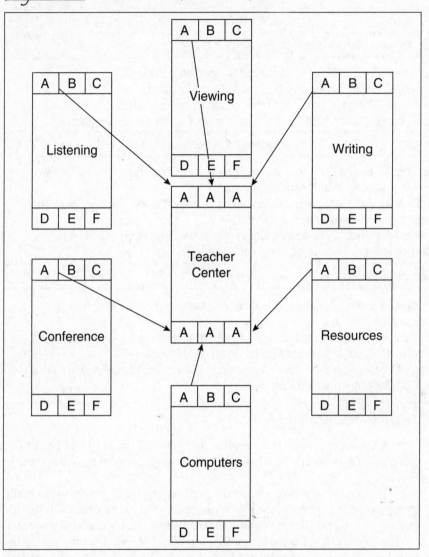

discussion. One instructional arrangement for doing so is a *jigsaw* (Aronson, 1978).

The readings used in a jigsaw may be chosen because they each offer similar perspectives of the same concept or event (*complementary*), or because they present very different views (*conflicting*) (Hartman & Allison, 1996). A third arrangement divides a concept or idea into smaller elements

Figure 2.3 Text sets for jigsaw.

TYPE	PURPOSE
Complementary	Texts focus on single concept
Example: California Gold Rush	Chambers, C. E. (1998). *California gold rush*. New York: Troll. Kalman, B. (1999). *The gold rush*. New York: Crabtree. Krensky, S. (1996). *Strike it rich!* New York: Scott Foresman. Schanzer, R. (1999). *Gold fever!* Washington, DC: National Geographic.
Conflicting	Texts focus on divergent perspectives of a concept
Example: Christopher Columbus	Osborne, M. P. (1997). *The story of Christopher Columbus: Admiral of the ocean sea*. New York: Gareth Stevens. MacDonald, F. (2004). *You wouldn't want to sail with Christopher Columbus!* New York: Franklin Watts. Schlein, M. (1992). *I sailed with Columbus*. New York: HarperCollins. Yolen, J. (1996). *Encounter*. New York: Voyager.
Divided	Concept is divided among texts
Example: Predators of North America	Berger, M. (2002). *Snap! A book about alligators and crocodiles*. New York: Cartwheel. Corrigan, P. (2001). *Cougars: Our wild world*. Chanhassen, MN: NorthWord. Gibbons, G. (1995). *Wolves!* New York: Holiday House. Hodge, D. (1999). *Bears: Polar bears, black bears, and grizzly bears*. Tonawanda, NY: Kids Can Press.

so that the topic is only fully understood after all the readings have been discussed (Aronson, 1978). Examples of these types of text sets appear in Figure 2.3.

The jigsaw is accomplished through two types of groups—the home group and the expert group. First, members of a home group divide the task of reading multiple texts among themselves. Each reader is responsible for identifying and reporting the important elements of the text to the home group. Students then meet in an expert group of students reading the same text to discuss the reading, and take notes for use in the home group. Finally, students reconvene in their home group to learn and share information from each of the readings. A procedural map for jigsaw is illustrated in Figure 2.4.

Collaborative Strategic Reading

Collaborative Strategic Reading (CSR) is a technique used by small groups of heterogeneously grouped students to read and comprehend text

Figure 2.4   Jigsaw.

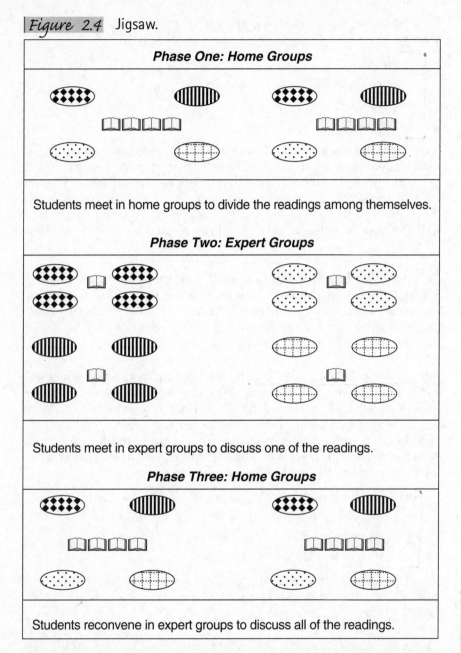

Phase One: Home Groups

Students meet in home groups to divide the readings among themselves.

Phase Two: Expert Groups

Students meet in expert groups to discuss one of the readings.

Phase Three: Home Groups

Students reconvene in expert groups to discuss all of the readings.

(Klinger & Vaughn, 1998). Typically used in groups of five, it is well suited for use with informational text. A text is divided into sections that indicate when the group should stop to discuss what they know so far and what they find confusing or unclear. The strength of this approach is in the use of cooperative learning principles to practice sound

Heterogeneous does NOT mean random—teachers often assign students to their mixed-ability groups to ensure that the group membership works.

comprehension strategies. The group uses four strategies to understand the text:

- Preview
- Click and clunk
- Get the gist
- Wrap up

Each of these strategies is taught and practiced as a whole group until students are able to use it without teacher support. A study of CSR in fourth-grade classrooms found that students who had been carefully taught each of the strategies focused the majority of their talk (65%) on the content of the reading, and another 25% on the procedural aspects of CSR (Klinger, Vaughn, & Schumm, 1998). Only 2% of their talk was off-task.

Before the Reading: Preview. This step is performed before the reading. Students discuss what they already know about the topic of the reading and make predictions about what may be learned in the reading. By creating prediction questions, students can begin to anticipate the information they may encounter during the reading.

During the Reading: Click and Clunk. "Clicks" is the term used by the authors to describe smooth reading that makes sense to the student—much like the hum of a well-oiled machine. On the other hand, "clunks" are the times when a reader encounters an unfamiliar word or concept. Together, clicks and clunks represent self-monitoring behaviors used by fluent readers. The clunks signal the readers that fix-up strategies are needed. After noticing that a problem has occurred, the reader can

- *Reread* the sentence or paragraph
- *Read ahead* until the end of the sentence or paragraph
- *Analyze* the word for familiar affixes or root words
- *Ask* his or her partner what it means

During CSR, students read a passage from the text, then discuss their clunks. Using their collective knowledge, they clarify each other's understanding of the word or concept in question.

During the Reading: Get the Gist. At the end of each section of the passage, students summarize the main ideas and important facts. Like prediction and self-monitoring, summarizing is a comprehension behavior used by more-fluent readers (Brown & Day, 1983). Both click and clunk and get the gist are repeated several times until the entire reading has been completed.

Figure 2.5 Student task sheet for collaborative strategic reading.

When?	What?	Sounds Like?
Before the Reading	Preview	What do we know about this topic? What do we expect to find out in this reading?
During the Reading	Click and Clunk	What can I do to fix this clunk? **Reread** the sentence or paragraph. **Read ahead** until the end of the sentence or paragraph. **Analyze** the word for familiar affixes or root words. **Ask** your partner what it means.
During the Reading	Get the Gist	What do we know so far? What is the main idea? What are the important facts?
After the Reading	Wrap Up	What did we learn?

Adapted from Klinger, J. K., & Vaughn, S. Using collaborative strategic reading. *TEACHING Exceptional Children, 30*(6), 32–37. Copyright 1998 by The Council for Exceptional Children. Reprinted with permission.

After the Reading: Wrap Up. Once the group has finished with the reading, they revisit the predictions made before the piece to check for accuracy. They also generate questions and answers that focus on the main ideas and important facts.

Students are assigned roles for CSR so that the discussion will flow more smoothly (Klinger & Vaughn, 1998). These roles include the following:

- *Leader*—makes sure the strategies are used and seeks help from the teacher when needed
- *Clunk expert*—leads discussion on how to figure out unknown words or concepts
- *Announcer*—makes sure everyone has a chance to participate
- *Reporter*—shares the group's work
- *Timer*—monitors the time so the group can complete the task

A student task sheet for CSR can be viewed in Figure 2.5 (on page 31). These task sheets aid students in performing their roles.

Reciprocal Teaching

Reciprocal teaching is used in student-directed groups of four to jointly understand a common piece of text (Palincsar & Brown, 1986). The text is segmented into smaller chunks, allowing students to check their understanding periodically throughout the reading. This is accomplished by using a structured discussion format, which is performed several times until the piece is complete. The teacher may create the stopping points for discussion in advance, or the group may decide how best to break up the text. At each stopping point, students use four kinds of comprehension strategies to understand the text:

- *Questioning* the text by asking literal and inferential questions of one another
- *Clarifying* understanding through discussion of how a confusing point might be cleared up (for example, using a dictionary, checking the glossary, asking the teacher)
- *Summarizing* the main ideas of the passage
- *Predicting* what the author will discuss next, based on what is known so far

Like CSR, the strength of this approach is in the consolidation and use of sound comprehension practices during the reading process. These four steps do not need to be performed in a fixed order, but rather can be discussed in the order the group decides.

Research on Reciprocal Teaching. The use of this instructional strategy is widespread in schools; therefore a considerable number of studies have been conducted on its effects. It has been found to be motivating for students who are considered to be at risk (Carter, 1997). Rosenshine and Meister (1994) reviewed 16 separate studies on reciprocal teaching and found the strategy to be effective in a wide range of classroom settings. In particular, they noted that reciprocal teaching was found to positively impact standardized testing results on reading comprehension.

Introducing Reciprocal Teaching. Like the other peer partner reading strategies, the techniques used in reciprocal teaching must first be taught, so that students are comfortable using them in collaborative groups. Each role is modeled until all roles have been introduced. We advise practicing each role separately until students are ready to use all the strategies together in a group meeting. This means that a series of lessons are presented in which everyone in the group uses prediction, followed by a series on summarizing, and so forth.

Role Sheets.   Many teachers use role sheets in the beginning to support student dialogue within the group. Because the text is not read in advance, but rather is chunked, read, and discussed in the same sitting, these question stems can be useful when group members are at a loss as to what to say next. These role sheets can be seen in Figure 2.6.

Think-pair-share, learning centers, jigsaw, CSR, and reciprocal teaching constitute a continuum of peer learning techniques for reading and understanding informational texts. Beginning in kindergarten with think-pair-share and learning centers, young children learn the skills of collaborative learning as they exchange ideas and share work with one another. By first grade, students can read and discuss expository readings on a shared topic. This is a valuable way for emergent readers to understand that to be well informed about a topic, it is likely that more than one book will be needed. Second-grade students are developing their oral language skills and can begin CSR. This is an excellent format for teaching readers about the roles in a group process. CSR also prepares them for reciprocal teaching in third grade and beyond. If you think your students are not ready for reciprocal teaching, consider introducing jigsaw and CSR as preparation. Figure 2.7 describes the continuum of peer learning strategies students can use in elementary school.

Learners like Adrianna, Rangina, and Charles possess a variety of strengths and areas of need. Using peer learning and grouping arrangements provides each of them with opportunities to refine their skills as they learn to read for information. At the same time, they are able to provide valuable assistance to one another. Each time we use these grouping techniques, we are reminded that there not just one teacher in the classroom—there are 25. Our job as teachers is to figure out how to use those resources to everyone's advantage.

School-Wide Conversations That Promote Learning

The conversations that occur when students have many opportunities to read together for information lead to improved understanding of those texts. Likewise, when educators engage in conversations about their practice, students profit. We advocate a school-wide approach to reading for information, accompanied by responsive professional development to meet the changing needs of teachers. We also know that parents are an important resource as students read for information.

Figure 2.8 contains an informational sheet that teachers can provide parents to engage them as partners in education.

Figure 2.6   Role sheet for reciprocal teaching.

Prediction

We look and listen for clues that will tell us what may happen next or what we will learn from the text. Good predictions are based on . . .
* what we already know
* what we understand from the text
* what pictures, charts, or graphs tell us

I think . . .
I predict . . .
I bet . . .
I wonder . . .

Question

We test ourselves about what we just read by asking ourselves questions. We see if we really understand and can identify what is important. We ask different kinds of questions:
* Factual questions:
    Who, what, when, where?
* Interpretive questions:
    How, why?
* Beyond the text questions:
    I wonder if . . .
    I'm curious about . . .

Clarify

We clear up confusion and find the meaning of unfamiliar words, sentences, ideas, or concepts.

This is confusing to me . . .
    I need to reread, slow down, look at the graphs or illustrations, or break the word apart.
When I began reading this, I thought . . .
Then, when I read this part, I realized . . .
It didn't make sense until I . . .

Summarize

We restate the main ideas, events, or points.
A good summary includes . . .
* key people, items, or places
* key words and synonyms
* key ideas and concepts

The main point is . . .
If I put the ideas together, I now understand that . . .
The most important thing I read was . . .

Source: Fisher, D., & Frey, N. (2003). *Improving adolescent literacy: Strategies at work,* 1st Edition, © 2004, pp. 72, 73, 109, 110, 125, 156, 170. Used by permission of Pearson Education, Inc., Upper Saddle River, NJ.

Figure 2.7 A grade-level continuum of collaborative reading techniques.

	Think-Pair-Share	Learning Centers	Jigsaw	Collaborative Strategic Reading	Reciprocal Teaching
K	📖	📖			
1	📖	📖	📖		
2	📖	📖	📖	📖	
3	📖	📖	📖	📖	📖
4	📖	📖	📖	📖	📖
5	📖	📖	📖	📖	📖

Does a School–wide Approach Matter?

The evidence is mounting. A study by Fisher (2001) suggests that a school-wide focus on literacy instruction could impact school-wide achievement. In fact, this book grew out of the desire of teachers to share their successes in teaching students to read for information.

Further evidence can be found in Reeves' (2000) study of highly effective schools. Schools described as 90/90/90 (90% receive free/reduced lunch, 90% are ethnic minorities, and 90% are at or above mastery level on standardized achievement tests) were analyzed for common factors. The results are encouraging for schools everywhere. Shared characteristics included a school-wide focus on achievement, agreed-upon curriculum choices, and an emphasis on writing (Reeves, 2000). It is possible that many schools that have not achieved the same levels of success as the 90/90/90 schools share these same characteristics. However, we believe that the key to success lies in another part of the report. All of these high-achieving schools shared another important element—they stick with their plans. These schools "are not lurching from one fad to another . . . they are consistent" (p. 193).

Students appreciate this level of consistency as well. Keep this in mind as you introduce literacy strategies to your classroom.

Figure 2.8 Eight tips to improve reading.

8 Tips to Improve Reading

No matter where your child is on the journey to becoming a reader, use the following tips to help point the way.

1. Talk to your child's teacher about reading instruction. Ask what students are learning in class and how you can support that learning at home. The teacher may have suggestions for good books, reading games, and activities. Be sure to ask whether your child is participating or is directed to other activities during reading time. In order to learn to read, children with disabilities (like all children) must receive reading instruction. If your child struggles with reading, ask what supports might help your student.

2. Read in front of your child. Studies have shown that children who often see family members read become better readers themselves. Try reading letters, newspapers, magazines, email messages, books, recipes, or even the comics. When reading, share something with your child that you liked. Let your child see that you think reading is important and fun.

3. Read to your child. All children benefit from listening to a parent reading out loud. Not only is it a great bonding activity, but it teaches concepts about letter shapes and sounds, words, grammar, books, and print. Keep it fun by using different voices for different characters. Capture your child's attention with a variety of books including tales that are funny, suspenseful, or poetic.

4. Encourage your child to read to you. Even when your child is too young to read, he or she can pretend to read by telling you what is happening in the pictures. Your child may memorize favorite books or phrases and can "read" those to you. Let your child read a character's name or a simple word every time you point to it. As your child becomes a better reader, take turns reading different parts or every other page. Try poetry written for two voices. Listening to your child read to you builds your child's confidence and desire to read.

5. Talk to your child about reading. Talking about books helps children build comprehension skills (the ability to understand what they've read). When reading a book together, have your child tell you about their favorite character or ask what they think is going to happen next. Tell them what you liked about a story, or how it reminds you of something in your own life. You can also practice this skill by talking about TV programs.

6. Find the best books for your child. Keep your child's age, interests, and experiences in mind when choosing books (for example, a love of soccer, a new pet, or a trip to Grandma's). If your child has a favorite TV character or movie, look for a book based on that. Reluctant readers can often be drawn in with a book of jokes or even a comic book. Ask a librarian for book ideas. To find resources (including accessible books) for children with all types of disabilities, go to:
http://www.nichcy.org/resources/literacy2.asp#disability

Figure 2.8   (continued)

7. Build a library of favorite books. Children benefit from reading and re-reading books. Having a library of your own is important, but it does not need to be expensive. Go to used bookstores, garage sales, and thrift shops. Try swapping books with family or friends. Auctions and booksellers on the Internet often have bargains on children's books.

8. Try games and activities that support reading. Games and activities make reading fun. Try creating your own alphabet book . . . cut pictures out of catalogs, newspapers, and magazines and make a page with items for each letter of the alphabet. When riding in the car, look for things that start with the letter "S." Try rhyming games. Look for computer reading games online or in your library. Get new ideas by searching for "reading games" on the Internet.

Finally, enjoy the reading journey with your child. As a parent, you are your child's first teacher and you can set the course for success.

Source: PEAK Parent Center. (2005, spring) 8 tips to improve reading. See www.peakparent.org. Used with permission.

Teaching Strategies That Are Transportable and Transparent

The strategies outlined in this book are designed to fit easily into the school day. While we identify them as "literacy strategies," most could really be called "content-area instructional approaches." The strategies in this book have a research base and a practical foundation for ensuring that students understand the content that they are being taught. Your students, like Adrianna, Rangina, and Charles, need guidance through informational texts, not simply an assignment to "read pages 34 to 46 for homework tonight." We like to think of these literacy strategies as being transportable across content areas. Each is elastic enough to be applied to a variety of learning situations.

> For example, a strategy is transportable when a student uses vocabulary skills learned during a social studies lesson about the centennial of the United States to determine what centimeter means in mathematics.

Another important goal of a school-wide approach to instruction is that over time these strategies become transparent to learners. As teachers, we are thrilled when we hear students murmur in recognition when we speak of graphic organizers or anticipation guides. It tells us that our colleagues have done a great job in creating a common vocabulary across the grade levels. It also means that when we collectively teach these strategies, we end up spending less time mired in the mechanics of getting the lesson under way. Setting up a graphic organizer becomes an instructional routine that takes seconds, rather than half the morning. In other words, it allows us to use an instructional shorthand that gives us more time to actually teach the content. Ultimately, we hope that these strategies become transparent in our students' learning lives as they become aware of how they learn.

We concur with this approach and see the evidence in our own school experiences. We believe that it takes time and collegial conversations to

> Metacognition is the ability to understand and act upon one's own learning and thinking.

Current news about what teachers and administrators around the nation are doing is published weekly in Education Week at www.edweek.org.

develop a shared vocabulary of teaching and learning. These conversations spring from a habit of reflective teaching. In other words, it is not a program, a set of books, or a box of materials that creates a high-achieving school. It is always teachers who matter, and what they do that matters most.

What Do We Mean by Reflective Teaching?

When we use the term reflective teaching, we are speaking of the habits of mind of effective educators who practice a recursive cycle of self-questioning and self-assessment to improve teaching and learning. Reflective teachers take the time to stand back from the fray and ask

- How effective was I today?
- What can I learn about my teaching by looking at today's lesson?
- How can I improve my teaching?

Teaching is both an art and a science, and each of these perspectives requires that we take a step back from what we have been doing to analyze the efficacy of our practice. At best, teaching is inexact because the context keeps changing—student needs never remain static but always demand shifts in how we create meaningful learning opportunities for them. Therefore, it is impossible to replicate a lesson exactly. You need only look to your own variation in teaching the same lesson content in two different school years. As a reflective teacher, you make adjustments and improvements to suit the needs of your students. We often hear teachers remark that they taught a small group lesson more effectively for the second group. This is reflective teaching in action, because these teachers are self-questioning and self-assessing. This not only applies across lessons, but across entire years as well. We believe that a strong repertoire of strategies for your instructional toolkit can help you arrive at solutions to these reflective questions.

Two organizations committed to the teaching profession are the American Federation of Teachers at www.aft.org and the National Education Association at www.nea.org.

Conclusion and a Professional Invitation

The point is a simple one, but often overlooked in the busy world of a teacher: to enjoy and flourish in your job, you can never stop learning.

It is ironic that those of us in the business of learning may forget the importance of our own learning. We may be caught up in the delivery of information and the orchestration of the classroom, with little time left to engage in our own learning. After all, the teacher is the oldest in the room and by tradition's unspoken and timeless decree, the one who is supposed to know what he or she is doing.

Figure 2.9   Professional organizations for teachers.

American Alliance for Health, Physical Education, Recreation and Dance
1900 Association Drive
Reston, VA 20191-9527
www.aahperd.org

Association for Supervision and Curriculum Development
1703 North Beauregard Street
Alexandria, VA 22311-1714
www.ascd.org

International Reading Association
800 Barksdale Rd.
PO Box 8139
Newark, DE 19714-8139
www.reading.org

National Art Education Association
1916 Association Drive
Reston, VA 20191-1590
www.naea-reston.org

National Association for Bilingual Education
1030 15th Street NW, Suite 470
Washington, DC 20005-1503
www.nabe.org

National Association for Music Education
1806 Robert Fulton Drive
Reston, VA 20191
www.menc.org

National Council for the Social Studies
8555 16th, Suite 500
Silver Spring, MD 20910
www.ncss.org

National Council of Teachers of English
111 W. Kenyon Road
Urbana, IL 61801-1096
www.ncte.org

National Council of Teachers of Mathematics
1906 Association Drive
Reston, VA 20191-1502
www.nctm.org

National Science Teachers Association
PO Box 90214
Washington, DC 20090-0214
www.nsta.org

PEAK Parent Center–Education of students with disabilities
611 North Weber, Suite 200
Colorado Springs, CO 80903
www.peakparent.org

TASH–Education of students with disabilities
29 W. Susquehanna Blvd., Suite 210
Baltimore, MD 21204
www.tash.org

We recognize that other resources are essential, too. For that reason, we have included a list of professional organizations, web sites, and publications for you to access in your efforts to refine your practice. They are listed in Figure 2.9.

The remainder of this book focuses on instructional strategies and planning tools that you will find useful in ensuring that your students can read for information. Specific instructional strategies are highlighted in different grade levels and in different content areas. That does not mean, however, that the strategy would not work in another content area or grade level. For example, word sorts are highlighted in a first-grade class while studying science, but word sorts can be used to teach vocabulary in other grades and with other content areas. This holds true for all of the major strategy chapters—the examples in this book are not tied to a specific content area or grade level.

We provide examples across the content areas and grade levels for the following strategies:

Before Reading

- anticipatory activities (Chapter 3)
- vocabulary instruction (Chapter 4)
- read alouds and shared reading (Chapter 5)

During Reading

- questioning (Chapter 6)
- graphic organizers (Chapter 7)
- notetaking and note making (Chapter 8)

After Reading

- writing to learn (Chapter 9)
- assessing student learning (Chapter 10)

We provide information about assessing students on their progress in learning to read for information as part of the "after reading" section. We also address how teachers prepare students for standardized tests. In particular, we will discuss how the literacy practices profiled in this book better prepare students for such tests.

We invite you then to consider the flexibility and applicability of these research-based literacy strategies in a variety of content areas. We also urge you to consider the experiences of Adrianna, Rangina, and Charles. Every day students like them traverse the landscape of elementary schools in the United States, bringing unique perspectives to the classroom. Their presence in your classroom will inspire you to apply these strategies in ways we have never considered—because you, the teacher, matter most.

References

Allington, R. L., & Johnston, P. H. (2000). *What do we know about effective fourth-grade teachers and their classrooms?* (Report Series 13010). Albany, NY: National Research Center on English Learning and Achievement.

Aronson, E. (1978). *The jigsaw classroom.* Beverly Hills, CA: Sage.

Bloome, D., & Egan-Robertson, A. (1993). The social construction of intertextuality in classroom reading and writing lessons. *Reading Research Quarterly, 28,* 305–333.

Brown, A. L., & Day, J. D. (1983). Macrorules for summarizing texts: The development of expertise. *Journal of Verbal Learning and Verbal Behavior, 22,* 1–14.

Calweti, G. (Ed.). (2004). *Handbook of research on improving student achievement* (3rd ed.). Arlington, VA: Educational Research Service.

Carter, C. J. (1997). Why reciprocal teaching? *Educational Leadership, 54*(6), 64–68.

Darling-Hammond, L. (1999). Target time toward teachers. *Journal of Staff Development, 20*(2), 31–36.

Fisher, D. (2001). We're moving on up: Creating a schoolwide literacy effort in an urban high school. *Journal of Adolescent and Adult Literacy, 45,* 92–101.

Frey, N., & Fisher, D. (2006). *Language arts workshop: Purposeful reading and writing instruction.* Upper Saddle River, NJ: Merrill Prentice Hall.

Hartman, D. K., & Allison, J. (1996). Promoting inquiry-oriented discussions using multiple texts. In L. B. Gambrell & J. F. Almasi (Eds.), *Lively discussions! Fostering engaged readings* (pp. 106–133). Newark, DE: International Reading Association.

Joyce, B. R., Showers, B. (1995). *Student achievement through staff development: Fundamentals of school renewal* (2nd ed.). New York: Longman.

Klinger, J. K., & Vaughn, S. (1998). Using collaborative strategic reading. *TEACHING Exceptional Children, 30*(6), 32–37.

Klinger, J. K., Vaughn, S., & Schumm, J. S. (1998). Collaborative strategic reading during social studies in heterogeneous fourth-grade classrooms. *Elementary School Journal, 99,* 3–20.

Lapp, D., Fisher, D., & Flood, J. (1999). Does it matter how you're grouped for instruction? Yes! Flexible grouping patterns promote student learning. *The California Reader, 33*(1), 28–32.

Lapp, D., Flood, J., & Goss, K. (2000). Desks don't move—students do: In effective classroom environments. *The Reading Teacher, 54,* 31–36.

Lyman, F. T. (1981). The responsive classroom discussion: The inclusion of all students. In A. Anderson (Ed.), *Mainstreaming digest* (pp. 109–113). College Park: University of Maryland Press.

Marzano, R. J., Pickering, D. J., & Pollock, J. E. (2001). *Classroom instruction that works: Research-based practices for increasing student achievement.* Beauregard, VA: Association for Supervision and Curriculum Development.

Oakes, J. (1985). *Keeping track: How schools structure inequality.* New Haven: Yale University Press.

Oakes, J., & Wells, A. S. (1998). Detracking for high student achievement. *Educational Leadership, 55*(6), 38–41.

Opitz, M. F. (1999). *Learning centers.* New York: Scholastic.

Palincsar, A. S., & Brown, A. L. (1986). Interactive teaching to promote independent learning from text. *The Reading Teacher, 39,* 771–777.

Reeves, D. B. (2000). *Accountability in action: A blueprint for learning organizations.* Denver, CO: Advanced Learning.

Resnick, L. (1995). From aptitude to effort: A new foundation for our schools. *Daedalus, 124*(4), 55–62.

Rosenshine, B., & Meister, C. (1994). Reciprocal teaching: A review of the research. *Review of Educational Research, 64,* 479–530.

Vygotsky, L. S.(1978). *Mind in society: The development of higher psychological processes* (M. Cole, V. John-Steiner, S. Scribner, & E. Souberman, Trans.). Cambridge, MA: Harvard University.

Before Reading Activities

Nancy Frey

Douglas Fisher

Kelly Moore

Chapter 3

Attention Getters:

Using Anticipatory Activities to Build Background Knowledge

A small kindergartner stands on his tiptoes, carefully peering through the blinds covering the large window. A voice calls out from across the room, "Do you need the Weather Glasses?" asks Mr. Giaquinto. "Will that help you see what is happening outside?"

Quickly, Mr. G. assists the child with a very special pair of pink and black glasses created especially for viewing the weather outside. Although the glasses have no lenses, the children in Tom Giaquinto's *kindergarten class use them as part of their daily weather report. Each day, the Weather Reporter dons the Weather Glasses to view the world of weather outside the classroom.*

Now comes their favorite part. After the child reports the current weather status, Mr. G. pulls his pants up to his chest, puts on the glasses, and assumes the personality of a weather nerd. The students view the weather symbols for the chart and vote on the correct choice. The information is then graphed on the daily weather chart. After the class has counted how many days they have experienced that type of weather, the children stand up and everyone sings, "Shake, shake, shake! Shake, shake, shake! Shake your booty! Shake your booty!" Mr. G., still sporting the Weather Glasses and hiked-up pants, may be having the most fun of all.

One of the most influential contributions to twentieth century educational theory was the development of the field of cognitive science. Before the advent of cognitive studies, the prevailing learning theory was behaviorism, which concentrated on the role of an outside stimulus as a mechanism for learning. The publication of *A Study of Thinking* (Bruner, Goodnow, & Austin, 1956) led the way for exploration of what happens inside the minds of learners and how they organize and use information. Over the course of the next 50 years, scientists, psychologists, and educators examined memory, emotion, schema, and experience as essential components of learning. In fact, the influence of cognitive science is so profound, that it now may be difficult to conceptualize how the process of learning was perceived in the first half of the 20th century. This book, for instance, is replete with learning approaches that reflect our profession's roots in cognitive science—scaffolding, metacognition, accessing background knowledge, and transfer of learning—to name a few.

> Anticipatory activities build background and create interest for students to read for information.

Types Of Anticipatory Activities

One aspect of learning theory that has received a great deal of attention is (please pardon us) "attention." Anyone who has ever taught a group of people can appreciate the importance of attention as a factor in learning. After all, if students aren't paying attention, how can they process new information?

When we speak of attention, we are not referring to behavior management, but rather to practices that elicit curiosity, provoke questions, and evoke recall of newly learned information. In addition, attention means activating students' background knowledge about the topic. This is really the very beginning of the learning process, although it is not bound in time to the beginning of a course, class, or lesson. Good and

Brophy (2002) remind us that effective teachers create memorable events throughout their lessons to capture student attention, much like the teacher in the opening vignette for this chapter. It is essential to note that gaining attention through anticipatory activities is not intended to provide entertainment for students, but rather to scaffold learning so that the responsibility for learning shifts to the student. A primary goal of classroom instruction is to move from teacher-directed instruction to student-centered learning. Anticipatory activities can ground new learning in meaning-based inquiry, because the student's attention is gained through an event that is connected to the purpose for studying the topic.

> What helps you remember? Do you remember more when your emotions are involved?

These memorable events may also use drama, humor, movement, or emotion to make an impression on learning. Eggen and Kauchak (2001) suggest four instructional strategies for gaining student attention:

1. demonstrations
2. discrepant events
3. visual displays
4. thought-provoking questions (p. 271)

We will discuss each of these in detail and then take a look inside classrooms to see how teachers across the content areas are using these "attention-getters" to stimulate curiosity, promote learning, and encourage students to want to read for more information.

Demonstrations

Classroom demonstrations are typically performed to display a theory, concept, or phenomenon. A demonstration of gravity is likely to involve dropping objects from a height; a demonstration of fractions and decimals might include several apples sliced into equal parts. The use of demonstrations is critical in the field of mathematics (Lee, 2000) and is associated with higher levels of learning in science (Beasley, 1982). They have been found to be effective for demonstrating scientific concepts such as air pressure (Shepardson, Moje, & Kennard-McClelland, 1994) and groundwater pollution (Schipper, Schipper, & Hornsby, 1993) to elementary students.

Demonstrations have become easier with the increased availability of technology in the classroom (Brooks & Brooks, 1996). We particularly like web sites portraying scientific concepts that could not otherwise be easily replicated in the classroom. For instance, students can manipulate variables such as energy and wind speed to watch a hurricane being formed (whyfiles.LARC.NASA.Gov/kids/problem-board/problems/weather/huricanebasics.swf). Demonstrations and Animations for Teaching

Astronomy (DATA) is a collection of Java applets and Flash animations. It is being developed at the Astronomy Department at the University of Illinois (http://www.astro.uiuc.edu/projects/data/MoonPhases/). These and many other web sites offer interesting ways for teachers to display a variety of science concepts. Using demonstrations to illustrate and augment lecture and readings is particularly effective for students with disabilities (Janney & Snell, 2000) and for English language learners because it is enhanced by physical and kinesthetic interaction.

> An applet is a small program automatically downloaded from the Internet.

Guest Speakers. Many educators acknowledge the role of experience in learning (Dewey, 1938, 1963). The transformative nature of experiences can assist learners in connecting knowledge to its application and variation in the larger world. Experiences can also provoke reflection as students begin to understand that knowledge is not fixed, but is constantly tested by new experiences (Kolb, 1984). This theory, called experiential learning, has its roots in the work of John Dewey and has been extended by the brain-based research of the past decade. Museum-based education is one example of experiential learning at the elementary level (Pumpian, Fisher, & Wachowiak, 2006). Teachers can also bring tenets of experiential learning into the classroom by introducing students to community members who apply the topics of study to their own work. This can be a unique form of demonstration, and can serve as an interesting means of introducing a course of study. When the experiences offered through guest speakers are introduced to the classroom, students can clarify their understanding through the eyes of another.

The use of guest speakers in social studies courses is very popular, perhaps because the study of the past and present often converge in the living examples of members of the communities. This is particularly true of older guests who can share their experiences about growing up decades earlier. Students studying world events can benefit from meeting a citizen of another country (Giannangelo & Bolding, 1998). Guest speakers who are experts on a topic, such as an entomologist who visited a classroom engaged in the study of insects (Fay, 2000), can also contribute to understanding by students.

Demonstrations should be used judiciously to prevent confusion. In particular, a demonstration is likely to fail if it is not grounded in the theoretical framework (Roth, McRobbie, & Lucas, 1997). In other words, an interesting demonstration does not replace the need for deep exploration of concepts. Also, don't overlook the importance of telling students that the demonstration is important to remember, and why. These simple statements of emphasis have been shown to be effective when coupled with demonstrations (Eggen & Kauchak, 2001; Larsen, 1991).

Discrepant Events

Discrepant events are demonstrations that involve a surprising or startling occurrence designed to command the students' attention. A performance may be staged—for instance, another teacher may be recruited to rush into the classroom with a copy of a telegram from 1869 Promontory Point, Utah, announcing the placement of the golden spike, thereby linking the Intercontinental Railroad. Hurst (2001) suggests that attention-grabbing events are a key element to content-area lesson planning, along with mini-lessons and comprehension instruction. She and others (e.g., Anderson & Pearson, 1984; Smith, 1998) remind us that attention is directly related to schema, the knowledge structure used to comprehend. Discrepant events can assist students in organizing new information, integrating it with prior knowledge, and increasing their ability to retrieve it later (Landauer, 1975).

Discrepant events can also expose students' misunderstandings. For example, young children may believe that a sweater has the capacity to warm, rather than to reduce heat loss. Older students often believe that the multiplication of fractions yields a larger number, because they have learned that multiplying increases the result. A lesson that includes a discrepant event can generate questions in the minds of learners, leaving them prepared for instruction. For example, the naïve theory of the warm sweater can be corrected by taking a temperature reading of the article of clothing.

Discrepant events also access a powerful aid to memory—emotional connection. As humans, we have a tendency to remember episodes connected to our emotional memories, such as a favorite celebration or a first kiss. The associations may be negative as well—most readers will recall where they were when they found out about the terrorist attack on the United States in 2001. While discrepant events in the classroom are unlikely to be connected to such intense emotions as these, it is important to recognize that they tap into the same neural pathways (Sylwester, 1995). Music, art, and dramatic play can provide a means for accessing students' emotional memory and can increase their ability to retrieve the information at a later time (McDonald & Fisher, 2006). Jorgensen (1998) calls these events "grabbers" because they command student attention and capture the imagination.

Visual Displays

Because visual displays such as graphic organizers are more thoroughly presented in Chapter 7, we will confine our discussion to what Hyerle refers to as "visual tools for constructing knowledge" (1996, p. 1). The rise of information technology in the last quarter of the twentieth century has fundamentally changed the way information is generated and shared.

> Many useful lesson plans are available at teachers.net/lessons.

> Integrated arts allows teachers to use visual and performing arts to teach content.

These same technologies—computers, CD-ROMs, web-based resources, and digital cameras, to name a few—are becoming an increasingly common means for classrooms to access information. Unlike earlier classroom technologies like televisions and video recorders, these newer advances are interactive and require the active participation of the learner.

No longer is visually presented information viewed as passive, to be absorbed by the learner. Rather, it is seen as a generative process in which the learner influences and changes the information. Exposure to these information technologies has influenced how our students learn as well. Young learners today are far more accustomed to processing multiple visual images in seconds (Jensen, 1998). If you doubt this, compare the editing style of a 1950s-era television show with a recent music video. The number of camera and scene changes is likely to be very different, suggesting that today's viewers can process a great deal of information, even during very rapid image changes.

WebQuests. WebQuests are another technology tool for gaining attention and supporting long-term learning (Dodge, 1995). A WebQuest is "an inquiry-oriented activity in which most or all of the information used by learners is drawn from the Web" (http://edweb.sdsu.edu/news/webeye) and is used to guide students in an investigation of a topic. The teacher plans the WebQuest in advance, and students are typically given a series of questions to guide their search. Specific web sites may be identified and bookmarked by the teacher to provide a frame for the learners to follow, much like lily pads strung across a pond. The good news is that you don't have to create your own WebQuest (although you may choose to do so later). Topics as varied as rain forests, pilgrim life, the food pyramid, and author studies are only a click away.

Mind Mapping. A favorite visual display is mind mapping (Buzan, 1979). Mind mapping is described by some as a method of notetaking; however, it is also a technique for learners to develop an organizational structure, or web. Typically, mind mapping relies on the use of color and simple line drawings and graphics to represent the concepts and connections associated with a topic. (A computer application called Kidspiration® makes it easy for elementary students to create mind maps and other webs electronically.) The mind maps are prepared in advance for display on an overhead. As the teacher introduces a new topic, the mind map provides a visual representation of the connections between and among concepts. Like semantic webs, they are typically organized around a word or phrase that represents the central idea. Pictures and words are connected by a series of lines representing linkages. The word *map* is important here, because this visual tool is meant to serve as a guide to help students negotiate their way around a topic.

Many museums post items from their collection on the Internet. Teachers can display these images in their classrooms using a video projector. The Louvre Museum Web Site is located at www.louvre.fr and the Metropolitan Museum of Art collection can be found at www.metmuseum.org.

The WebQuest site has hundreds of lesson plans and can be found at webquest.sdsu.edu.

If you are interested in learning more about mind–mapping techniques, take a look at Mapping Inner Space by Nancy Margulies (1991).

Figure 3.1   K–W–L chart.

What Do We Know?	What Do We Want to Know?	What Have We Learned?

Thought–Provoking Questions

Like mind mapping and WebQuests, thought-provoking questions are intended to assist students in organizing new information. Like discrepant events, they are meant to appeal to the emotional channels of learning. The use of a provocative question, particularly one that defies a simple answer, has been recognized as a method for promoting interest and sustaining learning by inviting students to formulate an understanding of the material (Brandt, 1992; Muncey, Payne, & White, 1999). These questions may be of a general investigatory nature, as in the K-W-L technique (Ogle, 1986). K-W-L stands for "What do I *know?* What do I *want* to know? What have I *learned?*" This organizer mirrors the process of scientific inquiry inherent in any investigation. Typically, a teacher will arrange these questions into three columns and then use them to prompt discussion about the new topic of study. Student responses are recorded and then become the guide for subsequent study. A K-W-L chart is featured in Figure 3.1.

This technique has been modified in a number of ways, including K-W-L-Plus (Carr & Ogle, 1987), which adds summarization and K-W-L-H (Wills, 1995), which adds "*How* do I know?" to focus on sources of evidence. The recursive nature of inquiry is emphasized through K-W-L-Q (Schmidt, 1999) when a fourth column, for further questions, is added at the end of the unit of study.

Thought-Provoking Questions Through Quick Writes. We refer to brief, timed writing activities intended to activate background knowledge and personal experience as quick writes. Students seem to like the term be-cause it connotes an event that is limited in duration, and teachers appear to honor the spirit of this anticipatory activity by indeed keeping it brief. We like the key contrasts that Daniels and Bizar (1998) offer between this type of writing event and other process pieces:

More information on the use of writing will be presented in Chapter 9.

- spontaneous vs. planned
- short vs. lengthy
- exploratory vs. authoritative
- expressive vs. transactional
- informal vs. formal
- personal vs. audience-centered
- unedited vs. polished
- ungraded vs. graded (p. 114)

Quick writes are frequently used when introducing a new reading to tap into prior knowledge and reader-related experiences, as well as to ini-tiate a reading/writing connection. In addition, they can be an excellent source of assessment information to gain insight into what students know and need to learn.

Quick Writes and Found Poems in Fifth Grade

Mr. Morrison wants his fifth-grade students to appreciate how difficult life could be for early settlers of the American West. He begins by reading aloud a short journal entry by an 11-year-old in 1851, describing her fam-ily's first "home" after arriving in the Colorado territory. As he reads, the students learn of the pioneer family's life in a cave. The writer describes life in the cave, including how the family ate, slept, and kept warm. After finishing, Mr. Morrison asks students to respond in the form of a quick write about what they may be feeling. In particular, he encourages them to make any personal connections they may see and to consider questions that come to mind. Students are familiar with this kind of writing and know that they have about 10 minutes to write as much as they can, as well as they can, about the topic. They also know that this piece is not going to be graded per se by the teacher but used as a springboard for later discussion.

Mr. Morrison may collect the quick writes to assess what knowledge and questions the students have about the topic being studied.

Harrison wrote the following after hearing the passage read aloud:

A cave? Wow! That must be cold. Sometimes it gets cold in my house but I wonder what it's like in a dark cave. It doesn't seem like a feather

Figure 3.2   Student chart for writer's block.

> **Room 28's Ideas for Beating Writer's Block**
>
> How does it make you feel?
> Why do you think the author wrote this?
> What does it remind you of?
> Describe the setting. Does it remind you
>   of anything in your community?
> Make a list of adjectives you remember
>   from the text.

mattress would be very comfortable. I have slept on the floor at my cousin's house and that seems like what it might be like to sleep on feathers. I wonder if anyone today still lives in a cave. Maybe it's like being homeless. That makes me worry.

For some students, putting ideas to words is difficult, so Mr. Morrison walks around the room having brief conversations with the students. The teacher can be overheard asking students, "How do you think it felt in the cave?" and "What chores do you think the children had to do? Are they like anything you are asked to do in your home?" He pauses at Ruben's desk because the boy appears to be stuck. Mr. Morrison and Ruben refer to a chart the class made several months ago containing ideas for overcoming writer's block. Some of the ideas on this chart can be found in Figure 3.2.

Mr. Morrison is able to get a good sense of what the students "bring to the table" in terms of the topic being studied. He knows how many students have a lot of prior knowledge about Colonial America and who has little knowledge about the life and times from long ago. He also knows if any personal connections have been made and whether he can rely on these students to make this topic come alive in today's world. Quick writes inform Mr. Morrison of what needs to happen in the coming unit. He asks himself the following questions:

- Who made a personal connection?
- Who was unable to get the gist of the passage?
- Who is struggling to find the words to match his voice?
- Who seems to know enough to research more about this topic independently?

He also knows that he has piqued his students' curiosity through the quick write. He has "hooked" many of his students by choosing an interesting reading passage and is now ready to begin the second phase of this anticipatory activity—Found Poems.

Mr. Morrison asks the students to reread their quick write and to underline phrases or adjectives that stand out to create a poem they have "found" in their writing. These fifth-grade students have written found poems before and know about the rhythm and feeling they are capable of evoking from their own writing. The following found poem is what Harrison created from his quick write.

A cave.
Cold.
Dark.
A feather mattress.
Comfortable?
I have slept on my cousin's floor.
A cave.
Cold.
Maybe like being homeless.

Mr. Morrison knows that by writing quick writes and turning them into found poems he is creating a mood in the classroom and a curiosity among his students. He has also learned more about his students and what they already know about the topic. He can tell what interests his students and knows how to build upon the lesson from the responses that have been shared. Just as these two anticipatory activities are intended to hook students into future learning, they are also rich sources of assessment information. Today's quick writes and found poems can and should guide tomorrow's lessons.

Anticipation Guides. An anticipation guide is a teacher-prepared list of statements that connects to a passage of text. The purpose is to activate prior knowledge, encourage predictions, and stimulate curiosity about a topic (Head & Readence, 1986). These guides are usually constructed for use with informational texts containing information that may be new or misunderstood by students. These guides are useful for promoting class discussion as well, because they can spark debate and foster the inevitable need to consult other sources of information. An example of a teacher-created anticipation guide for third-grade students on sharks can be located in Figure 3.3.

Perhaps the most challenging part of developing an anticipation guide is identifying a provocative text that will motivate your students to discuss, debate, disagree, and confront their own misconceptions. Once that is done, the steps to creating a guide are fairly simple (Head & Readence, 1986):

Step 1:   Identify the major concepts in the reading. What are the main ideas in the passage? Keep it to two or three so the guide won't be too long.

Step 2:   Consider your students' prior knowledge. What are they most likely to hold misconceptions about?

Step 3:   Write five or ten statements pertaining to the reading. Don't make them all factual—be sure to create open-ended statements as well. Look again at your major concepts to make sure you are creating statements that relate to larger concepts rather than isolated facts.

Figure 3.3 Anticipation guide for shark reading.

Name:_____ Date:_____

Let's Learn About Sharks!

Directions: Read the sentences and think about what you know about sharks. Write a "+" next to the sentences that are true. Write a "O" next to the sentences that are false. You will get to answer again after we read about sharks.

BEFORE WE READ	SENTENCES	AFTER WE READ
	All sharks eat people.	
	Sharks can grow up to 20,000 teeth in their lifetime.	
	All sharks live in the ocean.	
	Sharks use their sense of smell to hunt.	
	The great white shark sticks its head out of the water to look around.	

Introduce the anticipation guide and ask students to complete it before the reading. Encourage small-group discussions of the statements and invite them to read the text passage to confirm or disconfirm their beliefs. Let them know they can change their answers while they read. Follow up the reading with a class discussion of the items and the broader questions generated by the reading. This is an ideal opportunity to connect this activity with a strategy employed by critical readers—the self-assessment of beliefs and assumptions that may be supported or disputed by a reading. After all, it is this cognitive dissonance that challenges all of us to continually refine what we know.

> The anticipation guide helps students establish a purpose while they read for information.

Essential Questions. Other thought-provoking questions might be more specific to the unit and are likely to encourage an interdisciplinary study. A question like "What is a hero?" is far more interesting than a unit titled "Heroes of the 20th Century" and is likely to promote greater student interest. Jorgensen (1998) refers to these types of questions as "essential questions" because they are so difficult to answer succinctly. An example of an essential question discussed by Jorgensen is "Can you truly be free if you're not treated equally?"—an invitation to examine the U.S. civil rights movement of the 1950s and 1960s. Other essential questions used by educators include:

- What is the human need to celebrate?
- Why do people move to new lands?
- How much is a million?
- What would the world be like if there were no numbers?
- Does an apple a day keep the doctor away?
- Is there life on Mars?

When curriculum units are organized around thought-provoking questions, it provides the teacher with a means for establishing relevance. Learning is enhanced when the relevance of the material is made clear. In fact, information that is not attached to any larger meaning is likely to be quickly forgotten (Jensen, 1998). And remember that relevance is in the mind of the learner, not just the teacher. We know from our own teaching experience that we believe everything we teach is relevant; otherwise we wouldn't bother to talk about it. However, we can also appreciate the importance of relevance from our students' viewpoint. Therefore, it is up to us as instructors to make the relevance explicit. When a curriculum unit is organized around an essential question that is then connected to the assessments and culminating projects of the unit, students can begin to make meaning of the information. After all, when students understand that the information they are reading and writing about will ultimately be used to answer the question, they can appreciate the value of their inquiry.

> Again, this helps students focus on their purpose for reading for information.

We've discussed the importance of gaining and sustaining student attention to promote and extend learning. Now let's take a look at how teachers are using anticipatory activities in their content-area classrooms.

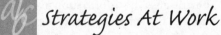 *Strategies At Work*

Visual Displays in Kindergarten Science

Visual displays offer students opportunities to learn complex information through photographs, diagrams, illustrations, and film. Like the other aspects of literacy (reading, writing, speaking, and listening), viewing is acknowledged as an essential component of communication (Flood, Heath, & Lapp, 1997). This is especially vital for emergent readers who cannot use the printed word at a level sufficient for learning detailed information. Visual displays can become an excellent means for communicating information to them. When paired with discussion, it becomes a venue for oral language development as well. Kindergarten teacher Dani Cole often uses visual displays to introduce content to her young learners.

As the students sit on the floor, Ms. Cole tells them she needs some paleontologists to help her out. "What's a 'colopist'?" asks one student?

"It's a big word—pa-le-on-tol-o-gist. Say it with me." The kindergartners solemnly repeat this new word.

"Does anyone know what a paleontologist is?" Ms. Cole inquires. To help them determine what the word means, she shows them large colored photographs of scientists at work. After viewing a few of these visual displays, one student raises his hand and responds, "Someone who finds stuff."

"That's right," Ms. Cole confirms. "A paleontologist digs for things, or tries to find things, that are from the past. Who wants to be a paleontologist this morning?" Twenty hands instantly shoot up in the air. "Great!" says Ms. Cole. "Then it's time for our first dig!"

The class lines up to be escorted outside to the sandbox. Ms. Cole tells all the eager learners that they need to be very careful when digging, so they don't accidentally destroy anything they find. Like the paleontologists in the photographs, these junior scientists work with small shovels. She demonstrates how the tool is used and reminds the students they will be working as partners in the project. "Just like a real paleontologist, you won't know exactly what you're looking for, so search carefully!" she offers. "Okay paleontologists, good luck! Begin your search."

"Look what I found!"

"It's an egg!"

"Ooohhh!"

"Be careful!"

"Cool!" Soon each child is holding a small plastic egg in his or her hands. Ms. Cole instructs the students to carefully walk back to class, so as not to damage what they have just found.

"Let's look at our photos again to see what paleontologists do with the relics they find," says Ms. Cole. They discuss the information available in the photographs and notice that many of the scientists are using paintbrushes to clean the items found on the dig. Ms. Cole explains that when something is buried it gets dirty from being underground for so long. It needs to be cleaned, so Ms. Cole takes a paintbrush and carefully dusts off the egg she found. After she models this, the students use paintbrushes to dust off their newly discovered eggs.

"Now it's time to see what's inside of our eggs," Ms. Cole says. The students carefully break apart the eggs. Student commentary abounds. "Ooooh, it's a dinosaur!"

"A T-rex!!"

"Check this out!"

Inside every egg was a small plastic dinosaur.

"You were all excellent paleontologists! For the next few weeks you're going to be paleontologists. A paleontologist is someone who studies all about dinosaurs." And so begins Ms. Cole's unit on the creatures who roamed the earth millions of years ago.

K–W–L Charts in First-Grade Art

A popular and effective anticipatory activity is K-W-L (Ogle, 1986). Remember that K-W-L (know/want to know/learned) is a method for activating prior knowledge and formulating questions to guide inquiry (see Figure 3.1). Teachers across content-area subjects have confirmed the usefulness and flexibility of this technique for introducing a unit of study. Brown, El-Dinary, Pressley, & Ogan (1995) identify it as one of the recommended instructional strategies for use by elementary educators, especially those working with students who struggle to read.

To introduce an integrated art and literature unit titled, "The Art in Our Picture Books," first-grade teacher Ramon Espinal displays several books illustrated by Eric Carle on the whiteboard ledge. These texts include *The Very Hungry Caterpillar* (Carle, 1994), *Brown Bear, Brown Bear What Do You See?* (Martin & Carle, 1996), *The Very Quiet Cricket* (Carle, 1997), *The Grouchy Ladybug* (Carle, 1999), and *The Very Busy Spider* (Carle, 1995). While these are narrative books, Mr. Espinal wants his students to use them as data to examine art and to read the illustrations in these books for information about the components of art, including the use of color, shading, lines, and perspective.

> Reading several books by the same person is called an Author Study.

Above the ledge is a chart paper divided into three parts labeled K-W-L. Students in this first-grade bilingual classroom are very familiar with this approach and before Mr. Espinal can even begin his lesson, the students are chatting about the texts.

"Oh, I know that book!" says one student, pointing to *The Very Hungry Caterpillar*.

"*Brown Bear, Brown Bear*! That's my favorite!" exclaims Juan Carlos.

"I know that he draws in a lot of books!" Cynthia chimes.

"Yeah, but where's the one with the polar bears?" questions Noemi.

"I wonder why he always writes about animals?" asks Jesus.

> Teachers and researchers continue to revise and update this time-honored instructional strategy.

Mr. Espinal smiles, as he knows many of his students are already hooked into this lesson. However, some of his students are quiet, and a few are not familiar with Eric Carle's books. To engage all his students in this lesson, which will teach the students about collage, the artistic medium used by Mr. Carle, Mr. Espinal wants to find out what students know about this illustrative style and what they want to learn. Later, they will return to this chart to record what they learned about this technique.

As he holds up the books, Mr. Espinal explains to his students that he wants them to think about what they already know about the pictures and illustrations and what they want to know. Mr. Espinal then instructs the students to talk with their partners on the rug before sharing with the whole class. Students are overheard saying:

"The pictures are so colorful."

"How does he do that? Does he use paint? Does he make it with a crayon?"

"He does it the same way in all the books."

Once students have had time to talk with their partners, Mr. Espinal asks for pairs to share what they have discussed. Mr. Espinal also reminds them to really think about their comments or questions and to tell him where the response should go (either in the K column or the W column). As students respond, Mr. Espinal writes their ideas on the chart paper. To encourage metacognitive awareness, Mr. Espinal prompts students with questions like "Is that a fact or a question?" "Is that something you don't know and want to find out?"

> These and other types of questions are discussed in depth in Chapter 6.

An important part of creating a K-W-L chart with students is asking them how they think they might find out the answers to their wonderings. After they complete the K and W columns, Mr. Espinal turns his attention to the research process. He generates another chart with his students titled, "What we will do to answer our questions." Mr. Espinal wants to teach his first graders about searching for answers on their own. Before students and the teacher read any of the Eric Carle books, the following ideas are generated on the supplemental chart (see Figure 3.4). Mr. Espinal writes the students' names after their ideas to empower the students and to acknowledge each child's contribution to the discussion. Mr. Espinal says that this sends the message, "Yes, that is a great idea and we are counting on you to help us find the answers to our questions." Students feel empowered to take the lead and to search out the answer when they see their name on K-W-L (and any other) chart in the classroom.

Figure 3.4 Student-generated chart for art.

What We Will Do To Answer Our Questions

Look through books – Marc
Look on the Internet – Sangeli
Write him a letter – Francis

During the week, Mr. Espinal shares Eric Carle books with his students and together they search for the answers to their questions. Over time, the L column of the chart is completed as students learn more about the artistic medium used in these texts. They discover that this style is called collage and that Eric Carle uses painted tissue paper to create the images. They also learn that he fills in spots that have not been covered with tissue paper using crayons and markers. They explore his use of color, lines, and perspective. As a culminating activity, students make a collage of their own using the same techniques as Eric Carle.

Visual Displays in Second-Grade Social Studies

Visual displays of objects are an effective means for building background knowledge and igniting the curiosity of young students who will want to read more for information. The use of realia (real objects) has long been recognized as an effective strategy for supporting the language development of English language learners (Krashen, 1987; Richard-Amato, 1988). Visual displays of realia are also used to introduce unfamiliar vocabulary to all students. Pam Pham-Barron uses visual displays of realia to engage students and build background knowledge.

She begins by showing the second graders three intriguing items—a brightly colored cloth, a basket woven from palm leaves, and a pair of chopsticks. As the students examine the items, she asks, "What are these things? Who uses them?" Several students offer their opinions about the objects and gradually conclude that the objects come from different parts of the world. "Would you be surprised if I told you I bought all of these things in our neighborhood?" The children nod.

Ms. Pham-Barron then refers the students to a language chart she has prepared for the lesson. "Boys and girls, we are going to be learning about how traditions from around the world are brought to new lands. I've written our Big Idea on this chart—'Where people live influences how they live.'" Like many of her colleagues in California, Ms. Pham-Barron organizes her social studies instruction around essential understandings, called Big Ideas. "Let me show you a book I found about people from all over the world. Some of them use these things," she says, gesturing to the cloth, basket, and chopsticks.

> Providing students with opportunities to discuss content with peers assists them in meeting oral language standards.

The teacher explains that the book, *How My Family Lives in America* (Kuklin, 1998), discusses the lives of three American families with ties to other countries. Although they live in the United States, they practice many of the traditions from their homelands.

The father of the first family is from Senegal. Ms. Pham-Barron reaches for a globe to show the children where the country is located. She notes that the text said that the child dressed in an African style for special occasions. She holds up the cloth and explains, "This cloth uses a pattern from Senegal."

The story emphasizes that the child's grandmother has taught her grandson about good manners. "Turn to your partner and tell him or her what you call your grandmother." Ms. Pham-Barron's students come from all over the world themselves, so they gleefully share their words for *grandmother*. "*Abuelita!*" announces a child from Mexico. A girl from Vietnam tells her partner she calls her grandmother *danh tu*. Her partner, whose family comes from Pakistan, calls his grandmother *daadi*.

Reprinted with the permission of Simon and Schuster Books for Young Readers, an imprint of Simon and Schuster Children's Publishing Division from *How My Family Lives in America* by Susan Kuklin. Jacket photographs copyright © 1992 Susan Kuklin.

When the children finish, Ms. Pham-Barron returns to the story. She calls their attention to the types of food featured in the book and explains that in this home everyone washes their hands and then eats from one big bowl using three fingers on their right hands. Ms. Pham-Barron asks the students, "Does your family prepare favorite dishes for special occasions?" She records their responses on the language chart.

The teacher shows them the photographs of the next family in the book and asks them to make predictions. A student says that the boy in the picture is from Mexico. Ms. Pham-Barron explains that the child's father came from Puerto Rico, and uses the globe to show them that it is an island nation. "In Puerto Rico," she says, "they play baseball, there are palm trees, it's warm, and the people speak Spanish." She shows them the basket again and then reads this portion of the book. Ms. Pham-Barron reminds the students that where people come from influences how they live. "What traditions does the boy in the story observe?" They tell the teacher that the boy speaks two languages, and eats rice, chicken, and beans. Ms. Pham-Barron writes down these details on the chart.

Before reading about the next family, she pauses to share a story about herself, where she came from, and a bit about the traditions practiced in her family. She shows them the chopsticks and tells the students that they are going to learn how to use them. She gives directions on how to hold them and demonstrates how to pick up popcorn from a cup. The children sit in pairs and practice using the chopsticks. After much giggling, Ms. Pham-Barron charts their responses about traditions and then finishes the story. Later that day, quite a few second graders can be seen using chopsticks to eat their lunches. More importantly, they have had a memorable introduction to a major concept in social studies and a desire to read for information.

Discrepant Events in Third-Grade Mathematics

Few things capture a child's attention like candy, and when content is paired with chocolate, it's a winning combination. Roberta Dawson used a popular trade book as a means for teaching an intriguing lesson in multiplication using, of all things, a chocolate candy bar.

Many states require that there be a balance of the types of foods discussed in classrooms and that there is not an exclusive focus on foods with sugar, caffeine, and nitrates.

The third-grade students in Mrs. Dawson's class arrive after lunch to find chocolate bars on their desks. "Whoa, that's awesome!" exclaim several students. After directing them to take their seats, she asks the students why they think she has given them a candy bar for math class. After some puzzled looks, there is a response. "So we can count how many bites it takes to eat it?" Then another. "Measure how long it is?" Mrs. Dawson asks the students to unwrap the candy bar and look at it. "What do you see?"

The students reply, "Lots of rectangles."

What if we use the rectangles to count? Not just regular counting, but really fast counting?" All the students agree that this would be a great thing to learn. Since learning the multiplication tables is an exciting milestone for third graders, using a candy bar makes it even more thrilling. She

Figure 3.5   Students working during Hershey's math.

instructs them to carefully break the candy bar apart into rectangles. Mrs. Dawson is certain she now has everyone's attention.

Mrs. Dawson then holds up the book, *The Hershey's Milk Chocolate Multiplication Book* (Pallotta, 2002), reads the title, and then turns to the first page. As she reads the book, she models on the overhead projector how to manipulate the candy bar pieces to understand the concept of multiplication. Using the book and their candy bars, Mrs. Dawson and her class manipulate the candy bar pieces to introduce the communicative property, multiplication and equal signs, and the vocabulary words *factors*, *product*, *horizontal*, *vertical*, and *equation*. Mrs. Dawson posts the vocabulary words on the Math Vocabulary Chart and on sentence strips that the students will use later for a matching activity as noted in Figure 3.5.

> Vocabulary instruction is the focus of Chapter 4.

Mrs. Dawson uses this anticipatory activity to introduce the concept of multiplication and its associated vocabulary in a way that is engaging and memorable. While the mastery of multiplication concepts will require many more lessons and experiences, it is likely that her students will recall their first exposure as a fun one. Especially when Mrs. Dawson finally announces what they have all been waiting to hear: "Eat your math lesson!"

Demonstration in Fourth-Grade Science

Perhaps there is no content area more perfectly suited to classroom demonstrations than science. A jaw-dropping demonstration can provoke wonder and inquiry and establish real purpose to the subsequent study of a scientific concept. These memorable occasions can also be considered discrepant events because they use the element of surprise to motivate (Wright & Govindarajan, 1995). They may be considered visual displays as well because they activate memory and retention through motion and light. We suspect that inside every good science teacher there is a young child who was mesmerized by a dazzling display of a mysterious scientific concept. In his autobiography, *Uncle Tungsten: Memories of a Chemical Boyhood*, Oliver Sacks (2001) recounts life in a household surrounded by parents and siblings deeply involved in the sciences. In a chapter titled "Stinks and Bangs," he writes of a demonstration he performed as a 10-year-old with his two older brothers:

> Attracted by the sounds and flashes and smells coming from my lab, David and Marcus, now medical students, sometimes joined me in experiments—the nine- and ten-year differences between us hardly mattered at these times. On one occasion, I was experimenting with hydrogen and oxygen, there was a loud explosion, and an almost invisible sheet of flame, which blew off Marcus's eyebrows completely. But Marcus took this in good part, and he and David often suggested other experiments. (p. 77)

Like young Oliver and his brothers, Mrs. Crandall appreciates the impact of a few "stinks and bangs." She has just announced the next unit of study to her fourth-grade class—volcanoes! Students think, pair, and share with one another for five minutes to activate prior knowledge and generate questions (Lyman, 1981). Student voices can be heard buzzing, and hands go up when the timer goes off and they have an opportunity to share what they know about the new topic.

One student, Zachary, explains what he knows about volcanoes from a book he has read called *Volcanoes and Earthquakes* (Van Rose, 2004). Furthermore, he says he has done an experiment from the book and would like to show the class how to create a volcano. The students are impressed with his expertise and begin begging Mrs. Crandall to conduct the experiment the following afternoon. Of course, she recognizes a teachable moment when she sees one and agrees to the suggestion. After meeting with Mrs. Crandall to discuss the details, Zachary forms a team of classmates to compile a list of materials needed and lets each member contribute to the experiment by bringing materials from home. He says they will need a tray, some sand, a small plastic bottle, red food coloring, vinegar, and baking soda. The team members write down their assigned item from the list and promise to bring the necessary materials.

The following day, Mrs. Crandall chooses two students to assist Zachary with the experiment. The plastic bottle must be cut down a bit—Mrs. Crandall does this for them. It is then centered on the tray and sand is brought in from the kindergarten sandbox. It won't stick around the bottle, so water is added and the sand is pressed evenly all around the outside of the plastic bottle. Then Zachary instructs his classmates to add the baking soda to the bottle; the food coloring and vinegar are mixed in a measuring cup. The class gathers around the table to watch Zachary carefully pour the red vinegar mixture into the "cone" of the volcano, but not before Mrs. Crandall asks them to predict what will happen next (see Figure 3.6). After discussion, the big moment arrives—Zachary adds the vinegar solution to the bottle. "Look out! Here it comes!" Red foaming liquid pours from the top of the volcano cone and streams down one side.

Students observe what has happened and hypothesize why the "lava" is not evenly dispersed around the cone. The class decides to do the experiment again to see if the same thing happens this time. They speculate that pressure could be part of the problem—maybe it is not evenly distributed inside the bottle. Perhaps if the liquid is poured carefully into the center of the bottle, it will come out more evenly. Mrs. Crandall smiles to herself because her first goal of instruction has been accomplished—inspire them to learn. After that, the rest is easy.

It is important to note that Mrs. Crandall's teaching is not all "stinks and bangs." She pairs discussion and writing with the demonstrations to give students an opportunity to clarify their understanding and support their inquiry about what is still unknown to them. She also ensures that there are a number of informational books related to the content she is teaching available

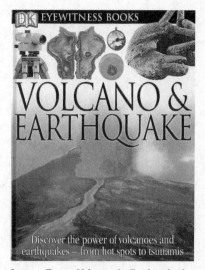

Source: From *Volcano & Earthquake* by Eyewitness Books. Copyright © 2004 by Dorling Kindersley Limited, London. Published by permission of Dorling Kindersley.

Figure 3.6   Students gathered around volcano.

in her classroom library. She is careful to ground her work in the theoretical underpinnings of each demonstration. Indeed, without this careful attention to the scientific concepts, students are likely to form misconceptions about what they have seen (Roth, McRobbie, & Lucas, 1997). But the powerful responses to anticipatory activities like this one are always part of the instructional repertoire of this teacher. "Learning is fun, especially science," says Mrs. Crandall. "No one ever said those two couldn't go together."

Freedman (2000) recommends several principles for designing effective science demonstrations:

- *Establish a clear purpose.* The demonstration must be directly related to the scientific concepts being studied.
- *Plan the demonstration carefully.* This is more than just assembling the materials. What other learning experiences will the students have in order to understand the theoretical basis for the demonstration? Plan the related lessons to support student connections to important concepts.
- *Plan for repeatability.* Students may need to see the demonstration again. Be sure to have extra materials on hand for this possibility. Also, be sure that the demonstration you've selected yields reliable and consistent results.
- *Plan for safety.* Although discrepant events like science demonstrations can enhance learning, your students don't need to witness you getting hurt.
- *Consider visibility.* A crowded classroom can make it difficult to see and fully appreciate the demonstration. It can become a safety issue as well for your students if they are jockeying for position. If the sight lines are obstructed in your classroom, consider dividing the class in half and performing the demonstration twice. If the phenomenon you are demonstrating needs to be seen from close range, then perform the demonstration with small groups of students.
- *Don't discount the importance of showmanship.* The literal and figurative "stinks and bangs" of science demonstrations can intrigue your students. Don't be afraid to play it up—your enthusiasm is infectious.

The anticipation guide provides a visual record of student learning as it scaffolds their growing understanding of the reading or information.

Thought-Provoking Questions in Fifth-Grade Social Studies

Anticipation guides are useful for activating background knowledge, encouraging prediction, and fostering questions. Typically, a series of true and false statements are constructed and students are invited to consider what it is they know (and do not know) about a topic of study. Aida Allen uses anticipation guides as a way to accomplish all these goals.

Ms. Allen's fifth graders are beginning a unit of study in social studies on the American Revolution. She gives them an anticipation guide with two columns labeled "before" and "after" and a series of statements about this time in American history (see Figure 3.7).

"Remember, you've done these before. Make sure to read each statement and think about what you already know. If you are not sure, make a prediction. What makes the most sense to you?" Because Ms. Allen's students have used anticipation guides in all content areas and are familiar with the task, they understand that it is not a competition and it isn't graded.

Figure 3.7 Anticipation guide for fifth-grade social studies.

Name:_____ Date:_____

Anticipation Guide — What Do You Know About the American Revolution?

Directions: Read each statement and put a "+" in the Before column for true statements and a "O" for false statements. You will answer again at the end of this unit.

BEFORE LESSON	IS THIS STATEMENT TRUE OR FALSE?	AFTER LESSON
	1. The British helped the first settlers protect themselves from some Native American tribes.	
	2. The Stamp Act was a law about collecting stamps.	
	3. Angry colonists dumped 342 crates of tea into Boston Harbor in an event called the Boston Tea Party.	
	4. Loyalists wanted to become independent from England.	
	5. Patriots wanted to be Americans and not citizens of England.	
	6. During the American Revolution, everyone chose a side.	
	7. There were 14 colonies involved in the American Revolution.	
	8. The Declaration of Independence made the colonies free from British rule.	

Joe and Tino are deep in discussion about the last item on the anticipation guide. "When we signed the Declaration, we got to be our own country," asserts Joe.

"I'm not sure. Did it mean we were free, or did it just mean that now there would be a war?" says Tino. Ms. Allen smiles to herself as she listens to this exchange. When she constructed the anticipation guide, she wanted to represent a range of knowledge, from basic facts to more complex concepts such as this.

After several minutes (and much discussion), Ms. Allen introduces a K-W-L chart. "I like using anticipation guides before [the K-W-L chart] because it sparks questions. Of course, these aren't the only questions I want on the chart, but they serve as good discussion-starters."

The completed anticipation guides and K-W-L chart are also useful to Ms. Allen as an assessment of her students' background knowledge. "There's so much to teach—the standards represent a lot of learning. If I can begin to determine what doesn't need to be retaught because they already know it, then I can use that instructional time to teach unfamiliar concepts. It's one of the best ways I know to buy some more time," Ms. Allen later remarks.

After the unit of study is completed, students revisit the anticipation guide and the K-W-L chart to see what they've learned. "Here's one more reason I like anticipation guides," Ms. Allen winks. "When their parents ask them, 'What did you learn today?' they usually answer, 'Nothing!' Anticipation guides prove them wrong, in their very own handwriting!"

Conclusion

Anticipatory activities can enhance the learning and retention of students in content-area classrooms. They can also serve to motivate and stimulate curiosity about the topics being studied. Demonstrations, discrepant events, visual displays, and thought-provoking questions are examples of the types of anticipatory activities used by effective teachers.

Demonstrations are typically used to display a theory, concept, or phenomenon. They are a staple of science instruction, but can be in any content area. Demonstrations are particularly useful for English language learners because they foster mental models for concepts. It is important to remember that a demonstration does not replace the need for the theoretical basis for understanding the phenomenon.

Discrepant events are useful for gaining attention and creating a lasting impression. These events are characteristically described as surprising or startling. Teachers have found success in using costumes and props to illustrate a character, setting, or era. The growing availability of technology makes it possible to include novel visual displays for illustrating ideas or concepts. Web-based programs can provide resources on a variety of phenomenon. Exciting examples of visual displays can be found through the growing number of available WebQuests. Thought-provoking questions are a primary tool for teachers to create anticipatory activities. Examples of thought-provoking questions in this chapter included essential questions, quick writes, found poems, anticipation guides, and K-W-L's.

References

Anderson, R. C., & Pearson, P. D. (1984). A schema-theoretic view of basic processes in reading comprehension. In P. D. Pearson, R. Barr, M. L. Kamil, & P. Mosenthal (Eds.), *Handbook of reading research* (pp. 255–292). Mahwah, NJ: Lawrence Erlbaum.

Beasley, W. (1982). Teacher demonstrations: The effect on student task involvement. *Journal of Chemical Education, 59,* 789–790.

Brandt, R. (1992). On Deming and school quality: A conversation with Enid Brown. *Educational Leadership, 50*(3), 28–31.

Brooks, H. B., & Brooks, D., W. (1996). The emerging role of CD-ROMs in teaching chemistry. *Journal of Science Education and Technology, 5,* 203–215.

Brown, R., El-Dinary, P., Pressley, M., & Ogan, L. (1995). A transactional strategies approach to reading instruction. *The Reading Teacher, 49,* 256–258.

Bruner, J. S., Goodnow, J. J., & Austin, G. A. (1956). *A study of thinking.* New York: Wiley.

Buzan, T. (1979). *Using both sides of your brain.* New York: E. P. Dutton.

Carr, E., & Ogle, D. (1987). K-W-L plus: A strategy for comprehension and summarization. *Journal of Reading, 30,* 626–631.

Daniels, H., & Bizar, M. (1998). *Methods that matter: Six structures for best practice classrooms.* York, ME: Stenhouse.

Dewey, J. (1938, 1963). *Experience and education.* New York: Macmillan.

Dodge, B. (1995). Some thoughts about WebQuests. Retrieved June 23, 2002 from http://edweb.sdsu.edu/courses/edtec596/about_webquests.html

Dodge, B. (1995). WebQuests: A technique for Internet-based learning. *Distance Educator, 1*(2), 10–13.

Eggen, P., & Kauchak, D. (2001). *Educational psychology: Windows on classrooms* (5th ed.). Upper Saddle River, NJ: Merrill/Prentice Hall.

Fay, J. (2000). Investigation—insects! *Science and Children, 38*(1), 26–30.

Flood, J., Heath, S. B., & Lapp, D. (1997). *Research on teaching literacy through the communicative and visual arts.* Newark, DE: International Reading Association.

Freedman, M. P. (2000). Using effective demonstrations for motivation. *Science and Children, 38*(1), 52–55.

Giannangelo, D. M., & Bolding, R. A. (1998). Ethnocentrism, geography, and foreign guest speakers: An attempt to change attitudes. *Journal of the Middle States Council for the Social Studies,* 122–126.

Good, T., & Brophy, J. (2002). *Looking in classrooms* (9th ed.). New York: Harper Collins.

Head, M. H., & Readence, J. E. (1986). Anticipation guides: Meaning through prediction. In E. K. Dishner, T. W. Bean, J. E. Readence, & D. W. Moore (Eds.), *Reading in the content* areas (2nd ed.) (pp. 229–234). Dubuque, IA: Kendall Hunt.

Hurst, B. (2001). ABCs of content area lesson planning: Attention, basics, and comprehension. *Journal of Adolescent & Adult Literacy, 44*, 692–693.

Hyerle, D. (1996). *Visual tools for constructing knowledge*. Alexandria, VA: Association of Supervision and Curriculum Development.

Janney, R., & Snell, M. E. (2000). *Modifying schoolwork: Teachers' guides to inclusive practices*. Baltimore, MD: Paul H. Brookes.

Jensen, E. (1998). *Teaching with the brain in mind*. Alexandria, VA: Association for Supervision and Curriculum Development.

Jorgensen, C. M. (1998). *Restructuring high schools for all students: Taking inclusion to the next level*. Baltimore, MD: Paul H. Brookes.

Kolb, D. (1984). *Experiential learning: Experience as the source of learning and development*. Englewood Cliffs, NJ: Prentice-Hall.

Krashen, S. D. (1987). *Principles and practice in second language acquisition*. Upper Saddle River, NJ: Prentice Hall.

Landauer, T. K. (1975). Memory without organization: Properties of a model with random storage and undirected retrieval. *Cognitive Psychology, 7*, 495–531.

Larsen, J. D. (1991). Pay attention! Demonstrating the role of attention in learning. *Teaching of Psychology, 18*, 238–239.

Lee, C. (2000). Modelling in the mathematics classroom. *Mathematics Teaching, 171*, 28–31.

Lyman, F. (1981). The responsive classroom discussion: The inclusion of all students. In A. S. Anderson (Ed.), *Mainstreaming Digest* (pp. 109–113). College park, MD: University of Maryland Press.

Margulies, N. (1991). *Mapping inner space*. Tucson, AZ: Zephyr.

McDonald, N., & Fisher, D. (2006). *Teaching literacy through the arts*. New york: Guilford.

Muncey, D. E., Payne, J., & White, N. S. (1999). Making curriculum and instructional reform happen: A case study. *Peabody Journal of Education, 74*, 68–110.

Ogle, D. (1986). K-W-L: A teaching model that develops active reading of expository text. *The Reading Teacher, 39*, 564–570.

Pumpian, I., Fisher, D., & Wachowiak, S. (Eds.). (2004). *Challenging the classroom standard through museum-based education: School in the park*. Mahwah, NJ: Lawrence Erlbaum Associates.

Richard-Amato, P. A, (1988). *Making it happen: Interaction in the classroom from theory to practice*. New York: AB Longman.

Roth, W. M., McRobbie, C. J., & Lucas, K. B. (1997). Why may students fail to learn from demonstrations: A social practice perspective on learning in physics. *Journal of Research in Science Teaching, 34*, 509–533.

Sacks, O. (2001). *Uncle Tungsten: Memories of a chemical boyhood*. New York: Alfred A. Knopf.

Schipper, A., Schipper, L., & Hornsby, A. (1993). Going underground: Demonstrating the underground part of the water cycle and the dangers of groundwater contamination with a simple aquifer model. *Science and Children, 31*, 16–18.

Schmidt, P. R. (1999). KWLQ: Inquiry and literacy learning in science. *The Reading Teacher, 52*, 789–792.

Shepardson, D. P., Moje, E. B., & Kennard-McClelland, A. M. (1994). The impact of a science demonstration on children's understandings of air pressure.

Journal of Science Teaching, 31, 243–258.

Smith, F. (1998). *The book of learning and forgetting.* New York: Teachers College Press.

Sylwester, R. (1995). *A celebration of neurons: An educator's guide to the human brain.* Alexandria, VA: Association for Supervision and Curriculum Development.

Wills, C. (1995). Voice of inquiry: Possibilities and perspectives. *Childhood Education, 71,* 261–265.

Wright, E. L., & Govindarajan, G. (1995). Discrepant event demonstrations. *Science Teacher, 62(1),* 24–28.

Children's Literature Cited

Carle, E. (1994). *The very hungry caterpillar.* New York: Philomel.

Carle, E. (1995). *The very busy spider.* New York: Philomel.

Carle, E. (1997). *The very quiet cricket.* New York: Grosset & Dunlap.

Carle, E. (1999). *The grouchy ladybug.* New York: HarperFestival.

Kuklin, S. (1998). *How my family lives in America.* New York: Aladdin.

Martin, B., Jr., & Carle, E. (1997). *Brown bear, brown bear, what do you see?* New York: Henry Holt.

Pallotta, J. (2002). *The Hershey's milk chocolate multiplication book.* New York: Scholastic.

Van Rose, S. (2004). *Volcanoes and earthquakes.* DK Publishing.

Chapter 4

Nancy Frey

Douglas Fisher

Sheryl Segal

Word for Word:

Vocabulary Development for Informational Texts

"*Einstein, James Dean, Brooklyn's got a winning team, Davy Crockett, Peter Pan, Elvis Presley, Disneyland . . ." (Joel, 1989). The familiar Billy Joel song "We Didn't Start the Fire" is being sung by Rachel Tuttle's fifth-grade history and geography students. These learners are making timelines of important events and people of the twentieth century, and Ms. Tuttle is using music to introduce new vocabulary. The song is rich in information expressed via vocabulary terms, people's names, and places. Ms. Tuttle wants her students to be able to identify their own place in history and realize that conflict and change occur when people of different cultures come into contact with one another.*

Today the class will work in groups of four to make their timelines, covering 4 to 5 years of history. The song lyrics are displayed on the overhead and each group is responsible for the events listed in one stanza. The students need to choose one person or event for each year, research the significance of that person or event, and place it correctly on the timeline.

Yesterday, Ms. Tuttle worked with a small group of students and pre-taught some of the vocabulary needed for today's lesson. She gave each of the six students a card with a photograph and an explanation of a person or event from the song; then they worked together to read and understand the historical importance. The whole class then read through the lyrics together and discussed the events.

"Has anyone heard of Joe DiMaggio?" asks Ms. Tuttle. "His name is next to the year 1949."

Angela, who had met with Ms. Tuttle the previous day, raises her hand. "He was a famous baseball player."

"Remember when we went to the Hall of Champions Sports Museum?" "Wasn't he famous for making home runs?" Jose chimes in. "Or was he a pitcher?"

"You'll need to find out what he's famous for and why 1949 was an important year for him. You can use the Internet, an encyclopedia, or a book on the history of baseball. And don't forget to ask other people in our class. Maybe someone in here knows who he is." Ms. Tuttle nods to Angela. "Does anyone know about Joe DiMaggio?"

Angela looks at her vocabulary card. "I know he played center field for the New York Yankees and he was inducted into the Baseball Hall of Fame in 1955," Janet replies. "His nickname was 'Joltin' Joe' because he was such a good hitter. But I don't know why 1949 is important in his life."

"Maybe something happened to him in 1949 or something important was going on in the world and he was part of it," Ms. Tuttle replies. "In your group you need to look up world events for that year and find out why Billy Joel chose that year to include in his song."

With the music playing in the background, the students move into groups and begin working.

The vocabulary demands on students are daunting. In the elementary school years, it is estimated that students must learn 3000 words per year by the time they reach third grade (Nagy & Herman, 1987). This is in contrast to the approximately 400 words directly taught by the teacher during the same year (Blachowicz & Fisher, 2002). While academic language demands are high, it is estimated that everyday speech consists of only 5,000 to 7,000 words (Klein, 1988). Therefore, it is unlikely that conversation and discussion alone can compensate for a limited command of the academic vocabulary. Taken together, these two figures demonstrate what most elementary teachers already know—the vocabulary gap for many students is so large that it is difficult to identify where to begin.

The Importance of Word Knowledge

This gap in word knowledge is problematic because of its impact on content learning (Flood, Lapp, & Fisher, 2003; Stahl & Fairbanks, 1986). Mastery of technical language has long been recognized as a predictor of success in any field. However, a causal relationship between vocabulary knowledge and reading comprehension has been less clear. In a study of fifth-grade students who were taught vocabulary strategies, the researchers found that although the students' word knowledge increased significantly, their reading comprehension of texts was mixed (Baumann, Edwards, Font, Tereshinski, Kame'enui & Olejnik, 2002). This is not to suggest that vocabulary knowledge has no effect on reading comprehension. On the contrary, the researchers note that "attempting to isolate just one of those factors [vocabulary] in the present study may have diminished the possibility of detecting effects . . . on text comprehension" (p. 170).

> In addition to vocabulary, comprehension is influenced by prior knowledge, fluency, text difficulty, and interest, among other things.

Given the academic vocabulary demands of the elementary school curriculum, it would seem logical to first identify and then explicitly teach the necessary words until the gap has been bridged. Indeed, vocabulary research through much of the twentieth century consisted of lists of words, such as *McGuffey's Eclectic Spelling-Book* (1879), Dolch's sight words (1936), and Thorndike and Lorge's (1944) *The Teacher's Word Book of 30,000 Words*. Vocabulary was viewed as a subset of either comprehension or spelling, but was rarely examined closely in its own right. Instead, the emphasis at the instructional level was to teach individual words, and these lists guided teachers in making word selections. Instruction often relied on rote memorization of definitions followed by weekly vocabulary tests. These words were rarely derived from texts the students were reading.

> Are there words in this text that you don't know? How are you adding them to your vocabulary?

Vocabulary Acquisition

Research in language acquisition in the 1980s had an important effect on trends in vocabulary instruction. Along with the studies about academic language demands and everyday usage, it was reported that students in grades 3 through 9 learn an average of 3,000 new words per year (Nagy & Herman, 1987), hardly an adequate pace for closing the vocabulary gap. Indeed, it appeared that teaching words exclusively in isolation was an inefficient way to foster word knowledge. At the same time, instructional approaches were influenced by a growing understanding of meaning as a component of vocabulary acquisition. Instructional practices shifted to culling vocabulary words from narrative and expository reading selections used in the classroom. Over time, teachers and educational researchers expressed dissatisfaction with this method as well, because of the hodgepodge nature of the word selection.

Vocabulary as Concepts or Labels. A vexing issue in vocabulary word selection relates to the usefulness of the word and its relation to the curriculum. Some words are concepts; others are labels. Given that students need to acquire a tremendous volume of vocabulary words each year, it seems careless to squander valuable instructional time on words that function only as labels in a particular reading. For example, in Lois Lowry's story *The Giver* (1994), a boy is faced with the challenge of confronting truth in his "perfect" community. The word *utopia* is a concept word, for it is central to the understanding of a society with no illness or poverty. On the other hand, the word *tunic* is a label describing the type of clothing worn by the characters. *Utopia* is well worth the instructional effort for students to think deeply about the complexities represented by this one word; *tunic* is a word that can be inferred through context clues and is not essential to comprehension. Students also benefit from instruction on the differences between concept and label words because it can prevent them from getting bogged down in minutia at the expense of big ideas.

> Context clues are hints about word meaning derived from phrases and sentences immediately around the word in question.

Self-Awareness of Current Knowledge. Teaching vocabulary is further complicated by the varying word knowledge levels of individual students. Even when the core reading is held in common, students bring a range of word understanding to the text. Rather than apply a "one size fits all" approach to vocabulary instruction, it is wise to assess students before the reading. This awareness is valuable for the student as well, because it highlights their understanding of what they know, as well as what they still need to learn to comprehend the reading. One method for accomplishing this is through *Vocabulary Self-Awareness* (Goodman, 2001). Words are introduced at the beginning of the reading or unit, and students complete a self-assessment of their knowledge of the words (see Figure 4.1). Each vocabulary word is rated according to the student's understanding, including an example and a definition. If they are very comfortable with the word, they give themselves a "+" (plus sign). If they think they know, but are unsure, they note the word with a "✓" (check mark). If the word is new to them, they place a "−" (minus sign) next to the word. Over the course of the reading or unit, students add new information to the chart. The goal is to replace all the check marks and minus signs with plus signs. Because students continually revisit their vocabulary charts to revise their entries, they have multiple opportunities to practice and extend their growing understanding of the terms. An excerpt from one student's

> Vocabulary development is recursive. For a term to become part of a student's vocabulary, they need opportunities to revisit it.

Figure 4.1   Vocabulary self-awareness chart.

WORD	+	√	–	EXAMPLE	DEFINITION

Procedure:
1. Examine the list of words you have written in the first column.
2. Put a "+" next to each word you know well, and can write an accurate example and definition of the word. Your definition and example must relate to the unit of study.
3. Place a "√" next to any words that you can write only a definition or an example for, but not both.
4. Put a "–" next to words that are new to you.
This chart will be used throughout the unit. By the end you should have the entire chart completed. Since you will be revising this chart, write in pencil.

Source: Goodman, L. (2004). Vocabulary self-check. In G. E. Tompkins and C. Blanchfield (Eds.), *Teaching vocabulary: So creative strategies, K–12* (pp. 44–46). Upper Saddle River, NJ: Merrill Prentice Hall. Used with permission.

vocabulary chart for *When Marian Sang* (Ryan, 2002) can be found in Figure 4.2.

Vocabulary Instruction

Current practices in vocabulary instruction seek to integrate these varied methods—choosing words from texts, teaching concepts as well as meanings, and teaching metacognitively. Word selection is essential for content-area language growth, and a growing number of teachers are identifying grade-level words for explicit instruction. However, reinforcement of understanding through meaning is also seen as critical to student learning. In addition, students who understand how they learn words can become

Figure 4.2 Vocabulary self-awareness example.

WORD	+	√	−	EXAMPLE	DEFINITION
Recital	+			Piano or dance recital	A show for your family so you can show them what you learned
Opera		√			A kind of music that tells a story
Harmony			−		

Source: Book cover from *When Marian Sang* by Pam Muñoz Ryan. Illustrated by Brian Selznick. Illustrations copyright © 2002 by Brian Selznick. Reprinted by permission of Scholastic Inc.

active participants in their own learning (National Research Council, 2005). Blachowicz and Fisher (2000) identified four principles for effective vocabulary instruction. They advise that students should

- be actively involved in word learning
- make personal connections

- be immersed in vocabulary
- consolidate meaning through multiple information sources

These researchers noted that while these principles applied to all learning, their experience has shown that they are vital for vocabulary acquisition and retention.

Elementary teachers must also consider the type of vocabulary used in their instruction. Vacca and Vacca (1999) suggest that there are three types of vocabulary to consider—*general, specialized,* and *technical.* General vocabulary consists primarily of words used in everyday language, usually with widely agreed-upon meanings. Examples of general vocabulary words include *annoying, difficult,* and *troublesome.* The meaning of these three words tends to be consistent across contexts, and the appearance of any one of these words would signal the reader that the subject of these adjectives would be bothersome indeed! In contrast, specialized vocabulary is flexible and transportable across curricular disciplines; these words hold multiple meanings in different content areas. For example, the word *table* has a common meaning—a flat piece of furniture with four legs—as well as a more specialized definition in mathematics—an arrangement of data in rows and columns. Finally, there are technical vocabulary words that are specific to only one field of study. *Opera* in music, *photosynthesis* in science, and *Asia* in social studies are all examples of technical vocabulary specific to a content area. These words can be more difficult to teach, because there is little association with previously known word meanings. In addition, they tend to be "dense" in meaning; that is, the level of knowledge necessary to fully understand the word is directly related to the content itself. Technical vocabulary, in particular, tends to be vexing for teachers because the fallback system for acquisition is often rote memorization.

Like other elementary educators, the teachers in this chapter work at explicit general, specialized, and technical vocabulary instruction that is grounded in the principles of effective word learning forwarded by Blachowicz and Fisher (2000). They also use a variety of other approaches to vocabulary development throughout the day. Before exploring vocabulary instruction in content areas, let's look at some of the practices held in common by all of the teachers featured in this book.

> Teachers must be aware of all three types of vocabulary to avoid teaching only the technical terms associated with the topic.

Sound Practices in Vocabulary Development

The literacy block is an important time for teaching language skills and strategies that are transportable across the learning day. Therefore, vocabulary instruction sometimes focuses on analysis of familiar words through word study (Lapp, Jacobson, Fisher, & Flood, 2000). In many classrooms, word walls are prominently displayed that are particularly useful for English language learners.

Word Walls to Develop Familiarity. Word walls (Cunningham & Allington, 2003) are alphabetically arranged (by first letter), high-frequency words displayed in a manner to allow easy visual access to all students in the room. As Cunningham and Allington remind us, however, it is essential to "do" a word wall, not merely display one. Teachers in primary grades often use the Dolch list of sight words. Because these words comprise much of the written texts of primary reading materials, mastery of these words promotes more fluent reading.

Teachers of older students may use high-frequency words such as the "500 Most Used Words List" (Harwell, 2001). These words are commonly used in speaking and writing (see Table 4.1). Although they are relatively simple words, many are misapplied (*knew/new*) or misspelled (*friend, neighbor,* and *when*) leading to unclear communication. In addition to high-frequency words, teachers also use word walls to highlight vocabulary that is related to a unit of instruction. For example, during a study of the Pilgrims, a teacher might include words like *Mayflower, settlement, persecution,* and *Wampanoag* on the word wall. These teachers "do" the word wall through brief (ten minutes or so) daily instruction around a particular set of words. Typically, five words are introduced and located on the word wall display. Novel games such as Guess the Covered Word (Cunningham & Allington, 2003), where a word is revealed one letter at a time, may be used. It is important that the words, once taught, remain in the same spot so students can reliably locate them.

Expanding Student Vocabulary. Another popular method for expanding written vocabulary is through specialized word lists, thesauri, and dictionaries. Many teachers have experienced the overuse of terms like *said* in their students' writing. This may occur because students have not explored the ways writers convey how a message is spoken by a character to illuminate the action. Teachers can adopt the "said" word list to help students use more descriptive terms in place of "said." Called " 'Said' is Dead" (Peterson, 1996), students have a list of words posted to help them use more interesting terms like *confided, quipped,* and *scoffed* in place of the aforementioned term when writing dialogue (see Table 4.2). These students also have a wealth of reference materials available to them to support their word choices. Student thesauri are useful for budding writers struggling to find the perfect word, but other specialized materials like a slang thesaurus, rhyming dictionary, and books of quotations are also popular with students.

Focusing on Words with Multiple Meanings. Confusion about words with multiple meanings can also confound English language learners. For example, the word *run* has 69 meanings, as defined by the *New Webster's*

Dolch sight words can be found at http://www.theschool bell.com/Links/Dolch/Dolch.html

Other good word lists include Dr. Fry's 1000 Instant Words (Fry, 1997), and the graded word lists in the Month by Month Phonics series (Cunningham & Hall, 1998).

The Internet has provided another important source of information on words and phrases. Teachers often bookmark web sites like http://www.rhymezone.com for resources on rhyme schemes, www.grammarbook.com for help with punctuation and grammar, and www.dictionary.com for an all-purpose site for word definitions.

Table 4.1 **500 Most Used Words List**

A	Best	Corner	F
Able	Better	Could	Face
About	Between	Country	Fall
Above	Big	Cow	Family
Across	Bird	Cried	Far
Afraid	Black	Cry	Farm
After	Blue	Cut	Fast
Again	Book		Father
Against	Both	**D**	Feed
Air	Box	Daddy	Feel
All	Boy	Dance	Feet
Almost	Bread	Dark	Felt
Also	Bring	Day	Few
Always	Brother	Deep	Finally
Am	Brought	Did	Find
And	Brown	Didn't	Finish
Angry	Build	Different	Fire
Animal	Built	Dig	First
Another	Busy	Dinner	Fish
Answer	But	Dirty	Five
Any	Buy	Do	Flew
Are	By	Does	Fly
Around		Dog	Follow
As	**C**	Doing	Food
Ask	Call	Done	For
At	Came	Don't	Found
Ate	Can	Door	Four
Away	Car	Down	Friday
	Carry	Draw	Friend
B	Cat	Dress	From
Baby	Catch	Drink	Front
Back	Caught	Drive	Fruit
Bad	Cent	Drop	Full
Ball	Chase	During	Funny
Be	Child		
Beautiful	Children	**E**	**G**
Because	City	Each	Game
Bed	Clean	Early	Garden
Been	Climb	Easy	Gave
Before	Close	Eat	Get
Began	Clothes	Eight	Girl
Begin	Cold	Enough	Give
Being	Color	Even	Glad
Believe	Come	Ever	Go
Below	Cook	Every	Goes
		Eye	

Table 4.1 500 Most Used Words List *(continued)*

Going	**I**	**M**	**O**
Good	Ice	Made	Ocean
Got	Idea	Make	Of
Grass	If	Man	Off
Great	Important	Many	Office
Green	In	May	Often
Grew	Is	Me	Old
Ground	It	Mean	On
Grow		Men	Once
Guess	**J**	Met	One
	Join	Might	Only
H	Jump	Mile	Open
Had	Just	Milk	Or
Hand		Mine	Orange
Happen	**K**	Monday	Other
Happy	Keep	Money	Our
Has	Kept	More	Out
Hat	Kick	Morning	Over
Have	Kind	Most	Own
He	Kitchen	Mother	
Head	Kitten	Mountain	**P**
Hear	Knew	Mr.	Page
Heard	Know	Mrs.	Paint
Help		Music	Paper
Her	**L**	Must	Park
Here	Land	My	Part
Herself	Large		Party
Hide	Last	**N**	Pass
High	Late	Name	Penny
Hill	Laugh	Near	People
Him	Learn	Neck	Pick
Himself	Leave	Need	Picnic
His	Left	Neighbor	Picture
Hold	Let	Never	Piece
Home	Letter	New	Plant
Hope	Life	Next	Play
Hot	Light	Nice	Please
Hour	Like	Night	Point
House	Listen	Nine	Pony
How	Little	No	Pretty
Huge	Live	Noise	Print
Hundred	Long	North	Prize
Hungry	Look	Not	Problem
Hunt	Lose	Nothing	Proud
Hurry	Loud	Now	Pull
Hurt	Lunch	Number	Puppy

(continued)

Table 4.1 **500 Most Used Words List** *(continued)*

Push	Should	They	Voice
Put	Show	Thing	
	Side	Think	**W**
Q	Since	Third	Wait
Question	Sing	This	Walk
Quick	Sister	Those	Want
Quiet	Six	Thought	Was
Quit	Sleep	Three	Wash
Quite	Slowly	Through	Watch
	Small	Thursday	Water
R	Snow	Time	We
Rabbit	So	To	Wednesday
Rain	Some	Today	Week
Ran	Soon	Together	Well
Reach	South	Told	Went
Read	Space	Tomorrow	Were
Real	Stand	Too	West
Red	Start	Took	What
Remember	Stay	Toward	When
Rid	Stop	Town	Which
Right	Store	Toy	While
River	Story	Travel	White
Room	Street	Tree	Who
Round	Such	Tried	Why
Run	Suddenly	Truck	Will
	Swim	True	With
S		Tuesday	Woman
Sad	**T**	Turn	Word
Said	Take	Two	Work
Same	Talk		World
Sat	Teach	**U**	Would
Saturday	Tell	Under	Write
Saw	Ten	Until	
School	Than	Up	**Y**
Second	Thank	Upon	Yard
See	That	Us	Year
Seem	The	Use	Yellow
Send	Their	Usually	Yes
Sentence	Them		Yesterday
Seven	Then	**V**	You
Several	There	Very	Young
She	These	Visit	Your
Short			

Source: Harwell, J. M. (2001). *Complete learning disabilities handbook: Ready-to-use strategies and activities for teaching students with learning disabilities* (2nd ed.). Paramus, NJ: Center for Applied Research in Education. Copyright © 2001 John Wiley. Reprinted with permission of John Wiley & Sons, Inc.

Table 4.2 Expanded Vocabulary Word List

"Said" is Dead
Enrich your dialogue writing with more descriptive terms like these:

added	mumbled
advised	objected
allowed	parroted
barked	pronounced
babbled	protested
begged	quipped
blurted	reported
cajoled	scolded
complained	scoffed
confessed	simpered
confided	snapped
demanded	swore
dithered	stuttered
droned	taunted
gasped	teased
groaned	wailed
howled	whimpered
interrupted	yammered
jeered	yelled
moaned	

Source: Peterson, A. (1996). *The writer's workout book: 113 stretches toward better prose.*
Berkeley, CA: National Writing Project. Used with permission.

Dictionary of the English Language (1981)! This small word can refer to a rapid form of ambulation, entrance into a political contest, or a migration of fish, and has dozens of other meanings. Interestingly, teachers report that it is often these humble words, not just those glamorous polysyllabic darlings strung like a necklace with multiple affixes that interfere with reading comprehension. For students to correctly interpret which definition should be applied, instruction must include pointing out such words and then using them in a variety of contexts. English language learners can build their specialized vocabulary through semantic instruction in multiple-meaning words like *run* and *bear*. By examining both the rules and the fluidity of meaning in language, students are positioned to make increasingly finer distinctions between words. As Mark Twain once said, "the difference between the right word and the almost right word is the difference between the lightning and the lightning bug"! (Twain, 1890).

For more information on unique and surprising uses of English, see Richard Lederer's Crazy English.

Studying Multiple-Meaning Words. Aida Allen's fifth-grade class studies multiple meanings through a series of activities. Using conversation about "crazy English," words like *hand, table, bill, change,* and *book* were first analyzed as multiple-meaning words. For instance, *hand* can mean the appendage at the end of the arm, or the indicator on a clock or dial. Students were then challenged to bring in ten other multiple-meaning words and present a lesson to the class on how the words can be used in a variety of contexts. These word challenges caused students to use online and traditional dictionaries and thesauri to locate novel examples. In the case of the multiple meanings for *run* discussed previously, students could appreciate that all the meanings referred to the act of traveling rapidly.

After many exposures to these words, she assessed their understanding of multiple meanings using a series of questions she presented on the overhead. Multiple choice questions were displayed, with possible answers appearing in red, blue, black, and green. Each student had similarly colored cards for responding to the questions. As each question appeared, students responded by holding up the color of the answer they chose. For example, they identified sentences that correctly used *bill*. "By using the response cards, I am able to do a quick pan of the class to see who is getting it and who is not," she explained.

Figure 4.3 Shades of meaning chart for *happy*.

Shades of Meaning
happy
pleased
delighted
overjoyed

Noticing Subtle Differences in Meaning. Relationships between words can be particularly challenging when discussing synonyms. The difference between *annoy* and *harass* is a fine but distinct one. Truly "the difference between the right word and the almost right word" can impact the ability of the student to use precise language. These "shades of meaning" can be taught in an imaginative way using paint chip cards from the local hardware store (Blanchfield, 2001). Students attach a paint chip card containing shades of color to notebook paper to illustrate a string of synonyms. Definitions are written to the right of the paint chip card on which the word has been written. For example, Mariana created the card in Figure 4.3 to illustrate synonyms for the word *happy*.

The work of vocabulary development transcends subject areas. Let's look inside classrooms to see how teachers address vocabulary teaching and learning across the curriculum.

Strategies at Work

Vocabulary in Kindergarten Science

One of the best ways to capitalize on the energy of kindergartners is to incorporate music and movement into their day. These kinesthetic expressions allow young learners to activate body memory to recall vocabulary. One example of kinesthetic expression in vocabulary instruction is role playing. This practice of "acting out" vocabulary extends from Total Physical Response, a method of language instruction used with students who are English language learners (Asher, 1969) and those who are deaf (Marlatt, 1995). When students are invited to "act out" vocabulary, they engage in physical movement and gestures to portray a word. It is likely that these movements assist the performer in remembering the word because he or she is required to think critically about the features of the word.

Music affords young children an opportunity to use their movements to learn new vocabulary. Look for repetition of key vocabulary in the songs chosen for use in the classroom. These songs not only reinforce the meaning of the words, they also allow children to practice saying the words, a critical component of oral language development. Expanded oral vocabularies serve emergent readers well. As Snow, Burns, and Griffin (1998) note, "Spoken language and reading have much in common . . . comprehension of connected text depends heavily on the readers' oral language abilities . . ." (p. 108).

Dani Cole begins each year with an "All About Me" interdisciplinary unit. Many of her students arrive in September unable to name common body parts. To teach her students this important vocabulary, Ms. Cole uses books that are also songs. She especially likes *Dem Bones* (Barner, 1996) and *Head, Shoulders, Knees, and Toes: And Other Action Rhymes* (Newcome, 2002). During her focus on the book and song "Head, Shoulders, Knees, and Toes," Ms. Cole combines music and movement, and students recite the vocabulary as they touch the corresponding body part. The song identifies eight body parts (head, shoulders, knees, toes, eyes, ears, mouth, nose). After singing the song repeatedly for several days, most of the students can correctly identify these eight body parts. Ms. Cole then teaches the students an extension of the song, using a new verse with new body part names: chin, shoulders, stomach, back, elbows, waist, legs, and ankles. This new song is recited daily, and like the original version, after about a week these new vocabulary words have been learned.

Source: Book cover used with permission by Chronicle Books.

As an extension, the students play a game to reinforce the new vocabulary learned. Ms. Cole uses flashcards with the name of each body part and an accompanying picture. Lara, a student in the class, comes to the front of the room and faces her peers.

"Remember, boys and girls—I am going to hold a flashcard of the name of a body part over Lara's head. Don't say the word! Let's act it out silently and see if Lara can guess our secret word."

Amid much giggling, Ms. Cole holds the word *chin* above Lara's head. The children point to their chins and Lara immediately guesses the correct word. They rapidly work through all 16 vocabulary words while incorporating the movements they initially learned through the music.

Word Sorts in First-Grade Science

The ability to manipulate words can be an important device in acquiring vocabulary. Unfortunately, committing words to paper often seems permanent and intractable to many students, as if the act of writing terms down means they must remain fixed and static. Word sorts can provide students with a way to arrange and rearrange words in ways that mimic the critical thinking processes they use to understand new words. Much like a key in search of a lock, readers try a variety of related words until they discover the one meaning that supports their ability to understand a passage.

Sorting words involves the manipulation of a set of words, usually written on individual cards, into a series of categories or related concepts. More than 25 years ago, Gillet and Temple (1978) described a process for helping students study the relationships between words. Word sorts typically consist of five to ten terms. Sorts can be closed or open. Closed sorting activities are performed using categories provided by the teacher. For example, the words *igloo, dogsled,* and *salmon* belong in the categories, respectively, of *shelter, transportation,* and *food,* which are furnished by the teacher to help students organize their understanding of the Inuit people. An open sort is similar, but students create a set of categories to reflect their understanding of the relationships between and among a set of words. Both of these examples represent conceptual word sorts, because students are using their semantic knowledge of terms. Other word sorts may focus word patterns (e.g., -at and -ag words), or derivations (words with the Latin root *vert* and *pend*).

Ramon Espinal uses word sorts to teach his first-grade students new vocabulary words in English and Spanish. During a unit on life sciences, Mr. Espinal constructs a closed conceptual word sort for students to complete in pairs. Using vocabulary cards featuring science terms in English and Spanish, learners discuss the characteristics of the animals they have been studying. Mr. Espinal has created categories like *Has a Tail* and *Lays Eggs,* and the children work with vocabulary cards that read *cow/vaca* and so on. While the children sort the vocabulary cards, Mr. Espinal circulates among the groups, listening for their use of academic language. "In my classroom, vocabulary instruction is an integral part of my daily schedule," explains Mr. Espinal. "I've learned throughout the years that when words are taught in relation to other words, my students have been actively drawn to the learning process." The science word-sort activity appears in Figure 4.4.

Figure 4.4   Word sort for first-grade science.

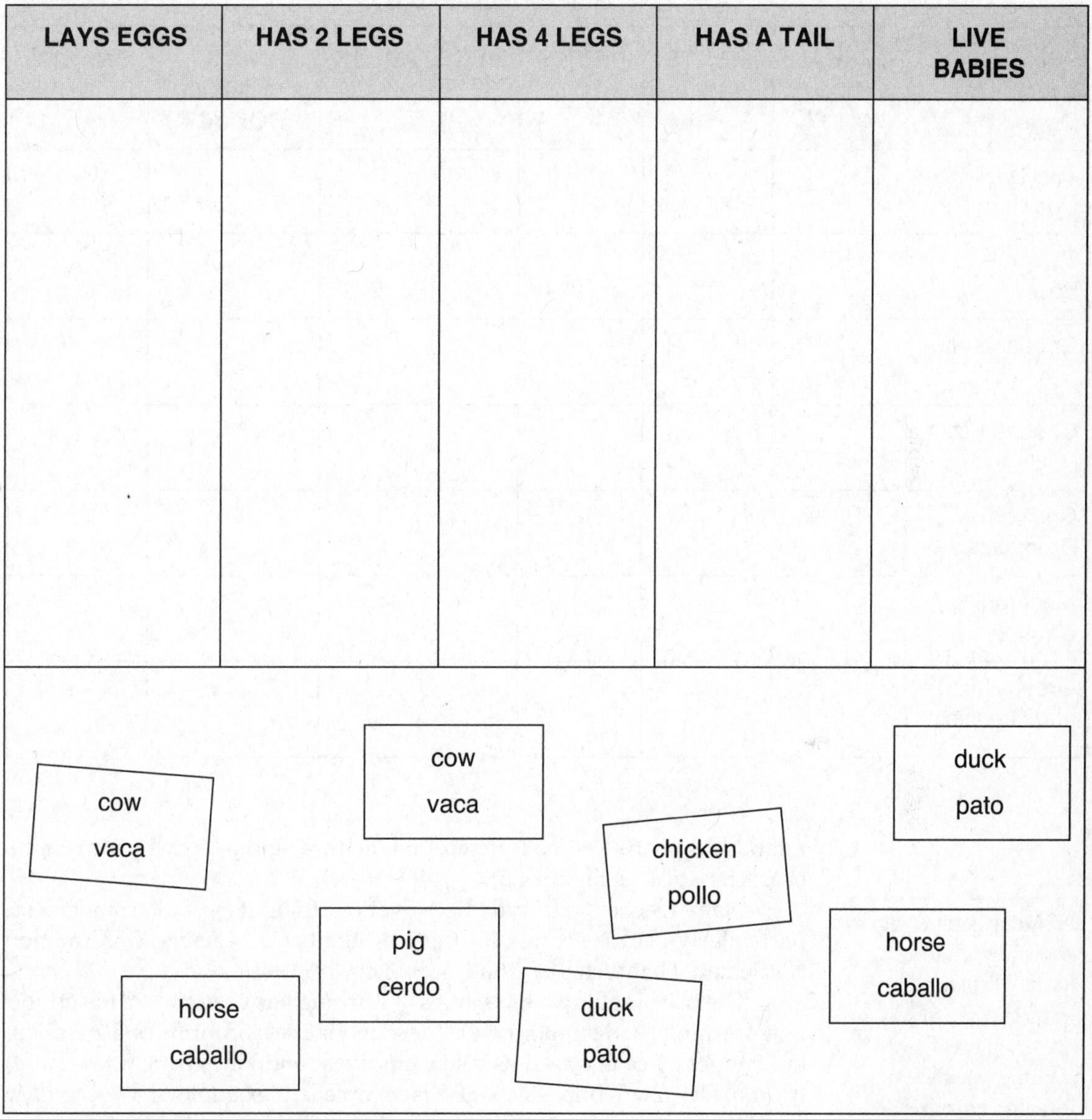

LAYS EGGS	HAS 2 LEGS	HAS 4 LEGS	HAS A TAIL	LIVE BABIES

cow
vaca

cow
vaca

duck
pato

chicken
pollo

pig
cerdo

duck
pato

horse
caballo

horse
caballo

Vocabulary in Second-Grade Science

A popular instructional strategy for categorizing terms by characteristics is semantic feature analysis (SFA) (Anders & Bos, 1986). This procedure assists students in assigning characteristics, or features, using a grid pattern. Vocabulary terms comprise the rows, and the features of those words make up the columns. Students place a "+" in each cell to indicate a

We do not recommend the use of a dash or minus sign as students can easily change it if they are wrong.

Figure 4.5 Semantic feature analysis in second-grade science.

Put a "+" or a "0" in each box.

MENU *Items*	CEREAL, RICE, PASTA	MEATS	FRUITS	VEGETABLES	MILK & MILK PRODUCTS	SNACKS
Turkey Hot Dog						
Tostada Boat						
Cheeseburger						
Cheese Pizza						
Chicken Drumstick						
Macaroni & Cheese						
Green Salad and Dressing						

> SFA draws on what we know about visual display of information: SFA is an example of a matrix type of graphic organizer, as discussed in Chapter 7.

relationship between the term and the feature, and a "0" when it is not a characteristic (see Figure 4.5).

Many teachers attribute the power of SFA to its visual arrangement, particularly because it mimics the way the brain organizes information (Pittleman, Heimlich, Berglund, & French, 1991).

The use of multiple modalities of learning has been shown to support new learning (Armstrong, 1994). These modalities, or forms of expression, are frequently categorized as visual, auditory, and kinesthetic (movement) (Carbo, Dunn & Dunn, 1991). SFA is an excellent example of a vocabulary strategy that taps into a student's visual learning modality. While conventional wisdom cautions against attempting to categorize students according to a particular learning style, educators widely recognize the value of integrating these forms of expression into instruction.

After studying how the body digests food, Pam Pham-Barron's second-grade class is learning about the importance of a balanced diet. The class has previously read from their science textbook about eating healthful foods. In particular, they learned about the components of the food pyramid.

Ms. Pham-Barron knows that this technical vocabulary is daunting for her students, so she plans to have her students use an SFA grid to analyze the day's school lunch menu.

Ms. Pham-Barron passes out the chart that has the lunch entrées listed in the first column and the six food groups across the top. Students working in small groups are to discuss their answers and complete an answer sheet for the whole group.

"Remember that you need to use the food pyramid in your science textbook," the teacher reminds her students. "That will help you decide how much you need to eat at lunch."

The teacher walks around and notices that one group can't agree on how to classify the Tostada Boat entree.

"We can't decide if we should put a plus sign or a zero under vegetables for the boat," complained Edward.

"What is the 'boat' made out of?" asks Ms. Pham-Barron.

"It's made out of corn," offers Jessica. "That's a vegetable."

"But I think it fits under the bread, cereal, rice, and pasta group because it's dried tortilla," counters Edward.

"Do you think it has the same vitamins and minerals whether it is fresh or dried?" asks Ms. Pham-Barron.

"Yes, because the tortilla is a corn without the liquid in it. Remember we read that when we learned about solid and liquid?" commented Lani.

"It might be helpful to think about what's inside the Tostada Boat, too," the teacher replies.

"That's right, it's got meat in it, too," exclaims Edward. "We need to put a plus under meat, too."

After the group work, the class shares what their group did and the teacher clarifies any misunderstandings. The students notice that the most balanced meal would be the turkey hot dog with the green salad and dressing, and a juice to drink.

Vocabulary in Third-Grade Mathematics

It has been a long-held tradition that explicit vocabulary instruction is an essential pre-reading activity to support students' subsequent comprehension (Moore; Readence, & Rickelman, 1989; Tierney & Cunningham, 1984). However, many teachers have experienced the dilemma of pre-teaching the vocabulary to such an extent that the student has little opportunity to apply it, relying instead on rote memorization at the expense of deeper understanding (Johnson & Pearson, 1984). Therefore, a "chicken-and-egg" conundrum results—what comes first, the vocabulary or the connected text?

Vocabulary in Context. Many teachers seek to resolve this argument by teaching both the vocabulary and the context for its use simultaneously. These teachers find success in timing the instruction of technical vocabulary

> Pre-teaching vocabulary is often called front-loading.

using a sequence of "introduce, define, discuss, and apply." Students are alerted to the necessity of a new word, provided a definition, given an opportunity to further refine their understanding through peer discussion, and then invited to experience the word within connected text. This sequence is particularly valuable when teaching technical vocabulary.

Vacca and Vacca (1999) believe that "vocabulary is as unique to a content area as fingerprints are to a human being" (p. 314). And few content areas are more defined by their vocabulary than the field of mathematics. Complicating matters further is the importance of what the National Council for Teachers of Mathematics (2000) calls the factual, procedural, and conceptual understandings that are inexorably woven together in the study of mathematics. This means that in mathematics, students must learn the definition of a term, the algorithms associated with the term, and the underlying principles that will allow them to apply a flexible understanding to solve unfamiliar problems.

> The National Council for Teachers of Mathematics web site can be found at www.nctm.org.

Developing Vocabulary Specific to a Content Area. Roberta Dawson, a third-grade teacher, uses an innovative approach to building flexible technical vocabulary for her students. She encourages students to define and apply their knowledge of the language of mathematics. She follows a sequence of instruction that begins with introducing and defining mathematical terms. Real-world examples and applications of the vocabulary are discussed at length in whole-class and small-group activities. Students apply the new algorithms through guided practice, and then extend their understanding by applying these concepts to novel problems. In addition, they record what they have learned in their mathematics journals (see Figure 4.6).

The vocabulary in the following geometry unit is extensive (54 words in all) and many are new words for the children. Prior to beginning the unit, Mrs. Dawson writes the vocabulary words, definitions, and diagrams on sentence strips and then cuts the vocabulary words apart from the definitions.

At the beginning of each lesson, Mrs. Dawson holds up vocabulary words, reads them aloud to the students, and discusses their common definitions for the words. Mrs. Dawson knows that many of the terms in this unit are complicated, such as *polygon* and *quadrilateral*. She records their predictions on a language chart and then places each word in a pocket chart.

"These are the words we'll be learning to use today," says Mrs. Dawson. She begins by introducing a definition for the term, which students record in their mathematics journals. They use the math textbook to understand examples, and work with manipulatives to understand the properties of plane and solid geometric figures. After rehearsing the words and definitions again using the sentence strips she has prepared, Mrs. Dawson distributes word cards written on tag paper. Working in pairs, students now roam the room looking for examples of today's geometric figures. When all the cards have been placed around the room, she asks each pair to explain their examples to the class. This extemporaneous speech provides

Figure 4.6   Sample page from mathematics journal.

Real Life: This is where I can find this shape:	Definition:
It is like _____ . It is not like _____ .	I can draw a diagram of this shape to help me remember.

students with additional practice in using the words and definitions in their oral language. Finally, students return to their seats and add real life examples and diagrams to their math journals.

Because the volume of vocabulary for this unit is so large, Mrs. Dawson knows that rehearsal is important if the students are to retain the vocabulary definitions. As a warm-up activity, she distributes the vocabulary cards, definitions, and diagrams to the children. They must find the people who possess the correct definition, word, and diagram to form a complete match. Mayra held a card that said *cube*. In a matter of a few minutes, she had located Ly, who held a sentence strip that said, *a solid figure with six equal sides*. Julia soon joined them, as she had a diagram of a cube in her hand.

"They need lots of repetition," says Mrs. Dawson. "This vocabulary is complicated and easy to forget unless they have many opportunities to use it. Math journals, illustrations, vocabulary cards, group matching games—these all allow them to say the words, write the words, read the words, and illustrate the concepts the words represent." An important element in mastering new vocabulary words is repetition and rehearsal with purpose (Baker, Simmons, & Kameenui, 1995). There is little evidence to indicate that students master vocabulary with traditional methods of rote memorization through oral and written drills (Anderson & Nagy, 1992; Gu & Johnson, 1996). Rather, it is repetition embedded in a meaningful context that supports vocabulary acquisition. By integrating vocabulary development into concept building, Mrs. Dawson is able to avoid rote memorization of terms.

"With purpose" is a key phrase. Student learning is greatly enhanced when connected to meaningful activities.

Vocabulary in Fourth-Grade Social Studies, Science, and Mathematics

The ability to deconstruct words to ascertain meaning is directly related to a student's knowledge of root words and affixes. Root words are morphemes (units of meaning) that compose the foundation of all words. Affixes (prefixes and suffixes) are attached to the root word to modify the meaning. For example, the word *dictionary* comes from the Latin *dictio* meaning "to speak." Other root words are derived from Greek words, such as *phonogram* from *phono* meaning "sound." Other root words are free morphemes, meaning that they can stand alone as a word. For example, *port*, *form*, and *act* are im*port*ant common root words that also serve as plat*form*s for *act*ivating word knowledge through the addition of a variety of affixes. By closely investigating the parts of a word, including root words, derivations, and affixes, students can acquire tools to use with unfamiliar words, thus expanding their general and specialized vocabularies.

Word study often begins with free morphemes like *port* because their meaning is generally more accessible. After discussing the meaning of *port* as a Latin word for "carry," and the common definition of the word as "a place where ships can safely dock," word extensions become more apparent. *Porter* means a person who carries an object; *airport* means a safe place for airplanes, and *import* means to carry something into an area.

In addition to root word analysis, instruction about prefixes and suffixes also occurs regularly. Understanding the morphological basis of affixes is critical to word knowledge. Cunningham (2002) estimates that "re-, dis-, un-, and in-/im- account for over half of all the prefixes readers will ever see . . . [and] -s/-es, -ed, and -ing account for 65% of all words with suffixes" (p. 4). Coupled with root word and derivational knowledge, students who understand common affixes possess a powerful set of skills for taking words apart and reassembling them to extract their meaning. This level of word analysis also appears to support reading as well because learners who can extract the morphological characteristics of the word will process and analyze across morphemes rather than syllables (Templeton, 1992).

Colleen Crandall focuses her word skill-building lessons on the challenging vocabulary words that students in her class use in mathematics, science, and social studies. Mrs. Crandall's goal is to teach her students to use prefixes, suffixes, and root words to help reduce spelling errors and to add meaning to new words her students encounter in fourth grade.

Using the grade-level textbooks as a base, Mrs. Crandall creates a word list each week of the school year with words from social studies, science, mathematics, and language arts. Her curriculum plan for the school year is mapped out prior to the beginning of each quarter of the school year. Her weekly plans are flexible, but she uses this master plan to keep herself on track through the school year.

> Like context clues, these morphological characteristics contribute to a student's understanding of the term and the ways it might be used.

Figure 4.7   Weekly vocabulary word list for fourth-grade.

May 17-21, 2007

Vocabulary words for the week: (SS) Levi Strauss, represent**ative**, conven**tion**, constitu**tion**, legisla**ture**, capital, (Science) volume, dens**ity**, (Mathematics) **bi**–two, **tri**–three, **penta**–five, **centi**–hundred, **kilo**–thousand, **circ**–around, **dis**–not, **poly**–many, **non**–not

As she begins the weekly plan, vocabulary words are organized into word-sort activities to set up strategies that will allow her students to develop spelling and vocabulary skills, and to increase comprehension of text material. The words are introduced and deconstructed to identify affixes that contribute to the meaning of the word. She begins this process in small groups during word-study center rotation time, and over time she has continued using the process with one student serving as the group facilitator. An example of a word list for the week might look like the one shown in Figure 4.7.

For Mrs. Crandall, the most exciting thing about using this kind of word study practice in the classroom is experiencing students' connections to new vocabulary experiences in real life. For example, when her class went to School in the Park (a unique program at her school where students spend part of the year at local museums), a number of hands went up when the museum education teacher used a new vocabulary term—*archaeology*.

Erik commented, "We've seen that word ending, *-logy*, in the Museum of Natural History—it means the study of something." As a result, the museum teacher only had to explain the meaning of the root *archae-*, which means *ancient*.

Erik laughed. "I get it—the study of ancient things. That's why there's all this old stuff around here!"

On a second trip to the Museum of Natural History, the word *geology* was used. Keyonna explained to the museum educator, "I think *geo-* means something about the surface of earth because we had that word in mathematics when we studied geometry. I also know that *-logy* means the study of something, because we had that here before."

"I teach vocabulary specific to the subject matter, but I also want them to understand that many of these words are related to one another across disciplines," Mrs. Crandall noted later. "When you understand how words work, science, math, and social studies become tools to understand the whole world, not just a sliver of it."

Vocabulary in Fifth-Grade Science

Visual representations can enhance student understanding of word meanings. Aida Allen uses specially designed vocabulary cards in her science class. These cards are based on the Frayer model of concept development, which posits that learning occurs when a definition, characteristics, examples, and non-examples are understood by the learner (Frayer & Klausmeier, 1971). These vocabulary cards are created using 4" × 6" index cards divided into quadrants. The concept word is written in the top left quadrant, and the definition in the student's own words is recorded in the upper right quadrant of the card. An opposite or non-example is written in the lower right quadrant, and a diagram or graphic symbol representing the term is drawn in the lower left quadrant.

These vocabulary cards serve several uses in the class. First, when placed on a binder ring, the cards become an easily accessible reference for the student when reading or completing science labs. The time involved in creating each card also provides an opportunity for students to spend an extended period of time concentrating on the meaning, use, and representation of the term, thereby increasing the likelihood that the term will become a part of their permanent vocabulary.

Ms. Allen uses a simple science experiment to introduce the vocabulary of the scientific method. "It's time for science," Ms. Allen announces to her fifth graders. "Today we are going to make a very cool vocabulary organizer to help you when you visit the science museum next week, and we'll be doing some experiments on matter. Scientists do their work in a very special way—they try to control certain things called variables to see what will happen. And they try to make sure that someone else can do the same experiment and get the same results. This is called the scientific method, and it helps scientists perform experiments that lead them to answers. Today I'm going to show you what the scientific method looks like and how it works when you're in a science laboratory. We'll make our vocabulary cards as we go along."

Proceeding with her demonstration, Ms. Allen instructs the students to hypothesize at their tables about how many pennies it will take to sink an aluminum-foil model of a boat and to record their guess on a sticky note. After writing their predictions, she explains what they have just done.

"How did you come up with your answer?" Ms. Allen asks Romel.

"I thought about how heavy pennies feel in my hand. I tried to decide how many I could put in the foil boat before it sank," he replies.

"Exactly! I want you to notice what you did to come up with your answer. You thought about what you knew about pennies and how much they might weigh. You didn't say '5000 pennies' because you knew from experience that would be very heavy. Instead, you made an educated guess. That's what a hypothesis is—an educated guess," she explains. "Now make your first vocabulary card for the word *hypothesis*."

The students get to work on their first card and within a few minutes they have created a good representation of what the concept of a hypothesis means to them. An example of a vocabulary card appears in Figure 4.8.

Ms. Allen calls one student to the overhead to act as the scribe, and as the experiment continues, she models aloud her thinking about each

Figure 4.8 Frayer model vocabulary cards in science.

Template

Vocabulary word	Definiton in students' own words
Graphic or picture	Sentence using word

Example

Hypothesis	A good guess (I know something)
 💡	A hypothesis is any old guess that doesn't make sense.

step. She is careful to include lots of descriptive words about each step of the experiment, so the students will be able to successfully describe the demonstration. Before long, they have created vocabulary cards for the concepts of *research, problem, hypothesis, experimentation,* and *conclusion.*

"We used these repeatedly throughout the week so that the students would get comfortable with this vocabulary. Because they are on binder rings, they were very easy to take with us to the science museum. As they performed experiments there, the students were able to make connections to the vocabulary and concepts we had first learned the week before," Ms. Allen remarked later.

Conclusion

The number of words students need in their academic vocabulary skyrockets during their elementary schooling years. The sheer volume of words students will encounter during their informational reading can be overwhelming. Isolated instruction in individual words is an ineffective use of instructional time, and is proven to be inadequate to keep pace with the content-area needs. Instead, effective teachers rely on a variety of approaches to foster learning of general, specialized, and technical vocabulary.

Common vocabulary can be successfully taught through word walls constructed from any of a number of sources for word lists. These visual glossaries can assist students in both usage and spelling. Interesting and innovative resource materials, such as rhyming dictionaries, thesauri, slang dictionaries, and web sites can expand students' knowledge and usage of words.

A particular challenge for English language learners is the array of multiple-meaning words. Often Anglo-Saxon in origin, these small words can offer a broad number of meanings across varied grammatical structures. Explicit instruction in multiple-meaning words can boost comprehension.

Specialized and technical vocabulary in the content area is also vital for learning. Vocabulary role-play and word sorts can introduce novel ways for students to experience a deeper understanding of a word and its relationship to other words. Teachers have also found success with structuring activities to invite students to write about words. Examples of these strategies include vocabulary journals and cards.

When vocabulary is taught and word knowledge is fostered, students gain more from the informational texts they read. It is hard to imagine that students can read for information when they don't know the words on the page.

References

Anders, P. L., & Bos, C. S. (1986). Semantic feature analysis: An interactive strategy for vocabulary development and text comprehension. *Journal of Reading, 29,* 610–616.

Anderson, R. C., & Nagy, W. E. (1992). The vocabulary conundrum.

American Educator: The Professional Journal of the American Federation of Teachers, 16(4), 14–18, 44–47.

Armstrong, T. (1994). *Multiple intelligences in the classroom.* Alexandria, VA: Association for Supervisors of Curriculum Development.

Asher, J. J. (1969). The total physical response approach to second language learning. *Modern Language Journal, 53*(1), 3–17.

Baker, S. K., Simmons, D. C., & Kameenui, E. J. (1995). *Vocabulary acquisition: Curricular and instructional implications for diverse learners.* Technical report no. 13. University of Oregon: National Center to Improve the Tools for Educators.

Baumann, J. F., Edwards, E. C., Font, G., Tereshinski, C. A., Kame'enui, E. J., & Olejnik, S. (2002). Teaching morphemic and contextual analysis to fifth-grade students. *Reading Research Quarterly, 37*, 150–176.

Blachowicz, C. L. Z., & Fisher, P. (2000). Vocabulary instruction. In M. L. Kamil, P. B. Mosenthal, P. D. Pearson, & R. Barr (Eds.), *Handbook of reading research* (Vol. III, pp. 503–523). Mahwah, NJ: Lawrence Erlbaum.

Blachowicz, C. L. Z., & Fisher, P. (2002). *Teaching vocabulary in all classrooms* (2nd/ed.). Upper Saddle River, NJ: Merrill Prentice Hall.

Blanchfield, C. (Ed.) (2001). *Creative vocabulary: Strategies for teaching vocabulary in grades K–12.* Fresno, CA: San Joaquin Valley Writing Project.

Carbo, M., Dunn, R., & Dunn, K. (1991). *Teaching students to read through their individual learning styles.* Boston: Allyn and Bacon.

Cunningham, P. M. (2002). *Prefixes and suffixes: Systematic sequential phonics and spelling.* Greensboro, NC: Carson-Dellosa.

Cunningham, P. M. & Allington, R. L. (2003). *Classrooms that work: They can all read and write* (3rd ed.). Boston: Allyn & Bacon.

Cunningham, P. M., & Hall, D. P. (1998). *Month by month phonics for the upper grades.* Greensboro, NC: Carson-Dellosa.

Dolch, E. W. (1936). A basic sight vocabulary. *The Elementary School Journal, 36,* 456–460.

Flood, J., Lapp, D., & Fisher, D. (2003). Reading comprehension instruction. In J. Flood, D. Lapp, J. M. Jensen, & J. R. Squire (Eds.), *Handbook of research on teaching the English language arts* (pp. 931–941). Mahwah, NJ: Lawrence Erlbaum.

Frayer, D. A., & Klausmeier, H. J. (1971). *Modeling as a technique for promoting classroom learning and prosocial behavior: Theoretical paper 39.* Madison, WI: University of Wisconsin Center for Research and Development for Cognitive Learning.

Fry, E. B. (1997). *Dr. Fry's 1000 instant words: The most common words for teaching reading, writing, and spelling.* Westminister, CA: Teacher Created Materials.

Gillet, J. W., & Temple, C. (1978). Word knowledge: A cognitive view. *Reading World, 18,* 132–140.

Goodman, L. (2001). A tool for learning: Vocabulary self-awareness. In C. Blanchfield (Ed.) *Creative vocabulary: Strategies for teaching vocabulary in grades K–12.* Fresno, CA: San Joaquin Valley Writing Project.

Gu, Y., & Johnson; R. K. (1996). Vocabulary learning strategies and language learning outcomes. *Language Learning, 46,* 643–679.

Harwell, J. M. (2001). *Complete learning disabilities handbook: Ready-to-use strategies and activities for teaching students with learning disabilities* (2nd ed.). Paramus, NJ: Center for Applied Research in Education.

Joel, B. (1989). We didn't start the fire. On *Storm front* [CD]. New York: Sony.

Johnson, D. D., & Pearson, P. D. (1984). *Teaching reading vocabulary* (2nd ed.). New York: Holt, Rinehart, & Winston.

Klein, M. L. (1988). *Teaching reading comprehension and vocabulary: A guide for teachers.* Upper Saddle River, NJ: Prentice Hall.

Lapp, D., Jacobson, J., Fisher, D., & Flood, J. (2000). Tried and true word study and vocabulary practices. *The California Reader, 33*(2), 25–30.

Lederer, R. (1998). *Crazy English: The ultimate joyride through our language.* New York: Pocket Books.

Marlatt, E. A. (1995). Language through total physical response. *Perspectives in Education and Deafness, 13*(4), 18–20.

McGuffey's Eclectic Spelling-Book. (1879). Rev. ed. New York: John Wiley and Sons. (Modern reproduction).

Moore, D. W., Readence, J. E., & Rickelman, R. J. (1989). *Prereading activities for content area reading and writing* (2nd ed.). Newark, DE: International Reading Association.

Nagy, W. E., & Herman, P. (1987). Breadth and depth of vocabulary Knowledge: Implications for acquisition and instruction. In M. G. McKeown & M. E. Curtis (Eds.), *The nature of vocabulary acquisition* (pp. 19–35). Hillsdale, NJ: Lawrence Erlbaum Associates.

National Council for Teachers of Mathematics. (2000). *Principles and standards for school mathematics.* Reston, VA: NCTM.

National Research Council. (2005). *How students learn: History, mathematics, and science in the classroom.* Committee on *How people learn: A targeted report for teachers,* M. S. Donovan and J. D. Bransford (Eds.). Division of Behavioral and Social Sciences and Education. Washington, DC: National Academies Press.

Peterson, A. (1996). *The writer's workout book: 113 stretches toward better prose.* Berkeley, CA: National Writing Project. Used with permission.

Pittleman, S. D., Heimlich, J. E., Berglund, R. L., & French, M. P. (1991). *Semantic feature analysis: Classroom applications.* Newark, DE: International Reading Association.

Snow, C. E., Burns, M. S., & Griffin , P. (Eds.) (1998). *Preventing reading difficulties in young children.* Washington, DC: National Academies Press.

Stahl, S. A., & Fairbanks, M. M. (1986). The effects of vocabulary instruction: A model-based meta-analysis. *Review of Educational Research, 56,* 72–110.

Templeton, S. (1992). Theory, nature and pedagogy of higher-order orthographic development in older children. In S. Templeton & D. Bear (Eds.), *Development of orthographic knowledge and the foundation of literacy: A memorial festschrift for Edmund H. Henderson* (pp. 253–278). Hillsdale, NJ: Lawrence Erlbaum.

Thorndike, E. L., & Lorge, I. (1944). *The teacher's words book of 30,000 words.* New York: Teachers College, Columbia University.

Tierney, R. J., & Cunningham, J. W. (1984). Research on reading comprehension. In P. D. Pearson, R. Barr, M. L. Kamil, & P. Mosenthal (Eds.), *Handbook of reading research* (pp. 609–655). Mahwah, NJ: Lawrence Erlbaum.

Twain, M. (1890). In G. Bainton (Ed.), *The art of authorship: Literary reminiscences, methods of work, and advice to young beginners, personally contributed by leading authors of the day* (pp. 85–88). New York: D. Appleton and Company.

Vacca, R. T., & Vacca, J. L. (1999). *Content area reading: Literacy and learning across the curriculum* (6th ed.). New York: Longman.

Children's Literature Cited

Barner, B. (1996). *Dem Bones*. San Francisco: Chronicle Books.

Lowry, L. (1994). *The giver*. New York: Laurel Leaf.

Newcome, Z. (2002). *Head, shoulders, knees, and toes: And other action rhymes*. New York: Candlewick.

Ryan, P. M. (2002). *When Marian sang: The true recital of Marian Anderson*. New York: Scholastic.

Steinbeck, J. (1939). *The grapes of wrath*. New York: Viking.

Chapter 5

Nancy Frey

Douglas Fisher

Maureen Begley

Read-Alouds and Shared Readings:

Building Vocabulary and Background Knowledge During Reading

"*T*he reading box!" exclaims Reynaldo. "Hey, she's got the read-ing box out today!" says fellow kindergartner Elaine. The other children catch sight of the box and grin. These children know that when their teacher Kerrie Keough has the reading box, a book is sure to follow. She dramatically shakes the box and listens for telltale noises that might reveal the contents. A jingling sound can be heard from within. "Should I open the box?" she asks. The children answer with a loud, collective "YES!"

"Now, remember," says Mrs. Keough, "all the items in the reading box are clues about the book."

The first item lifted from the box is a rose. One child says, "It's a flower!" Another child says, "Yeah, it's a rose, my mom has one." Next, a chocolate cookie is held aloft. Of course, most children immediately grab their stomachs and launch into a discussion about everyone's favorite cookies.

Next comes a hat made from newspaper, then a bone, and finally a fish. With each item, Mrs. Keough is introducing vocabulary and activating background knowledge. She shakes the box once more to see if there is anything left. Five shiny pennies tumble out. Mrs. Keough inquires about the name of the coin, its worth, and its purchasing power.

"I wonder what this story is about?" asks Mrs. Keough. "Put your imagination caps on." She holds up both hands and quietly counts to ten. The students formulate an idea and then turn to a partner at the count of ten. Each child begins sharing his or her predictions. Mrs. Keough charts their predictions so the children can see their ideas in writing.

"Your ideas are great!" says Mrs. Keough. "You're really thinking about this book and we haven't even read it yet. Let's read it to find out how these clues help us to understand the story." With that, she begins her mathematics lesson with a read-aloud of Benny's Pennies (Brisson, 1993). The children will soon be immersed in Benny's dilemma—how to best spend the five pennies. Should it be a rose for his mother, a cookie for his brother, a hat for his sister, a bone for the dog, or a fish for the cat?

Interest in the practice of read-alouds and shared readings in content-area classrooms has increased substantially in the last decade. As early as 1925, William S. Gray was advocating the importance of literacy in geography, history, and mathematics instruction. That said, it was rare to find trade books used in content instruction, and at various times there has been some resistance to instruction of any reading strategies during content lessons (Price, 1978; Rieck, 1977; Smith & Otto, 1969). However, deeper understandings of the connections between reading and learning have caused content-area teachers to reexamine sound literacy practices in their classrooms (McKenna & Robinson, 1990; Ornstein, 1994).

Two literacy practices borrowed from developmental reading theory and customized for content instruction are read-alouds and shared reading. A *read-aloud* is a text or passage selected by the teacher to read publicly to a large or small group of students. A primary purpose for the read-aloud selection is to focus on the content of the text. A *shared reading* is a text or passage that is shared by teacher and student, but is read aloud by the teacher. In shared readings, the students can see the text also. It is usually chosen both for its content and to draw attention to a particular text feature or comprehension strategy.

> In both read-alouds and shared reading, the reading is done by the teacher, not the students.

Read–Alouds

The practice of reading aloud in public dates to the dawn of written language. Throughout history, town criers shared local news, religious orders proclaimed scriptures, and lectors, paid by the laborers themselves, read classical works and newspapers to Cuban cigar factory workers (Manguel, 1996). Even in widely literate societies, the act of being read to continues to enthrall. For example, demand for audiobooks rose 75% between 1995 and 1999, and some estimate that for every ten print books sold, one audio program is sold (Block, 1999).

A large body of evidence suggests that being read to by an adult enhances literacy development. For example, young children who are read to are more likely to enter school with higher literacy skills (Anderson, Hiebert, Scott, & Wilkinson, 1985). Likewise, a longitudinal study of students identified as precocious readers (before age 6) revealed that they were more likely to be read to by their parents (Durkin, 1974–1975). Correlation studies demonstrate an association between exposure to read-alouds and positive motivation to read (Greaney & Hegarty, 1987; Morrow & Young, 1997). Conversely, Rosow's (1988) interviews with illiterate adults demonstrated the negative effects when read-alouds are not available. Her data revealed that none of the interviewed adults had any recollection of being read to as a child.

> Do you remember being read to as a child? Who read to you?

Effectiveness of Read–Alouds

While read-alouds have been shown to be effective for young children's literacy development, they can also be used to motivate older readers to become interested in a topic (Ivey, 2003). Students themselves have reported that a preferred instructional practice is having teachers read portions of text aloud to introduce new readings and promote interest (Worthy, 2002). It appears that students appreciate the read-aloud event as an opportunity to share the teacher's enthusiasm and interest in the topic.

> Teachers should monitor student interest in reading and topics associated with the content. This can be accomplished using an interest survey as described in Chapter 10.

Vocabulary and Comprehension. Read-aloud instruction has been demonstrated to be effective at the word and text level as well (Schippert, 2005). Cohen (1968) demonstrated that second-grade students in classrooms where read-aloud occurred daily outperformed their peers on standardized measures of vocabulary and comprehension. Cohen's findings were further supported by subsequent work on the effects of repeated readings of books by the teacher (Martinez & Roser, 1985). So powerful are teacher read-alouds that a study found that when struggling fifth-graders were read to once a week for 12 weeks, they outscored peers on a standardized achievement test (Ouellette, Dagostino, & Carifio, 1999). While we do not advocate such infrequent and short-lived read-alouds, we are impressed with the vigor of this instructional practice in even limited use.

Text Complexity.   Another advantage to the use of read-alouds is the level of text complexity that can be used. When text is read aloud by the teacher, students can access books that might otherwise be too difficult for them to read independently. This is essential in content instruction when students are trying to read for information and learn from increasingly complex texts. Text complexity rises rapidly during the elementary years, and students who have reading difficulties often find themselves unable to comprehend the information in textbooks. A vicious cycle then begins; these students fail to assimilate the information, which further impacts their ability to use it as prior knowledge for new content. Thus, the gap continues to widen as students with reading difficulties fall further behind their classmates. The well known "fourth-grade slump" is associated with the increased informational-text demands (Chall, Jacobs, & Baldwin, 1990). Indeed, these researchers and others suggest it may be possible to reduce the fourth-grade slump by using more informational text in the primary grades (Duke, 2000; Kristo & Bamford, 2004).

While read-alouds alone cannot compensate for these gaps, they can be used to introduce important texts that some students might not otherwise be able to read and comprehend independently (Wang, 1996). In other words, read-alouds are a viable strategy for clarifying difficult text and are motivating for students.

The Benefits for English Language Learners

English language learners benefit from exposure to read-alouds as well. Any child acquiring a new language is subjected to a bewildering array of social, pragmatic, and academic language patterns (Nieto, 1992). Read-alouds create opportunities for the teacher to use multiple pathways to promote understanding of the content of the text, including intonation, facial expressions, and gestures (Cummins, 1980).

This also helps students meet and exceed the English language arts standards for listening.

Read-alouds also support language acquisition for English language learners because they provide fluent language role models (Amer, 1997). At the same time, it introduces new and unfamiliar language in a context that is pleasant and supportive for young English language learners (Ghosn, 2002). The text choice for the read-aloud is also crucial for English language learners. Selecting books that use engaging illustrations or photographs adds another dimension to assist students in creating new schema (Early & Tang, 1991). Schema building for English language learners is enhanced by a preview-review approach (Ulanoff & Pucci, 2001).

Planning for Read–Alouds in Content Instruction

The successful use of read-alouds in content instruction has been well documented. It has been shown to be effective in science (Campbell, 2001), social studies (Farris & Fuhler, 1994), and mathematics (Maxim, 1998). In addition, it is a useful tool for fostering discussion on informational topics

Regardless of where you find your readings, make sure they are connected to the content you are teaching.

(Schifini, 1996). However, text selection can also be daunting for teachers who are unfamiliar with the range of possibilities associated with content areas of social studies, mathematics, science, and the visual and performing arts. Several excellent teacher resources on text selection are available, including *Read All About It!* (Trelease, 1993) and *The Read-Aloud Handbook* (Trelease, 2002). The author of these books has compiled an array of short stories, poems, and newspaper articles suitable for a number of classroom applications. We've created a list of great read-aloud picture books for content instruction. This list can be found in Figure 5.1.

There are several elements to consider in planning and delivering read-alouds to elementary students. These elements also serve as indicators of effective instructional practice for administrative observations. A self-assessment rubric of these same elements appears in Figure 5.2.

1. *Select readings that are appropriate to content, to students' emotional and social development, and to their interests.* Read-alouds can be especially useful for activating background knowledge and connecting to student experiences.

2. *Practice the selection.* You wouldn't go on stage without rehearsing, would you? Think of the read-aloud as a performance. Rehearsal allows you to make decisions about inflection, rate, and pitch.

3. *Model fluent oral reading.* In addition to exposure to content information, a read-aloud also serves as a place for students to hear fluent oral reading. Reading acquisition for students with reading difficulties, as well as some English language learners, can be inhibited by their own disfluent reading.

See Chapter 3 for information on using anticipatory activities.

4. *Engage students and hook them into listening to the text.* Creating anticipation for the reading, as the teacher did in the *Midnight Ride of Paul Revere* scenario, can activate student interest and increase meaning. When appropriate, pair read-alouds with other supporting materials such as props, diagrams, manipulatives, or illustrations.

5. *Stop periodically to ask questions.* Talk within the text enhances student understanding. Plan questions in advance for critical thinking and write them on a sticky note to remind yourself. Don't rely only on "constrained questions" (Beck & McKeown, 2001) that can be answered in a few words. For example, "What do you believe was the author's purpose for writing this story?" allows for a more detailed response than, "Where did the story take place?" Create inferential questions that invite connections beyond the text as well.

See Chapter 6 for more information on questioning strategies.

6. *Engage students in book discussions.* This is related to the questioning that is done during the reading. Choose read-alouds that foster further discussion once the reading is complete. You might ask students why you chose this particular reading, or how it relates to the current topic of study.

Figure 5.1 Read-aloud book list by subject.

Read-Alouds for Mathematics

Carle, E. (1996). *The grouchy ladybug.* New York: HarperCollins.

Cuyler, M. (2000). *100th day worries.* New York: Simon & Schuster.

Friedman, A. (1996). *The king's commissioners.* New York: Scholastic.

Hutchins, P. (1986). *The doorbell rang.* New York: Greenwillow.

Masurel, C. (1997). *Ten dogs in a window.* New York: North-South.

McKissack, P. (1996). *A million fish . . . . more or less.* New York: Dragonfly.

Merriam, E. (1993). 12 ways to get to 11. New York: Aladdin.

Neuschwander, C. (1997). *Sir Cumference and the first round table.* Watertown, MA: Charlesbridge.

Pappas, T. (1991). *Math talk: Mathematical ideas in poems for two voices.* San Carlos, CA: Wide World.

Pinczes, E. J. (1993). *One hundred hungry ants.* Boston: Houghton Mifflin.

Pinczes, E. J. (1995). *A remainder of one.* Boston: Houghton Mifflin.

Rumford, J. (1998). *The-island-below-the-star.* Boston: Houghton Mifflin.

Schwartz, D. (1985). *How much is a million?* New York: Lothrop, Lee & Shepard.

Schwartz, D. M. (1999). *If you hopped like a frog.* New York: Scholastic.

Tang, G. (2001). *The grapes of math: Mind stretching math riddles.* New York: Scholastic.

Tompert, A. (1998). *Grandfather Tang's story: A tale told with tangrams.* New York: Dragonfly.

Viorst, J. (1978). *Alexander, who used to be rich last Sunday.* New York: Aladdin.

Wells, R. (2000). *Emily's first 100 days of school.* New York: Hyperion.

Zimelman, N. (1992). *How the second grade got $8,205.50 to visit the Statue of Liberty.* Morton Grove, IL: Albert Whitman.

Read-Alouds for Science

Brisson, P. (1994). *Wanda's roses.* Honesdale, PA: Boyds Mill Press.

Cole, J. (1995). *Spider's lunch: All about garden spiders.* New York: Grosset & Dunlap.

Cole, J. (1999). *The magic school bus and the electric field trip.* New York: Scholastic.

Cole, J. (2001). *The magic school bus explores the world of senses.* New York: Scholastic.

Darian, S. (1996). *Grandpa's garden.* Nevada City, CA: Dawn.

Gibbons, G. (1991). *From seed to plant.* New York: Holiday House.

Glasser, L. (1992). *Wonderful worms.* Brookfield, CT: Millbrook.

Pascoe, E. (1996). *Earthworms.* Woodbridge, CT: Blackbirch.

Pfeffer, W. (1997). *A log's life.* New York: Simon and Schuster.

Preiss, J., & Preiss, R. (1998). *You can't take a balloon in the Metropolitan Museum.* New York: Dial.

Ryder, J. (2003). *Wild birds.* New York: HarperCollins.

Schwartz, D. *Q is for quark.* New York: Tricycle.

Simon, S. (1990). *Oceans.* New York: Morrow.

Weisner, D. (2001). *June 29, 1999.* Sagebrush.

(continued)

Figure 5.1 Read-aloud book list by subject. *(continued)*

Read-Alouds for Social Studies

Appelt, K. (2005). *Miss Lady Bird's wildflowers: How a first lady changed America.* New York: HarperCollins.

Blumenthal, K. (2002). *Six days in October: The stock market crash of 1929.* New York: Athenum.

Clinton, C. (2005). *Hold the flag high.* New York: HarperCollins.

Freedman, R. (2000). *Give me liberty! The story of the Declaration of Independence.* New York: Holiday House.

Krull, K. (1998). *Lives of the presidents: Fame, shame (and what the neighbors thought).* San Diego: Harcourt Brace.

Macaulay, D. (1975). *Pyramid.* Boston: Houghton Mifflin.

Macaulay, D. (2003). *Mosque.* Boston: Houghton Mifflin.

Maestro, B., & Maestro, G. (1991). *The discovery of the Americas: From prehistory through the age of Columbus.* New York: HarperTrophy.

McPherson, J. M. (2002). *Fields of fury: The American Civil War.* New York: Athenum.

Schanzer, R. (1997). *How we crossed the west: The adventures of Lewis & Clark.* Washington, DC: National Geographic.

St. George, J. (2000). *So you want to be president.* New York: Penguin Putnam.

Wheeler, J. C. (2002). *September 11, 2001: The day that changed America.* Edina, MN: ABDO & Daughters.

Read-Alouds for the Visual and Performing Arts

Carle, E. (1996). *I see a song.* New York: Scholastic.

Curtis, G. (1998). *The bat boy and the violin.* New York: Simon and Schuster.

Jabar, C. (1992). *Shimmy shake earthquake: Don't forget to dance poems.* Boston: Little, Brown.

Krull, K. (1993). *Lives of the musicians: Good times, bad times (and what the neighbors thought).* San Diego: Harcourt Brace.

Levine, R. (2000). *Story of the orchestra: A child's introduction to the instruments, the music, the musicians, and the composers.* New York: Black Dog and Leventhal.

Littlesugar, A. (1999). *Marie in the fourth position: The story of Degas' "The Little Dancer."* New York: Paperstar.

Martin, B., & Archambault, J. (1986). *Barn dance.* New York: Henry Holt.

Moss, L. (1995). *Zin! Zin! Zin! A violin.* New York: Simon and Schuster.

Pickney, A. (1993). *Alvin Ailey.* New York: Hyperion.

Waldman, N. (1999). *The starry night.* Honesdale, PA: Boyds Mill.

Winter, J. (1998). *My name is Georgia.* San Diego: Harcourt Brace.

Wu, N. (1997). *Fish faces.* Isle of Wight, England: Owlet.

Figure 5.2 Rubric for read-alouds.

	SUCCESSFULLY IMPLEMENTED	MODERATELY SUCCESSFUL	JUST GETTING STARTED	NOT EVIDENT
Text chosen appropriate for students' interests and level				
Selection has been previewed and practiced				
Clear purpose established				
Teacher provides fluent reading model				
Students are engaged in listening				
Teacher stops periodically and questions thoughtfully (literal, interpretive, and evaluative)				
Students engaged in discussion				
Connections to reading and writing				

COMMENTS:

7. *Make explicit connections to students' independent reading and writing.* A read-aloud should relate directly to the content—otherwise, it might have limited applicability in the curriculum. It should also connect to other literacy experiences. For instance, the end of a read-aloud event might signal an ideal time to invite students to write a response. Questions raised through the discussion following the reading might also prompt further research and outside reading by students.

Shared Reading

In addition to read-alouds, teachers also extend literacy experiences through shared reading. Shared reading is the practice of reading collaboratively with students. Unlike read-alouds, where only the teacher can see the text, an important feature of a shared reading experience is that students can follow along silently as the teacher reads aloud. Shared-reading lessons specifically focus on a comprehension strategy, text feature, or reading behavior, while read-aloud lessons sometimes focus only on the content itself. As with read-alouds, the practice of shared reading has its roots in emergent literacy practices for young children (Holdaway, 1982).

Shared reading serves as an instructional bridge between the teacher-directed read-aloud and student-directed independent reading. While read-alouds are teacher-controlled and independent reading is student-controlled, these literacy activities provide little opportunity for teacher and students to alternately take and relinquish the lead. Pearson and Gallagher (1983) proposed a model for comprehension instruction called the gradual release of responsibility. They suggest that using guided practice as a method for instruction allows students to attempt new strategies for eventual use in their own reading. Thus, through instructional practices like shared reading, teachers move from modeling in read-alouds to helping their students apply those strategies during independent reading.

Shared reading is grounded in the sociocultural theory of Vygotsky's zones of proximal development (1978). This allows for scaffolding of information to extend learning through guided instruction. Vygotsky theorized that when students receive support just beyond what they can accomplish independently, they learn new skills and concepts. He defined the zone as

> the distance between the actual developmental level as determined by independent problem solving and the level of potential development as determined through problem solving under adult guidance or in collaboration with peers. (p. 86)

The scaffolded instruction of shared reading extends students' learning. In addition, the learner receives immediate feedback and further prompts to arrive at solutions (Tharp & Gallimore, 1989). While students

---

See Chapter 9 for more ideas on using writing to learn.

The concept behind the gradual release of responsibility is that students experience scaffolded instruction that moves them from teacher-modeled activities to student-directed work.

Vygotsky, a Russian psychologist, also theorized that humans learn when they transfer information to inner speech.

may not be able to initiate a new strategy alone, they can easily apply one with guidance, thereby advancing their zone of proximal development.

Shared-reading events allow teachers to address comprehension strategies through modeling. For instance, teachers who work with English language learners and students with reading difficulties recognize the power of a daily fluent reading model (Early, 1990). This allows teachers to model prosody (the use of rate, pitch, inflection, and tone) to demonstrate subtle language techniques that influence meaning (Pynte & Prieur, 1996). While read-alouds also present opportunities for modeling prosody, they lack the visual prompts that signal fluent readers. Because students can see the text in shared reading, they can associate the punctuation, layout, spacing, phrase boundaries, and other text cues used by the teacher to decide how the piece should be read and interpreted. Perhaps the most powerful endorsement of this effect comes from students. A survey of 600 students revealed that they attributed their literacy achievement growth to shared reading (Allen, 2001).

Implementing Shared Reading

As with all instruction, practical application is as important as the theoretical underpinning. One of the first decisions teachers make in shared reading is how students will interact with the reading. Teachers employ several methods to share the text with students, such as using an overhead projector to display enlarged print on a screen.

> E-books and audiobooks can be used together, sharing text with a laptop and data projector while being read by a professional reader.

This is particularly convenient for textbook passages, graphs, or charts. This technique also allows the teacher to highlight words or phrases using overhead markers. At other times, photocopies of a passage can be distributed to each student. This encourages students to become more actively involved with the reading, including making notations directly on the paper. While marking passages in a school textbook is usually discouraged for obvious reasons, this method provides students with guided practice for interacting with text. When teachers construct participatory approaches to text, they assist their students in moving away from ineffective beliefs about reading as a passive experience (Brown, Palinscar, & Armbruster, 1994; Wade & Moje, 2000).

Selecting Texts for Shared Reading

Text choice, which is equally important in shared reading, differs on several levels from text choice for read-alouds. Recall that a primary purpose for read-alouds is to build background knowledge, often through ancillary text that might otherwise be above the students' independent reading level. In shared reading, teachers focus on a comprehension strategy or a text feature that enables the learner to understand the content of the text. Therefore, the text selected should be at the independent or instructional level of the students. It should also offer the teacher an opportunity to discuss the identified strategy. Examples of comprehension strategies suitable for shared-reading instruction include:

- inferencing
- summarizing
- self-questioning and self-monitoring
- text structures (e.g., cause and effect, sequence, problem-solution)
- text features (e.g., headings and subheadings, captions, directions)
- interpreting visual representations (charts, graphs, diagrams)

Notice that these comprehension strategies are not the exclusive domain of any one content area; rather, they transcend reading for meaning in any discipline, with any text. Figure 5.3 contains a list of various reading comprehension strategies that are common in shared reading lessons. Figure 5.4 contains ideas for implementing think-alouds during shared-reading lessons.

Want to discuss inferencing? Then choose a text that implies attitudes or opinions without stating them outright. Text features and interpretation of visual representations are easily modeled using the course textbook. Self-questioning and self-monitoring (that small insistent voice inside every fluent reader's head that keeps asking, "does this make sense?") can be demonstrated through the teacher's own questions as a reading is shared. If the word "ancillary" in the previous paragraph was a little vague to you (and you noticed) then you are self-monitoring!

As with read-alouds, we find that a self-assessment rubric can be useful for organizing lessons (see Figure 5.5). Some of the elements on this rubric overlap with the features of the read-aloud (for instance, practicing the reading), so we will focus on the unique elements of the shared reading:

1. *Choose text that is appropriate for the purpose.* In the case of shared readings, not only should the text be associated with the content of the class, but it should also provide clear illustrations of the strategy or reading behavior being modeled. For example, a passage about how the biceps muscle of the arm contracts to move a lever (the radius) on a fulcrum (the elbow) is an excellent example of cause-and-effect text, especially if it contains signal words like accordingly, therefore, as a result, or since.

2. *Make the purpose of the reading explicit.* If you are modeling a particular strategy, tell your students what it is before you read. Remind them each time you model the strategy.

3. *Decide how the text will be accessible to all students.* If you are projecting the reading on the overhead, make sure the font is large enough for students in the back row to read.

Figure 5.3   Reading comprehension glossary of terms.

Cause and effect — text structure used to explain the reasons and results of an event or phenomenon. Signal words for cause include *because, when, if, cause,* and *reason.* Words like *then, so, which, effect,* and *result* signal an effect.

Compare and contrast — text structure used to explain how two people, events, or phenomena are alike and different. Some comparison signal words are *same, at the same time, like,* and *still.* Contrast signal words include *some, others, different, however, rather, yet, but,* and *or.*

Connecting — linking information in the text to personal experiences, prior knowledge, or other texts. This is commonly taught using three categories:
- ❑ Text to self — personal connections
- ❑ Text to text — connections to other books, films, etc.
- ❑ Text to world — connections to events in the past or present

Determining importance — a comprehension strategy used by readers to differentiate between essential information and interesting (but less important) details.

Evaluating — the reader makes judgments about the information being read, including its credibility, usefulness to the reader's purpose, and quality.

Inferencing — the ability to "read between the lines" to extract information not directly stated in the text. Inferencing is linked to a student's knowledge of vocabulary, content, context, recognition of clues in the text, and experiences.

Monitoring and clarifying — an ongoing process used by the reader to ensure that what is being read is also being understood. When the reader recognizes that something is unclear, he or she uses a variety of clarifying strategies, including rereading, asking questions, and seeking information from another source.

Predicting — the reader uses his or her understanding of language, content, and context to anticipate what will be read next. Prediction occurs continually during reading, but is most commonly taught as a pre-reading strategy.

Problem/solution — text structure used to explain a challenge and the measures taken to address the challenge. Signal words for a problem include *trouble, challenge, puzzle, difficulty, problem, question,* or *doubt.* Authors use signal words for a solution like *answer, discovery, improve, solution, overcome, resolve, response,* or *reply.*

Question-Answer Relationships (QAR) — Question-answer relationships were developed to help readers understand where information can be located. There are four types of questions in two categories.

(continued)

Figure 5.3 Reading comprehension glossary of terms. *(continued)*

(1) *In the Text*—these answers are "book" questions because they are drawn directly from the text. These are sometimes referred to as *text explicit* questions:
- ❑ *Right There*—the answer is located in a single sentence in the text
- ❑ *Think and Search*—the answer is in the text but is spread across several sentences or paragraphs

(2) *In Your Head*—these answers are "brain" questions because the reader must generate some or all of the answer. These are sometimes called *text implicit* questions:
- ❑ *Author and You*—the reader combines information from the text with other experiences and prior knowledge to answer the question
- ❑ *On Your Own*—the answer is not in the text and is based on your experiences and prior knowledge

Questioning — a strategy used by readers to question the text and themselves. These self-generated questions keep the reader interested and are used to seek information. Specific types of questioning includes QAR, QtA, and ReQuest.

Questioning the Author (QtA) — an instructional activity that invites readers to formulate questions for the author of the text. The intent of this strategy is to foster critical literacy by personalizing the reading experience as they consider where the information in the textbook came from and what the author's intent, voice, and perspectives might be.

Synthesizing — the reader combines new information with background knowledge to create original ideas.

Summarizing — the ability to condense a longer piece of text into a shorter statement. Summarizing occurs throughout a reading, not just at the end.

Temporal sequence — a text structure used to describe a series of events using a chronology. Signal words and phrases include *first, second, last, finally, next, then, since, soon, previously, before, after, meanwhile, at the same time*, and *at last*. Days of the week, dates, and times are also used to show a temporal sequence.

Visualizing — a comprehension strategy used by the reader to create mental images of what is being read.

Source: Frey, N., & Fisher, D. (2006). *Language arts workshop: Purposeful reading and writing instruction.* Upper Saddle River, NJ: Merrill Prentice Hall. Used with permission.

Figure 5.4 Tips for effective think-alouds.

Choose a Short Piece of Text.
Think-alouds are often the most effective when they are focused and well paced. A brief think-aloud delivered using a passage of one to four paragraphs will have more impact because student interest is maintained. It also prevents the temptation to model too many strategies.

Let the Text Tell You What to Do.
Don't plan to think aloud using cold text because your teaching points will be unfocused. Read the text several times and make notes about the comprehension strategies you are using. These will provide you with ideas for the content of your think-aloud. Annotate the text so you will have something to refer to as you read.

Keep Your Think-Alouds Authentic.
It can be a little disconcerting to say aloud what's going on in your head. Most teachers adopt a conversational tone that mirrors the informal language people use when they are thinking. An overly academic tone will sound contrived. It's better to say, "Hey — when I read this part about the penguins, right away I see a penguin in my mind," rather than, "I am metacognitively aware and activated my visualizing strategy to formulate an image of a penguin as I read that paragraph."

Think Like a Scientist, Mathematician, Historian, Artist, Literary Critic . . .
Your shared reading texts are chosen because they have content value. Thinking aloud doesn't mean that everyone suddenly has to be a reading or English teacher. Make your think-alouds authentic by telling students how you process text through the lens of your content expertise. This elevates the think-aloud because you are showing them how your understanding of content text is influenced by what you know about the content.

Tell Them What You Did.
Using an authentic voice doesn't mean you can't name the strategy. Tell your students what strategy you used to help you comprehend. This allows them to begin to form schemas about reading comprehension. Underline or highlight words or phrases that helped you understand and encourage students to do likewise, if possible.

Resist the Urge to "Over-Think."
The meaning of the passage should not be sacrificed for the sake of the think-aloud. Don't insert so many think-alouds into the reading that the intended message is lost. Fewer well-crafted think-alouds will have far more impact than a stream-of-consciousness rap that leaves the students bewildered by what just happened.

Figure 5.5 Rubric for shared reading.

	SUCCESSFULLY IMPLEMENTED	MODERATELY SUCCESSFUL	JUST GETTING STARTED	NOT EVIDENT
Choice of text is appropriate for purpose				
Selection has been previewed and practiced				
Purpose of reading made explicit and reflective of student needs				
Text visible to students				
Model provided of fluent reader				
Lesson design reflects scaffolding for student success				
Questions elicit thoughtful response				
Students are aware of what they are expected to do with new knowledge				

COMMENTS:

4. *Scaffold, scaffold, scaffold.* This is the foundation of shared reading. Don't assume that they "got it"—teach the strategy or reading behavior explicitly and provide multiple examples. Then have them do it with you during the course of the reading. This leads to the last element of a shared reading. . . .

5. *Make sure students are aware of what they are supposed to do with the new knowledge.* Teachers are frustrated when students ask questions like, "Is this going to be on the test?" when the teacher really wanted them to see the usefulness and practicality of what they had been taught. Our experience has been that when students ask questions like this, it is because we have not made it clear what they should do with the new information. After you have modeled a strategy and given them guided practice in using the strategy, you must connect it to their independent reading. When students can apply the strategy independently, the instructional cycle of shared reading is complete.

Strategies at Work

Interactive Read–Alouds in Kindergarten Mathematics

While read-alouds are effective for building topical knowledge (Hoffman, Roser, & Battle, 1993), their role in oral language development is also important. Several studies have demonstrated the power of interactive read-alouds to extend the oral language skills of first and second language learners (e.g., MacLure, 1988; Nelson, 1981). It appears that when an engaging text is strategically used by a teacher to elicit responses from students, their ability to master the academic vocabulary and inherent concepts increases. In a comparative study of the practices of teachers, it was found that educators who were expert at interactive read-alouds could be identified by their ability to create opportunities for response through the use of questioning, discussion, and writing (Fisher, Flood, Lapp, & Frey, 2004).

Dani Cole understands the role of student talk in interactive read-alouds. Many of her kindergarten students are English language learners, and a focus of her instruction is on acquiring academic vocabulary. Her class has been learning how to tell time in mathematics. There have been discussions about the clock components, such as the hour and minute hands, and the numbers on the face of the clock. During past lessons, the children had worked in small groups to manipulate the hands on individual clocks to represent specific times. After a few days of practice, most students can adjust their clocks to tell time to the hour. Today, they have brought their paper plate clocks to the reading rug for a special event.

Ms. Cole plans to read aloud Eric Carle's (1996) *The Grouchy Ladybug*, an engaging story of a mean ladybug who threatens to fight each animal she meets, all much larger than she. Ms. Cole is using a narrative text to encourage students to read for information related to telling time. In the text, the ladybug encounters 13 animals at different times (all on the hour) throughout one day. The book, Ms. Cole explains, includes many different times. "As I read, listen for the time. When you hear me say that time, I want you to move the hands on your clocks to match the time the Grouchy Ladybug meets another animal. "Let's practice. If I said 'At 12:00 I ate lunch,' show me what you would do." The students all position the big and little hands on the twelve. Then, as instructed, they hold the clocks up in the air so Ms. Cole can check for understanding.

And so she begins the story. "At six o'clock in the morning, the sun came up," she reads (Carle, 1996, p. 3). "Boys and girls, set the time on your clock and check with your neighbor. Tell him or her what time your clock says, and be sure to use full sentences," says Ms. Cole. Figure 5.6 shows the children displaying their clocks.

The students move the hands on their clocks to the appropriate position, and then hold them aloft. Children can be heard saying, "My clock says it's six o'clock." A few students look at their classmates' clocks before setting the time, and Ms. Cole assists any student who has the hands misplaced. When she is satisfied, she rereads the page from the beginning.

| *Figure 5.6*   Kindergarten class with clocks.

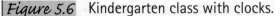

This continues throughout the entire book, with the students setting the time twelve more times over the course of the story. "I like the repetition that a story like this offers my students," remarks Ms. Cole. "It's so important that they get lots of opportunities to use this academic vocabulary."

Cross–Age Peer Tutoring in First–Grade Social Studies

"Risk taking is a crucial factor in literacy learning," says first-grade teacher Ramon Espinal. "In order to deepen their participation and build confidence, I use different groupings." One of his innovative grouping methods is cross-age peer tutoring. Every Friday morning, the students from Rachel Tuttle's fifth-grade class come to Mr. Espinal's first-grade classroom to share an important hour with his students. Paired up with their "reading buddies," the fifth-graders read to his children using both read-aloud and shared-reading strategies.

A Rationale for Cross-Age Tutoring. Cross-age peer tutoring involves an older student, under a teacher's guidance, helping younger students learn or practice a skill or concept (Cassady, 1998; Giesecke, 1993). Though features vary from program to program, cross-age tutoring provides individualized and personal attention, high levels of interaction, and immediate feedback. The effects of cross-age peer tutoring on the older students are particularly intriguing. A study of 21 students participating in a cross-age peer tutoring program found significant growth in the tutors' reading scores on standardized measures (Jacobson, Thrope, Fisher, Laff, Frey, & Flood, 2001).

According to Gaustad (1993) and Cobb (1998), cross-age tutoring is beneficial because the process provides tutors with expanded opportunities to review material, reiterate the purpose of the assignment, and expand their communication skills. A meta-analysis of 65 studies on cross-age tutoring revealed that the practice of students helping one another enhanced classroom instruction and led to higher academic achievement (Cohen, Kulik, & Kulik, 1982). Through purposeful engagement, cross-age tutoring provides the older learners with an authentic reason for practicing in order to improve their reading performance (Haluska & Gillen, 1995; Juel, 1991). Tutoring has been shown to be effective within classrooms as well. Referred to as peer tutoring, classmates are paired to support each other's learning and problem solving. In addition, cross-age or peer tutoring has been found to promote positive reading attitudes and habits (Caserta-Henry, 1996; Newell, 1996). Cohen (1986) suggests that the act of planning instruction for another aids the student in understanding the text.

It is likely that the relatively small difference in ages between tutor and tutee contributes positively to the success of the younger students.

Sensitivity and responsiveness to tentative understandings of a concept are seen frequently in cross-age tutoring (Schneider & Barone, 1997). The ability of older students to effectively communicate with younger children may be because they are cognitively closer to the tutee, and likely to have experienced similar situations in the recent past (Jenkins, Mayhall, Peschka, & Jenkins, 1974). Feldman and Allen (1979) demonstrated that sixth-graders were more likely to accurately determine understanding through the nonverbal behavior of their third-grade tutees than experienced teachers.

Student-Conducted Read-Alouds and Shared Readings. An understanding of the reading process is essential in Ms. Tuttle's fifth-grade class. They receive instruction on read-alouds and shared-reading techniques, principles of reading, and child development. Because they work with emergent and early readers, they pay particular attention to directionality, accessing prior information, rereading for fluency, making predictions, and phonics. Mr. Espinal is an important resource for information about the reading development of his first-graders. In addition to working with the younger students, Ms. Tuttle also emphasizes the fifth-graders own literacy development, particularly through writing. Tutors are expected to maintain reflective journals, develop lessons, and communicate with Mr. Espinal.

Today the fifth-graders have chosen biographies about famous Americans in history. Ms. Tuttle's students have practiced reading the books aloud in class, as well as to their families and friends. They have written questions and connections on post-it notes to indicate specific places for predictions and comprehension strategies and have placed them next to the appropriate passages. Additionally, they have identified vocabulary that they think might give their reading buddies difficulty. These words are written on index cards and are introduced before the reading. This reinforces the meaning of the words in the context of the story.

Rosie, a student in Ms. Tuttle's class, is working with her first-grade buddy, Angelica. This month Angelica's class has been studying famous Americans, so Rosie has chosen the book *A Picture Book of Abraham Lincoln* (Adler, 1990). She is excited to share this book with Angelica because she thinks the illustrations will help Angelica understand the story.

"Hi Angelica! Look at the book I brought today. It's all about one of the famous people your class has been learning about," says Rosie.

"Oh, let me see! Can I guess who it is?" Angelica asks as she looks closely at the cover. " I know who that is! It's Abe Lincoln. He wore a tall hat and kept secret messages in it!"

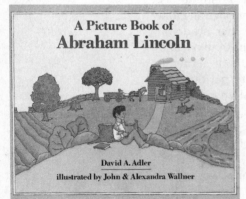

Source: Book cover used with permission of Holiday House.

"Wow! You remember that story about him? Do you think there may be some more fun stories about him in this book? Let's look at the cover and see if we can guess some more interesting things about Abe," says Rosie.

Using the think-aloud technique (Davey, 1983) that she has been taught by Ms. Tuttle and Mr. Espinal, Rosie points to the cover and says, "He's leaning up against that tree that someone chopped down. He is also reading a book. I know that Abe Lincoln was president. I wonder if this helped him become president.

"Yes, yes it did! His mother taught him to read and he used it to write laws!" Angelica beams at her knowledge of the sixteenth president.

"You're right, Angelica. He lived a long time ago. How does the cover illustration remind us of that? Do you see some things that we might see in our front yards?"

"There is a horse and a wagon and a wood house. There is smoke coming from the house. I wonder if his mom is cooking his dinner," says Angelica.

"That's a great observation. Let's remember that and see if we read about his dinner in the book," Rosie replies.

As the conversation continues, Rosie asks many questions to make personal connections for Angelica. "Look at the wagon. That's like the family car. Does your family have a car? What does your family use the car for? Hmmm, I wonder if Abe's family used their wagon for the same things your family uses your car for," says Rosie.

Satisfied with the connections she helped Angelica make and the prior knowledge that she had about Abraham Lincoln, Rosie begins to read the book aloud to Angelica. As she reads, she stops to explain vocabulary, either relating it to the meaning of the story or using the word in a sentence that makes sense to Angelica. Rosie also uses a think-aloud strategy to show Angelica how she figures out an unfamiliar word. To recall the questions she developed before the lesson, Rosie has earmarked specific pages with a post-it and stops to ask Angelica the questions she had written on the note.

By the time the hour comes to a close, Rosie has read the entire book to Angelica. The vocabulary is listed on index cards, predictions have been confirmed or disconfirmed, and questions have been answered. The closeness of the one-to-one tutoring gives Angelica the storybook lap time needed. This time also allows Rosie to help Angelica understand the story and the specific supporting vocabulary. When Rosie returns to her classroom, Ms. Tuttle has the students write in their tutoring journals about their reading lessons. The students write down successes, challenges, and two things they might do differently the next time. Finally, they record their next steps and their plans for the next week.

"Shared reading and read-alouds not only allow educators to scaffold their teaching, and build a community of fluent readers with good comprehension skills, but also to build a bridge between them and their students," says Mr. Espinal. In this case, some of the best educators can be found in the fifth grade.

Reader's Theatre in Second-Grade Science

A critical aspect of reading is fluency, the ability to decode and understand words, sentences, and paragraphs in a way that is smooth and accurate. Fluency is closely related to the concept of prosody discussed earlier in this chapter. While the rate of reading alone is not the only indicator of a good reader, consider the labored reading of a struggling student (Rasinski, 2000). When reading is choppy and disfluent, it becomes difficult to attend to the message behind the words. Meaning for the reader (and listener) is lost in a string of pauses, false starts, and hesitations.

Rereading. An effective instructional strategy for building fluency is repeated readings (Mastropieri, Leinart, & Scruggs, 1999). Repeated readings are just that—the repeated reading of the same text passage. There is a great deal of evidence to suggest that repeated readings lead to a practice effect. If you are skeptical, try it yourself. Select a passage from this chapter and read it aloud for one minute—be sure to time yourself. When the timer rings, count the number of words you read and record it. Now read the same passage again, beginning at the same starting point, and count the number of words you read during this second one-minute interval. Repeat this cycle one more time and then compare your results. If you are like most readers, you read more words at cycle 3 than you did at cycle 1. Many of you may have read more during each cycle.

If you completed the above exercise, then you have also identified a difficulty with repeated readings. Many students, and especially adolescents, are not terribly motivated to reread. In fact, we often hear them say something like, "I read this before! Why do I have to read it again?" And indeed, less-able readers often believe that any text only needs to be read once, with no new information being gained from subsequent readings (Alvermann, 1988). However, good readers recognize that rereading is an important tool for comprehending text (Garner & Reis, 1981).

Reader's Theatre. A popular method for engaging in repeated readings to build fluency and comprehension is Reader's Theatre (Martinez, Roser, & Strecker, 1998–1999). Reader's Theatre is the public performance of a scripted text, but unlike traditional theatre, the lines are not memorized and props, movement, and other acting devices are not used. Instead, students read the text using prosodic elements while their classmates follow along silently using their own copies.

The success of Reader's Theatre for promoting repeated reading and conversations about meaning seems to be related to the performance itself. Think about what motivates you—if you know that you will be presenting an oral reading for your peers, you are probably going to rehearse, reread, and discuss the methods of performance with your fellow actors. That is precisely what happened in Pam Pham-Barron's second-grade science class.

"Today's our day to be actors!" announced Ms. Pham-Barron. The students in her class know what this means and have their yellow markers out ready to highlight their parts in the Readers' Theatre script their teacher is about to hand out. These seven- and eight-year olds have been studying the sequential life-cycle stages of several animals, including frogs. Ms. Pham-Barron has adapted portions of the book *Frogs* (Gibbons, 1994). Since this has been used before as an informational text in the classroom, students have become familiar with the language and phrasing. The students will bring Gibbons' text to life with this script adaptation.

She begins by conducting a picture walk of the author's dynamic watercolor illustrations. As she displays each page, she talks through the content to access the students' background knowledge. "Look closely at this picture. The tadpoles are hatching from their eggs. As soon as they hatch, they wiggle their tails back and forth to swim away in search of algae. That's the small plant they eat to grow."

After reviewing the content, she distributes the script. "I'll read through the script while you read in your heads. Listen to how I use my voice to make it sound like talking," says Ms. Pham-Barron. She begins, "One by one the tadpoles hatch from their eggs." (Gibbons, 1994, p. 3). After modeling the reading, she assigns the parts in groups of four.

"Remember to highlight your part and practice your lines before we read it together," reminds Ms. Pham-Barron. As the students practice their lines, she visits each group to answer any questions regarding tricky vocabulary. She coaches students to support expressive reading.

"Can you read that line again stopping only at the period?" Ms. Pham-Barron asks a group. After they read it again, she inquires, "Does that make more sense when you pause only at the period?" When they nod in the affirmative, she moves to the next group.

"Ms. Pham-Barron, how do you say this word?" asks Eric pointing to the script.

"What part of that word do you already know?" she replies. "Take that word apart."

Eric covers part of the word and answers, "Out . . . side . . . outside!"

"There you go! You knew it all along. Just remember to use what you know and you'll get it."

The following day, the students perform their Reader's Theatre script with confidence. Every student has a part and, as with all such performances,

> Remember that the emphasis of Reader's Theatre is on oral language development and fluency, not on props, costumes, or dramatic performance.

Source: Book cover used with permission of Holiday House.

> Many Reader's Theatre scripts are available at www.aaronshep.com/rt/index.html

they tour other classrooms to share their efforts. After the reading, Ms. Pham-Barron asks each group to illustrate a portion of the book for the classroom library. "I like to rewrite books we've been using in the class during read-alouds and shared-reading because it moves the words from me to them. They've heard me read it—with Readers Theatre they get to make the words their own," says Ms. Pham-Barron.

Think-Alouds in Third-Grade Visual Arts

Many teachers use read-alouds and shared-readings to demonstrate a think-aloud strategy for explicit modeling (Davey, 1983). The purpose of a think-aloud is to model how comprehension strategies are used to understand text. As Wilhelm (2001) explains, "When a teacher says aloud—reports out—all he is noticing and doing as he reads, students finally 'see' all the steps and motions of an expert reader" (p. 45).

> A think-aloud is a metacognitive process that allows students to hear what goes on "inside the head" of a fluent reader.

Like all instructional strategies, using a think-aloud process requires planning in advance of the reading. We find that using sticky notes with specific comments written on them is useful when we read to students because it helps us remain focused on a particular set of strategies. Think-alouds that consist of a stream-of-consciousness riff on a text are more likely to confuse than to clarify. As you read a text, look for the opportunities it provides to highlight a strategy. A surprise ending to a story? It might be an excellent candidate for noticing foreshadowing. Lots of descriptive passages? It could be a terrific chance to model visualizing as a comprehension strategy.

Once you have identified the strategy or strategies you'll model, don't forget to tell your students. When you begin by stating the purpose of your think-aloud, you signal your learners about what they should be noticing. After all, the goal of a think-aloud is to transfer the responsibility to them. Over time, the think-alouds should become "think alongs" as students participate with you as fellow readers (Wilhelm, 2001). Roberta Dawson used this approach to model prediction and visualizing with her third-grade students.

Her students were preparing to visit the San Diego Museum of Art as part of a unique program called School in the Park (Pumpian, Fisher, & Wachowiak, in press). Mrs. Dawson's students attend school in one of the museums in Balboa Park for one week a month throughout their third-, fourth-, and fifth-grade school years. Because this will be the first time many of her students have been to the museum, she wants to build their background knowledge about both art and the institution. She has selected the book *Jack in Search of Art* (Boehm, 1999) and has identified making and changing predictions as her target strategy.

"Come over to the gathering rug," Mrs. Dawson announces. After the 20 third-graders settle into their spots, she tells them she will be reading a book about a mixed-up bear who wanders around an art museum looking for something. "I'm also going to tell you what I'm thinking about as I read the story. You know, boys and girls, good readers talk to themselves inside their heads when they read—that's their reader voice. I'm going to tell you what my reader voice is saying inside my head. I want you to pay attention to how I make predictions and sometimes change my mind as I read."

With that, she displays the book cover and reads them the title. "*Jack in Search of Art*. Hmm, I know that searching means you're looking for something. I wonder what he's looking for? The title says he's searching for art, and I can see by the picture that he's standing in front of a big brick building. That building is too big to be a house. There's a statue, too. Maybe this is an art museum."

Now she encourages them to think along with her. "Tell me what you're predicting. What is your reader voice saying inside your head?" asks Mrs. Dawson. She records their predictions on a language chart, along with their names (see Figure 5.7). "Let's read the book and check our predictions."

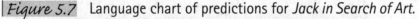

| *Figure 5.7*   Language chart of predictions for *Jack in Search of Art*.

Jack in Search of Art
Predictions:
  I think the book will be about...
· the bear looking for art. (Brian)
· the bear looking at art. (Chase)
· the bear looking at pictures. (Jessenia)
· Jack, the bear going into the museum to see art. (Diem)

What is art?   a museum?
· Drawing pictures. (Marcos)   · a place to see art
· Coloring pictures. (Erik)   (all students)
· Painting pictures. (Vivian)

Revised Predictions:
· Jack is going to learn art is not a person. (Ana)
· Jack is going to find out what art is. (Jose)

What is art?
· Paintings. (Erik) · Sculpture (Diem) · Pictures of people. (Jenny)
· Messed up pictures (Abstract art) (Jose) · Pictures of trees mountains, lakes. (Christian)

After reading a few pages, it is clear that the main character, a bear named Jack, thinks that "Art" is a person. Mrs. Dawson pauses to think aloud. "I didn't expect this! I thought Jack would know that art is not the name of a person. I'm going to have to change my prediction. Now I think that the author is going to tell us more funny things this bear does and says because he is confused." Again, she shifts responsibility to them. "What is your reader voice telling you?" she asks. "He's going to miss all the art in the museum!" exclaims one student. She records this on the language chart and continues. Sure enough, Jack overlooks art by Calder and Wyeth, among others, reproduced using digitalized photography.

After reading the story, Mrs. Dawson asks the students to form a circle. During circle talk, her students discuss questions about the book they have just heard. After discussing the purposes for museums, she asks them about art. "How do we know something is art?" she inquires. Mrs. Dawson discovers that her students' view of art is limited to two-dimensional works. She returns to the picture book to locate examples of sculpture. "Is this art?" she asks. They readily agree that it is art and she adds it to the language chart.

"We use predictions in lots of ways," she reminds them. "What do we expect to see at the San Diego Museum of Art?" Again, she records their predictions. "We'll use our list next week to see if we can find these in the museum. Just like Jack, we'll be in search of art, too!"

Read-Alouds in Fourth-Grade Mathematics

While read-alouds are frequently used to build background knowledge, they can also be useful for activating prior knowledge to reteach, reinforce, and introduce new information. Colleen Crandall finds that the use of a favorite book from third grade serves as a good tool for reteaching fractions in mathematics. Because fractions are among the most difficult concepts for students to grasp (Cramer, Behr, Post, & Lesh, 1997), Mrs. Crandall wants to make sure they are certain of this mathematics concept before she introduces new skills. The National Council of Teachers of Mathematics (NCTM) recommends that learners have multiple opportunities to use physical manipulatives to investigate concepts of order and equivalence as a means to understand operations (NCTM, 1989).

In this case, her beginning of the year lesson starts with a read-aloud of a familiar book from last year, *The Hershey's Milk Chocolate Fractions Book* (Pallotta, 1999). Her objective is to clarify student understanding about what the numerator and denominator parts mean in fractions. As part of the daily routine, students have composition books and a pencil out on their desks so when they come in from recess, they are ready to begin math.

Mrs. Crandall walks around the room carefully laying out one whole Hershey's candy bar on each student's desk, as well as an envelope filled with paper strips. The children are thrilled. "Do we get to eat these?" say several students. Mrs. Crandall walks to the front of the class and gives the quiet signal with all five fingers on her hand palm out to her students. A hush falls upon the room, so she announces, "Today, I've brought in a story about fractions using a Hershey's chocolate bar. We're going to revisit fractions using the chocolate bars and paper strips. We're going to review what we know about fractions and make sure we understand what a fraction represents. At the end of today's lesson, you will be welcome to enjoy eating your candy bar, fraction by fraction! Please get ready to draw pictures and write down any ideas that come to you as we go through this read-aloud."

After Mrs. Crandall reads a page, she stops and draws exactly what she has just finished reading to her class on an overhead projector. The students open their composition books and take pencils in hand to copy into their books what Mrs. Crandall has just drawn on the overhead. The read-aloud continues and students break the candy bar into 12 pieces and see that all 12 pieces make one whole candy bar whether the pieces are attached or separate.

Students then place all 12 of the pieces into one whole stack and see that this stack is also one whole, or 12/12ths. As the story continues, students illustrate each fraction and write it in mathematical notation. Equivalent fractions are also found throughout the story and students stack their pieces of chocolate to show fractional equivalents for 1/2. "How can we represent 1/2 using our chocolate bars?" she asks. "Work with your partners to figure it out." Within moments, the pairs are recording 6/12ths into their notebooks.

Another page in the book shows students how they can add fractional parts of $1/3 + 2/3 = 3/3$ or one whole. Students are asked to stack their fractions to show how this is a true statement in mathematics. They do the same thing again, adding $4/12 + 8/12 = 12/12$ or one whole. Satisfied that they are accurately using these simple operations, she now moves to new information.

The next page features cows, rather than chocolate bars. "You'll need your paper strips for this part," Mrs. Crandall tells the class. "This page says 1/5. Why has the author chosen that fraction to represent the information on the page?"

As she walks around the room, students take a closer look at the picture. Suong is the first to respond. "One of the cows has red spots on it and the other four cows have black spots. Maybe the whole group of cows is 5 so one out of the five cows on the page isn't the same."

"Talk to your partners about that idea. What do you think of Suong's suggestion?" asks Mrs. Crandall. After discussing this, students hold up a fist if they disagree or an open hand if they agree with Suong. Most of the students have up an open hand. Mrs. Crandall asks Gregorio why he and his partner agree. Gregorio responds, "Five cows are the whole amount—the denominator. One cow is different than the others—this cow is the numerator—the part of the whole group that doesn't look the same. But there are still five cows, even if that one is not the same color as the others."

"That's it! You also used two important vocabulary words to explain your answer—numerator and denominator. Now let's try something new. Please take your paper strips out of the envelope. Let's try folding a strip to represent the concept of 1/5."

Familiar stories can be useful for activating prior knowledge. "This book is a big hit with students in third grade. Since fractions can be confusing for my students, I like to tap into what they already know by using familiar lessons. September curriculum always has a lot of review so we can begin with a good foundation. I find that I need to reteach less because they have this set of common experiences. Very handy for math!"

Nontraditional Texts in Fifth–Grade Social Studies

While many of the informational texts used in content-area instruction come from picture books, trade books, and textbooks, effective teachers recognize the advantages of using less-traditional materials to teach important concepts. These innovative materials include comic strips and cartoons, wordless books, and song lyrics. A growing body of research indicates that classroom use of such nontraditional texts can promote engagement and increase motivation (e.g., Cary, 2004; Cassady, 1998; Frey & Fisher, 2003).

Comic Strips and Cartoons. The sequential nature of comic strips and comic books provides a natural link to story grammar and inferencing. Young children can assemble comic strip panels that have been cut apart, reinforcing the basic story grammar of beginning, middle, and ending. Students of all ages who are English language learners can use storyboarding as part of their composition process (Cary, 2004). In this approach, students create a series of panels to illustrate an original story. Cary also recommends storyboarding as a means for assessing comprehension. After listening to or reading a story, learners draw a series of cartoon panels to serve as a "roadmap" for oral retelling (2004, p. 35).

Political cartoons are useful for teaching history because they represent the sentiments of the time. These cartoons are primary source documents, a key part of an effective social studies curriculum (National Council for the Social Studies, 1994). Editorial cartoons can also be useful for modeling document-based questioning (DBQ) during shared reading. DBQ is an instructional approach that invites students to generate and respond to questions prompted by the close analysis of a primary source document. The National Archives and Records Administration offers teaching materials online that promote DBQ for use with cartoons, photographs, artifacts, and documents at www. archives.gov/digital_classroom/analysis_worksheets/worksheets.html

Wordless Books. Over the past decade, the number of wordless books for younger and older readers has significantly increased. Once the domain of preschoolers, wordless books have become teacher favorites for their unique ability to portray concepts while offering oral language development opportunities. There are engaging wordless books about the environment (*Window* by Jeannie Baker), the harrowing journey of enslaved Africans (*White Ships, Black Cargo* by Tom Feelings), and mathematical comparatives (*More, Fewer, Less* by Tana Hoban). Wordless books have proven effective for students with disabilities (Cassady, 1998) and English language learners (Dame, 1993). A list of wordless books appears in Figure 5.8.

Figure 5.8 Wordless and nearly wordless picture books.

BOOK	CONTENT AREA	DESCRIPTION
Baker, J. (1991). *Window.* Greenwillow.	Social Studies	A boy watches the environment outside his window change for the worse as development and pollution choke out plants and animals.
Fain, K. (1995). *Handsigns: A sign language alphabet.* San Francisco: Chronicle.	Language	Beautiful portraits accompany each American Sign Language alphabet letter.
Hutchins, P. (1983). *Rosie's walk.* New York: Simon & Schuster.	Mathematics	Rosie takes a walk, unaware that a fox is following. Great for teaching geometry and spatial sense.
Feelings, T. (1995). *Middle passage: White ships, black cargo.* New York: Dial.	Social Studies	The illustrations tell the story of the suffering of enslaved Africans on their forced journey to America.
Hoban, T. (1998). *More, fewer, less.* New York: Greenwillow.	Mathematics	Photographs of familiar objects portray comparative concepts of size, quantity, and distance.
Rohmann, E. (1994). *Time flies.* New York: Crown.	Science	A bird flies through a natural history museum while illustrating the evolutionary relationship between birds and dinosaurs.
Weitzman, J., & Weitzman, R. (1998). *You can't take a balloon in the Metropolitan Museum.* New York: Dial.	Visual Arts	A balloon serenely sails through this great art museum, playfully highlighting the great works of art in the collection.

Wordless books offer a number of instructional opportunities to develop written and spoken language. A sample of these include:

- *Partner talk*—Invite students to turn to their partner and orally compose text for the page.
- *Partner retellings*—Use wordless books for students to retell stories to one another. As you listen in, you may be surprised at the level of academic vocabulary students use as they explain the story.
- *Writing dialogue*—Model writing dialogue during a shared-reading by recording possible dialogue on a language chart.

Song Lyrics. Songs offer a rich variety of texts related to content-area instruction. They are also appealing because their use practically demands repeated readings as students learn the tune. The somewhat limited volume of text is appealing to struggling readers, who welcome assigned texts that rarely exceed 100 words. Obvious choices include the *Schoolhouse Rock* series, which features songs on science, history, mathematics, and grammar. These engaging songs are accompanied by short cartoons, originally produced for viewing between Saturday morning cartoons in the 1970s.

Popular music can also provide opportunities for teaching. "You've Got to Be Carefully Taught" from the musical *South Pacific* is a powerful introduction to the type of prejudices that are passed from generation to generation (Hammerstein, 1958). "Buffalo Soldier" chronicles the challenges met by African-American soldiers in the American west (Marley, 2002). Be sure to take a look at Chapter 4 on vocabulary to find out how Rachel Tuttle introduces late 20th-century American history through Billy Joel's song, "We Didn't Start the Fire" (1989).

Song lyrics can be used like any other shared reading text. It is advisable to introduce the purpose, then let the students hear the song uninterrupted so they can first listen and read for meaning. Next, discuss the main ideas and move to targeted skills such as vocabulary development. When the lyrics are complex, consider practicing the song a stanza at a time. This allows students to master portions of the music before bringing it all together. Many songs lend themselves to gestures and movements. Encourage students to choreograph the song based on their growing understanding of the lyrics, rather than teaching them a preconceived set of dance moves. Finally, don't forget the performance aspect that song lyrics offer. Like Reader's Theatre, the power of song lyrics lies in the repeated readings necessary for a good performance.

Aida Allen uses song lyrics for shared reading with her fifth-grade students. She selected songs that the students were familiar with or thought were "cool" Top 40. Of course, she screened songs carefully to ensure that the lyrics did not contain any inappropriate content or language. These songs were used as part of a social studies unit on the impact of media in the 20th century.

One song selected for the unit of study is "Where Is the Love?" by the Black Eyed Peas (2004). Ms. Allen gives each student his or her own copy of the song lyrics to use while she displays the text on the overhead projector. "Do you sometimes hear a song on the radio but you really don't know all the words?" she asks. Many students nod in agreement. She continues. "I know most of you have heard this song. I'd like for you to follow along while we listen. There are some good words in here that I thought we could discuss."

While the song plays on the boom box, the students read the song independently. Many are surprised by some of the words. "I didn't know that's what it said!" remarks Mariana.

"What's this song's big idea? What's the message?" asks Ms. Allen. "Before we discuss it, please take three minutes to do a quickwrite." The students get to work on writing their ideas. When the time has elapsed, Ms. Allen says, "Please turn to your neighbor and share your idea. Make sure that you listen closely to your partner's ideas as well."

Ms. Allen listens to several partners and writes ideas she overhears on a transparency she has placed on a clipboard. When they finish, she places the transparency on the overhead projector.

"Here are ideas I heard during your conversations. Leo and Tino said they thought the song was about making peace because the world is getting dangerous. Karen said that she thought they wrote the song to tell people to be nicer to each other. Miriam said it reminded her of a song they sing in her church." The other students giggle.

"Well, not the way it sounds, but what the words say. That you have to give love to the world," Miriam says quickly.

After discussing the ideas in the song for a few more minutes, Ms. Allen says, "Let's take the song apart and look more closely at the lyrics. I'm going to read the first stanza aloud while you follow. I'd like for you to circle any vocabulary you don't understand."

Coriama circles the words *trauma*, *irate*, and *meditate*. The class nominates words to add to the language chart Ms. Allen has started. Using a variety of contextual and structural analysis skills, they identify the meaning of each of the words. Sensing that they are ready to move on, she ends the lesson with the students' favorite part—singing the song. Over the next few days, they return to new stanzas of the song. Each time they focus on main ideas and vocabulary. "It's a great strategy for building fluency at the same time we are learning content. They reread all the time and plan their choreography. In the meantime, I get a chance to introduce important ideas they need to know," says Ms. Allen.

ab Conclusion

> The decision to use a read–aloud or a shared reading is based on the purpose and the text selected. Teachers do both, but often at different times of the day or on different days.

Read-alouds and shared reading are two instructional practices borrowed from elementary reading practice and customized for use across content areas. A read-aloud is a text or passage selected by the teacher to read publicly to a small or large group of students. A primary purpose for the read-aloud selection is to focus on the content of the text. A shared reading is a text or passage that is jointly shared by teacher and student. In shared readings, the students can also see the text, and it is usually chosen both for its content and as a way to draw attention to a particular text feature or comprehension strategy. A summary of tips for using read-alouds and shared readings in the classroom appears in Figure 5.9.

Figure 5.9   Summary of effective strategies for using read–alouds and shared reading.

TIPS FOR SUCCESSFUL READ-ALOUDS AND SHARED READINGS
❑ Read-alouds and shared-reading events do not need to be long to be effective. A short, powerful passage has far more impact than a long, dull reading. Plan short lessons initially and build students' stamina for listening through daily practice.
❑ Rehearse in advance of the reading. Remember that one goal is to provide a fluent language model. That requires a bit of rehearsal so that you can bring the proper expression and inflection to the text.
❑ Choose readings that are meaningful to you and are connected with the content you are teaching. Comprehension increases with connections that are made, so don't assume that your students understood the relevance of your selection. Be explicit.
❑ Determine in advance where you're going to stop when reading longer texts. Look for natural breaks in a piece. Selected passages can either be read in a single reading, or extended over a few lessons. If the reading will continue on another day, stop at a point where you can elicit predictions about what is yet to come.

When considering read-alouds and shared readings for your own practice, always keep in mind the focus of your content. While we believe strongly that students should see their teachers regularly engaged in the act of reading for pleasure, we do not suggest that large portions of instructional time should be spent on using readings that are unrelated to your instructional purposes.

The teachers in this chapter made a strong case for their purposes in selecting a particular piece, and clearly saw these experiences as an important way to advance student learning. Having said that, do not underestimate the influence of a teacher who shares a newspaper story that concerned them, an email that made them laugh, or a cartoon that made them think. When students see their teachers reading a variety of genres, they begin to see possibilities in their own literate lives.

> Read–alouds and shared readings increase content knowledge.

References

Allen, J. (2001). *Yellow brick roads: Shared and guided paths to independent reading 4–12*. Portland, ME: Stenhouse.

Alvermann, D. (1988). Effects of spontaneous and induced lookbacks on self-perceived high- and low-ability comprehenders. *Journal of Educational Research, 81,* 325–331.

Amer, A. A. (1997). The effect of the teacher's reading aloud on the reading comprehension of ESL students. *ELT Journal 1997, 51*(1), 43–47.

Anderson, R. C., Hiebert, E. H., Scott, J. A., & Wilkinson, I.A.G. (1985). *Becoming a nation of readers,* Washington, DC: U.S. Department of Education.

Beck, I. L., & McKeown, M. G. (2001). Text talk: Capturing the benefits of read-aloud experiences for young children. *The Reading Teacher, 55,* 10–35.

Black Eyed Peas. (2004). Where is the love? On *Elephunk* [CD]. Santa Monica, CA: A&M Records/Interscope.

Block, D. G. (1999, November 11). Spoken word still a stronghold. *TapeDisc Business: The International Business Magazine for Media Manufacturers.* Retrieved April 13, 2002, from http://www. tapediscbusiness.com/tdb_nov99/ 11spoken.htm.

Brown, A. L., Palinscar, A. S., & Armbruster, B. B. (1994). Instructing comprehension-fostering activities in interactive learning situations. In R. B. Ruddell, M. R. Ruddell, & H. Singer (Eds.), *Theoretical models and processes of reading* (4th ed., pp. 757–787). Newark, DE: International Reading Association.

Campbell, R. (2001). *Read-alouds with young children.* Newark, DE: International Reading Association.

Cary, S. (2004). *Going graphic: Comics at work in the multilingual classroom.* Portsmouth, NH: Heinemann.

Caserta-Henry, C. (1996). Reading buddies: A first-grade intervention program. *The Reading Teacher, 49,* 500–503.

Cassady, J. K. (1998). Wordless books: No-risk tools for inclusive middle-grade classrooms. *Journal of Adolescent and Adult Literacy, 41,* 428–432.

Chall, J., Jacobs, V., & Baldwin, L. (1990). *The reading crisis: Why poor children fall behind.* Cambridge, MA: Harvard University Press.

Cobb, J.B. (1998). The social contexts of tutoring: Mentoring the older at-risk student. *Reading Horizons, 39,* 50–75.

Cohen, D. H. (1968). The effect of literature on vocabulary and reading achievement. *Elementary English, 45,* 209–213, 217.

Cohen, J. (1986). Theoretical considerations of peer tutoring. *Psychology on the Schools, 23,* 175–186.

Cohen, P. A., Kulik, J. A., & Kulik, C. C. (1982). Educational outcomes of tutoring: A meta-analysis of findings. *American Educational Research Journal, 19,* 237–248.

Cramer, K., Behr, M., Post, T., & Lehr, R. (1997). *Rational number project: Fraction lessons for the middle grades: Level 1, grades 4–5.* Dubuque, IA: Kendall-Hunt.

Cummins, J. (1980). The cross-lingual dimensions of language proficiency: Implications for bilingual education and the optimal age issue. *TESOL Quarterly, 14,* 175–187.

Dame, M. A. (1993). *Serving linguistically and culturally diverse students: Strategies for the school library media specialist.* New York: Neal-Schuman.

Davey, B. (1983). Think aloud–modeling the cognitive processes of reading comprehension. *Journal of Reading, 27*(1), 44–47.

Duke, N. (2000). 3.6 minutes per day. The scarcity of informational texts in first grade: *Reading Research Quarterly, 35,* 202–224.

Durkin, D. (1974–1975). A six year study of children who learned to read in school at the age of four. *Reading Research Quarterly, 10,* 9–61.

Early, M. (1990). Enabling first and second language learners in the classroom. *Language Arts, 67,* 567–575.

Early, M., & Tang, G. M. (1991). Helping ESL students cope with content-based texts. *TESL Canada Journal, 8*(2), 34–44.

Farris, P. J., & Fuhler, C. J. (1994). Developing social studies concepts through picture books. *The Reading Teacher. 47,* 380–387.

Feldman, R. S., & Allen, V. L. (1979). Student success and tutor verbal and nonverbal behavior. *Journal of Educational Research, 72,* 142–149.

Fisher, D., Flood, J., Lapp, D., & Frey, N. (2004). Interactive read alouds: Is there a common set of implementation practices? *The Reading Teacher, 58,* 8–17.

Frey, N., & Fisher, D. (2003). Using graphic novels, anime, and the Internet in an urban high school. *English Journal, 93*(3), 19–25.

Garner, R., & Reis, R. (1981). Monitoring and resolving comprehension obstacles: An investigation of spontaneous text lookbacks among upper-grade good and poor readers' comprehension. *Reading Research Quarterly, 16,* 569–582.

Gaustad, J. (1993). Peers and tutoring. ERIC Digest, 79. Office of Educational Research and Improvement. [ERIC Document Reproduction Service No. ED 354 608].

Ghosn, I. K. (2002). Four good reasons to use literature in the primary school ELT. *English Language Teaching Journal, 56,* 172–79.

Giesecke, D. (1993). Low-achieving students as successful tutors. *Preventing School Failure, 37,* 34–43.

Greaney, V., & Hegarty, M. (1987). Correlates of leisure-time reading. *Journal of Research in Reading, 10*(1), 3–20.

Haluska, R., & Gillen, D. (1995). Kids teaching kids: Pairing up with cross-grades pals. *Learning, 24*(3), 54–56.

Hammerstein, O. (1958). You've got to be carefully taught [Recorded by John Kerr]. On *South Pacific* [Album]. New York: Sony.

Hoffman, J. V., Roser, N., & Battle, J. (1993). Reading aloud in classrooms: From modal to "model." *The Reading Teacher, 46,* 496–503.

Holdaway, D. (1982). Shared book experience: Teaching reading using favorite books. *Theory into Practice, 21,* 293–300.

Ivey, G. (2003). "The teacher makes it more explainable" and other reasons to read aloud in the intermediate grades. *The Reading Teacher, 56,* 812–814.

Jacobson, J., Thrope, L., Fisher, D., Laff, D., Frey, N., & Flood, J. (2001). Cross-age tutoring: A literacy improvement approach for struggling adolescent readers. *Journal of Adolescent & Adult Literacy, 44,* 528–536.

Jenkins, J. R., Mayhall, W. F., Peschka, C. M., & Jenkins, L. M. (1974). Comparing small group instruction and tutorial instruction in resource rooms. *Exceptional Children, 40,* 245–250.

Joel, B. (1989). We didn't start the fire. *On Storm Front* [CD]. New York: Sony.

Juel, C. (1991). Tutoring between student athletes and at-risk children. *The Reading Teacher, 45,* 178–186.

Kristo, J. V., & Bamford, R. A. (2004). *Nonfiction in focus: A comprehensive framework for helping students become independent readers and writers of nonfiction, K–6.* New York: Scholastic.

MacLure, M. (1988). Oracy: Current trends in context. In M. MacLure, T. Phillips, & A. Wilkerson (Eds.), *Oracy matters: The development of talking and listening in education* (pp. 1–10). Milton Keynes, UK: Open University Press.

Manguel, A. (1996). *A history of reading.* New York: HarperCollins.

Marley, B. (2002). Buffalo soldier [Recorded by Bob Marley and the Wailers]. On *Legend* [CD]. New York: Island.

Martinez, M. & Roser, N. (1985). Read it again: The value of repeated readings during storytime. *The Reading Teacher, 38,* 782–786.

Martinez, M., Roser, N. L., & Strecker, S. (1998–1999). "I never thought I could be a star:" A reader's theatre ticket to fluency. *The Reading Teacher, 52,* 326–334.

Mastropieri, M. A., Leinart, A., & Scruggs, T. E. (1999). Strategies to increase reading fluency. *Intervention in School and Clinic, 34,* 278–283, 292.

Maxim, D. (1998). Math reading aloud. *New England Reading Association Journal, 34*(1), 3–5.

McKenna, M. C., & Robinson, R. D. (1990). Content literacy: A definition and implications. *Journal of Reading, 34,* 184–186.

Morrow, L. M., & Young, J. (1997). A collaborative family literacy program: The effects on children's motivation and literacy achievement. *Early Child Development and Care, 127–128,* 13–25.

National Council for the Social Studies. (1994). *Expectations of excellence: Curriculum standards for social studies.* Silver Spring, MD: Author.

National Council of Teachers of Mathematics. (1989). *Curriculum and evaluation standards for mathematics.* Reston, VA: Author.

Nelson, K. (1981). Individual differences in language development: Implications for development and language. *Developmental Psychology, 17,* 170–187.

Newell, F. M. (1996). Effects of a cross-age tutoring program on computer literacy learning of second-grade students. *Journal of Research on Computing in Education, 289,* 346–358.

Nieto, S. (1992). *Affirming diversity: The sociopolitical context of multicultural education.* White Plains, NY: Longman.

Ornstein, A. C. (1994). Curriculum trends revisited. *Peabody Journal of Education, 69*(4), 4–20.

Ouellette, G., Dagostino, L., & Carifio, J. (1999). The effects of exposure to children's literature through read aloud and an inferencing strategy on low reading ability fifth graders' sense of story structure and reading comprehension. *Reading Improvement, 36*(2), 73–89.

Pearson, P. D., & Gallagher, M. (1983). The instruction of reading comprehension. *Contemporary Educational Psychology, 8,* 317–344.

Price, R. D. (1978). Teaching reading is not the responsibility of the social studies teacher. *Social Education, 42,* 312, 314–315.

Pumpian, I., Fisher, D., & Wachowiak, S. (Eds.). (in press). *Challenging the classroom standard with museum-based education: School in the park.* Mahwah, NJ: Erlbaum.

Pynte, J., & Prieur, B. (1996). Prosodic breaks and attachment decisions in sentence parsing. *Language and Cognitive Processes, 11,* 165–191.

Rasinski, T. V. (2000). Speed does matter in reading. *The Reading Teacher, 54,* 146–151.

Rieck, B. J. (1977). How content teachers telegraph messages against reading. *Journal of Reading, 20,* 646–648.

Rosow, L. V. (1988). Adult illiterates offer unexpected clues into the reading process. *Journal of Reading, 32,* 120–124.

Schifini, A. (1996). Discussion in multilingual, multicultural classrooms. In L. B. Gambrell & J. F. Almasi (Eds.), *Lively discussions!*

Fostering engaged reading (pp. 39–51). Newark, DE: International Reading Association.

Schippert, P. (2005). Read alouds and vocabulary: A new way of teaching. *Illinois Reading Council Journal, 33*(3), 11–16.

Schneider, R. B., & Barone, D. (1997). Cross-age tutoring. *Childhood Education 1997, 73,* 136–143.

Smith, R. J., & Otto, W. (1969). Changing teacher attitudes toward teaching reading in the content areas. *Journal of Reading, 12,* 299–304.

Tharp, R. G., & Gallimore, R. (1989). *Rousing minds to life: Teaching, learning, and schooling in social context.* New York: Cambridge University Press.

Trelease, J. (1993). *Read all about it! Great read-aloud stories, poems, and newspaper pieces for preteens and teens.* New York: Penguin.

Trelease, J. (2002). *The read-aloud handbook* (5th ed.). New York: Penguin.

Ulanoff, S. H., & Pucci, S. L. (2001). Learning words from books: The effects of read aloud on second language vocabulary acquisition. *Bilingual Research Journal, 23*(4), 364–378.

Vygotsky, L. S. (1978). Mental development of children and the process of learning. In M. Cole, V. John-Steiner, S. Scribner, and E. Souberman (Eds. and Trans.), *Mind in Society: The development of higher psychological processes.* Cambridge: MA: Harvard University Press.

Wade, S. E., & Moje, E. B. (2000). The role of the text in classroom learning. In M. L. Kamil, P. B. Mosenthal, P. D. Pearson, & R. Barr (Eds.), *Handbook of reading research* (Vol. III, pp. 609–628). Mahwah, NJ: Lawrence Erlbaum.

Wang, J. (1996). An empirical assessment of textbook readability in secondary education. *Reading Improvement, 33,* 41–45.

Wilhelm, J. D. (2001). *Improving comprehension with think-aloud strategies.* New York: Scholastic.

Worthy, J. (2002). What makes intermediate-grade students want to read? *The Reading Teacher, 55,* 568–569.

Children's Literature Cited

Adler, D. A. (1990). *A picture book of Abraham Lincoln.* New York: Holiday House.

Boehm, A. P. (1999). *Jack in search of art.* Lanham, MD: Roberts Rinehart.

Brisson, P. (1993). *Benny's pennies.* New York: Dell Dragonfly.

Carle, E. (1996). *The grouchy ladybug.* New York: HarperCollins.

Gibbons, G. (1994). *Frogs.* New York: Holiday House.

Pallotta, J. (1999). *The Hershey's milk chocolate fraction book.* New York: Scholastic.

Part 3

During Reading Activities

Chapter 6

Douglas Fisher

Nancy Frey

Maureen Begley

Questions, Questions, Everywhere

"**A**re you ready, boys and girls? Here we go . . . which mammals have fur on their bodies?" Juan Velasco asks his first-grade students.

Mr. Velasco looks out upon a sea of blue cards with the word Bat written on them. Zabdy, Maya, Ali, and Emmanuel hold up their yellow cards emblazoned with Bird.

"Now I want you all to turn to your partner to talk about why you held up the colored card that you did," Mr. Velasco directs.

Shortly after turning to Jesus and discussing the differences between bats and birds, Maya blurts out, "Oh yeah, I forgot! It is a bat with fur, not a bird!"

Juan Velasco uses this method regularly to question his students. After reading the informational text Bat and Bird: Discover the Difference (Theodorou, 1997), Mr. Velasco wants to assess whether his students understand the differences between the two creatures. At first, Mr. Velasco asks questions while his students hold up response cards *(see Figure 6.1). Most students have a picture of a bat and a bird on their cards for extra support. The students who able to distinguish between the two words use cards without picture support.*

After Mr. Velasco poses several questions to his students, he turns the questioning over to his first-graders. "I want you to think of important facts about bats and birds and then ask questions about those facts," explains Mr. Velasco. Once again, students work in pairs to construct questions.

"Who's ready to begin?" asks the teacher.

Like many six-year-olds, Marcos relishes the chance to use a big word. "Which animal uses echolocation?"

"Ahhh, that's easy!" Students roar as they all hold up their blue Bat cards. "Ask something harder!" Mr. Velasco smiles at their response.

Mr. Velasco incorporates the use of response cards frequently in his class for quick assessment of content knowledge. "With all these students it is so difficult to meet with them individually. This way of questioning is so fast and tells me exactly what I need to know to plan the next steps in my instruction."

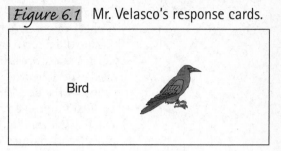

Figure 6.1 Mr. Velasco's response cards.

Bird

Bat

What's Mr. Velasco doing? What does he hope to accomplish by having students use response cards? Why does he value these interactions? The answer lies in the queries themselves: Mr. Velasco is using questioning as a means for instruction. If questions are not asked, then expected application to meaningful context is limited (Routman, 2000). We are reminded of Isidor Rabi. After winning the 1944 Nobel Peace Prize, he was asked by reporters, "What made you so successful?" Rabi responded that when he came home from school, his mother would ask him, "What good questions did *you* ask today?" Thinking of good questions had a very positive influence on this Nobel Peace Prize winner's development.

Why Use Questioning?

Traditionally, teachers use questioning more than any other method for developing comprehension. Questions help the teacher assess whether students understand the text (Durkin, 1978–1979). However, in organizing daily lessons, teachers are inclined to plan thinking activities where the learners' potential to question the text is diminished because the teacher dominates the questioning (Busching & Slesinger 1995). Conversely, less time is dedicated to student questioning. In addition, questioning loses its effectiveness when teachers require students to swallow and regurgitate

> Literal comprehension refers to information related to discrete facts like names and dates, rather than information that requires the student to draw inferences.

facts before they have had an opportunity to chew and digest information. Another drawback of teachers' routine questioning habits is that their questions too often focus on literal comprehension rather than critical thinking, even in content areas like mathematics (Wimer, Ridenour, & Thomas, 2001). This is especially true when working with students perceived as struggling readers (Allington, 1983; Durkin, 1978–1979; Gambrell, 1983).

Reading researchers report from their classroom observations at the elementary level that the majority of questions are teacher-generated and explicit, and require only one correct answer (Armbruster et al., 1991; Block, 2001). An important series of studies on the questioning habits of teachers was conducted by Cazden (1986, 1988). Like others before her, she found that classroom instruction is dominated by a particular cycle of questioning known as IRE: Initiate, Respond, and Evaluate (Dillon, 1988; Mehan, 1979). The IRE pattern of questioning is familiar to all—the teacher initiates a question, students respond, and then the teacher evaluates the quality and accuracy of the responses. Here's an example of IRE:

Teacher: Why was the Gold Rush important in California's history? (Initiate)

Student: Lots of new settlers came to California. (Respond)

Teacher: Good. (Evaluate) Why else was it important? (Initiate)

Here's the difficulty with that question—the student could have also answered that it sparked immigration from countries all over the world, or that it fueled the growth of cities like San Francisco, or that some people grew wealthy by developing businesses to support the hopeful miners. Instead, the question is low-level and consists of a teacher-directed query that excludes any discussion or debate among students. A classroom where IRE is the dominant form of discourse quickly becomes a passive learning environment dependent on the teacher for any kind of discussion. The danger, of course, in the overuse of an IRE pattern of questioning is that the teacher alone becomes the mediator of who will speak and who will not (Mehan, 1979). The students learn that the only questions worth considering are those formulated by the teacher. Ironically, the teachers in Cazden's study (1988) reported that they wanted a student-centered, constructivist classroom, yet clung to IRE as their dominant instructional method for inquiry. If you doubt the pervasiveness of this questioning pattern, then eavesdrop on kindergartners "playing school." Invariably, the five-year-old "teacher" will engage in this questioning pattern with his or her "students." If only all teaching behaviors were this easy to teach!

If you want to gain insight into how your students perceive you as a teacher, invite them to teach for a day!

How Do You Create Quality Questions?

From these studies, it is evident that many students have little practice in answering implicit questions in elementary school and may be poorly equipped to formulate and respond to questions requiring critical thinking. Beginning in kindergarten, it is imperative to create a classroom culture of inquiry. However, students are likely to require teacher modeling to engage in inquiry. One way teachers can accomplish this is through effective questioning strategies. The goal of these restructured questions should be to monitor and guide the ways that students construct and examine meaning in reading, writing, talking, listening, and reflecting.

Poor readers often fail to self-monitor understanding because they underutilize self-questioning (Paris, Wasik, & Turner, 1991). In turn, these struggling readers learn to dislike reading because it is unsatisfying and the concepts of textbook language are unfamiliar. Their comprehension skills then fail to advance because they do not read, reinforcing a cycle of failure (Stanovich, 1986). A basic expectation of reading for information is that students learn a variety of strategies and engage in a variety of activities in order to convert new information into learned information. We know that while learning to read for information, students develop meaningful understanding gradually, and not in a single brief and isolated experience (Marzano, Pickering, & Pollock, 2001). Therefore, instruction must routinely incorporate questioning techniques that encourage active participation and high response opportunities for students. Questioning is central to the two tools in every teacher's arsenal—scaffolding and coaching (Roehler & Duffy, 1991).

When teachers use these strategies to ask probing questions, students develop their thinking processes. At the same time, teachers should share with their students the reasons for their questions. Additional research suggests that instructional questioning strategies that focus on inferences and main ideas equip the students to respond with improved recall and understanding (Raphael, 1984). This is achieved through higher-order questioning.

> Scaffolding is an instructional approach that begins with what the students know, then extends their understanding through supported learning experiences. Scaffolding is especially useful when teaching English learners and struggling readers.

What Are "Higher-Order" Questions?

If you have read the previous pages, you have probably inferred that some questions are better than others. You have seen phrases like "low-level" and "higher-order" questions. But what distinguishes types of questions? How do you determine what sorts of questions are appropriate? A review of the work of Benjamin Bloom is helpful to understand questioning.

In 1956, Benjamin Bloom, an educational psychologist at the University of Chicago, published a series of handbooks on the domains of learning—psychomotor, affective, and cognitive. The handbook devoted to the cognitive domain outlined a classification system that described six levels of competence. This classification system, commonly referred to as Bloom's taxonomy, has become a cornerstone in the description of questions used in the classroom and on tests (Bloom, 1956). Bloom described these competencies; we've included a sample question to illustrate each one:

Level 1—Knowledge: States facts, terms, and definitions.
Sample question: What is the capital of California?

Level 2—Comprehension: Change the information to compare to another form.
Sample question: Explain why Sacramento was selected as the state capital.

Level 3—Application: Solve a new problem using information.
Sample question: What city in California would you choose as the state capital today?

Level 4—Analysis: Identifies components and infers causes or motives.
Sample question: Why do you believe that the legislature chose to move the state capital from San Jose to Sacramento?

Level 5—Synthesis: Create a new product using information in a novel way.
Sample question: Design a state capital for California that will be useful throughout the twenty-first century.

Level 6—Evaluation: Make judgments and defend opinions.
Sample question: Assess the suitability of the present state capital and make recommendations for future development.

The questions got more difficult, didn't they? This is where the terminology of higher- and lower-order questions comes from.

Knowledge and comprehension questions are sometimes referred to as literal questions because they require the student to draw upon memorization or location of facts. In other words, the answers to these types of questions are usually located verbatim in a text. They are also the easiest questions to compose and test. Guszak (1967) estimated that 70% of the questions asked in a typical classroom are knowledge or comprehension questions. That means that only 30% of the queries required students to apply knowledge in unique ways, or to construct understanding by assembling disparate information. It is the imbalance between literal and non-literal questions that is problematic, not the questions themselves. Brophy and Good (1986) noted that students who have experience with lower-order questions do well on tests of basic skills because these tests mirror this type of question.

Tests do not consist only of basic skills; they also demand that students can draw inferences, justify answers, and defend opinions. These same higher-order skills are also widely recognized as critical for adult success (Pithers & Soden, 2000). Therefore, classrooms should provide ample opportunities for students to generate and respond to questions

> Today's standardized tests not only assess basic skills, they increasingly demand that test takers use more sophisticated strategies like predicting, inferring, and synthesizing information.

that require them to analyze information, identify problems, develop original solutions, and formulate opinions.

Fostering Student-Generated Questions Through Question-Answer Relationships

Ultimately, questioning should not emanate only from the teacher; the true goal of questioning is to move it from an external source (the teacher) to an internal one (the student). After all, the power of questioning stems from the learner's use of it as a means to monitor, clarify, and extend his or her learning. An effective means for teaching students how to develop questions is through the question-answer relationships.

The question-answer relationship (QAR) strategy describes four types of questions: Right There, Think and Search, Author and You, and On Your Own (Raphael, 1982, 1984, 1986). It is based on the three question classifications described by Pearson and Johnson (1978): text explicit (the answer is directly quoted in the text); text implicit (the answer must be implied from several passages in the book); and script implicit (requires both the text and prior knowledge and experiences). A classroom poster on Question-Answer Relationships appears in Figure 6.2. These posters are best generated with students using questions they have developed.

QAR requires teachers to model the different levels of questions that are associated with a text. QAR should not be confused with Bloom's taxonomy of questions (Bloom, 1956) because QAR "does not classify questions in isolation but rather by considering the reader's background knowledge and the text" (McIntosh & Draper, 1996, p. 154). In addition to serving as a tool for teachers to develop questions, it is also a framework for students to apply in answering questions. QAR is a student-centered approach to questioning because it "clarifies how students can approach the task of reading texts and answering questions" (Raphael, 1986, p. 517). A comparison chart illustrating the relationship between these concepts of text questioning can be found in Figure 6.3.

It is advisable to pair "right there" and "think and search" questions to encourage the learner to self-assess for uncertainties. This inquiry interaction promotes more personal involvement than using questions with separate phrases of isolated facts. In contrast, "author and you" and "on your own" questions invite the reader to integrate personal experiences and prior knowledge into their responses. These inferential and evaluative questions require the reader to make connections among text, self, and world (Keene & Zimmerman, 1997). During this time, the reader must deduce, infer, connect, and evaluate (Leu & Kinzer, 1995; Raphael, 1982, 1986).

The instructional power of QAR lies in the explicit instruction of identifying what type of question is being asked, and therefore what resources are required to answer it. Raphael (1984) notes that less-effective readers are often puzzled by where to locate answers to questions based

> Posting comprehension tools like the QAR poster in the classroom assists students in applying the strategy after initial instruction has been completed.

> When students can connect texts with their own experiences or with other texts, they are able to understand and remember information efficiently.

Figure 6.2   Question-answer relationship classroom chart.

IN THE TEXT: Right There

How does the caterpillar get out of the egg?

Butterflies begin life as an egg. The caterpillar eats its way out of the egg. They eat to grow, then form a pupa. The butterfly hatches from the pupa's chrysalis as an adult and does not grow anymore.

Answers to Right There questions are in the text. The words in the question usually match a sentence in the text.

IN THE TEXT: Think and Search

What are the stages of a butterfly's life?

Butterflies begin life as an egg. The caterpillar eats its way out of the egg. They eat to grow, then form a pupa. The butterfly hatches from the pupa's chrysalis as an adult and does not grow anymore.

Answers to Think and Search questions are in the text. The answer is found over several sentences or paragraphs.

IN YOUR HEAD: Author and You

What are the similarities and differences between the life cycles of butterflies and frogs?

Answers to Author and You questions are not directly in the text. You need to think about what the author has told you and what you already know about the topic.

IN YOUR HEAD: On Your Own

If you were an entomologist, what part of the butterfly's life cycle would you study? Why?

Answers to On Your Own questions are not in the text. You need to think about your personal experiences to answer.

Adapted from Fisher, D., & Frey, N. (2004). *Improving adolescent literacy: Strategies at work.* Upper Saddle River, NJ: Merrill Prentice Hall. Used with permission.

on a reading. Some students rely only on the text, sometimes fruitlessly searching for an answer that is just not there. Conversely, other students rarely return to the text for any answers, believing that they can only depend on information they can recall from memory. By teaching the

Figure 6.3 Question-answer relationship comparison chart.

QAR STRATEGY	CATEGORY	DESCRIPTION
Right There	Text explicit	The question is asked using words from the text and the answer is directly stated in the reading.
Think and Search	Text implicit	The questions are derived from the text and require the reader to look for the answer in several places and to combine information.
Author and You	Script and text implicit	The question uses the language of the text, but in order to answer it the reader must use what he/she knows about the topic. The answer cannot be found directly in the text, but the text can provide some information for formulating the answer. The information may be implied and the reader infers what the author meant by examining clues in the text.
On Your Own	Script implicit	The question elicits an answer that comes from the reader's own prior knowledge and experiences. The text may or may not be needed to answer the question.

Source: Fisher, D., & Frey, N. (2004). *Improving adolescent literacy: Strategies at work.* Upper Saddle River, NJ: Merrill Prentice Hall. Reprinted with permission.

relationship between questions and answers, students can apply the framework to answer more efficiently and accurately.

The QAR framework can typically be taught in one lesson. We advise the teacher to read aloud a small segment of text and ask a question about what was read. The teacher reflects aloud on the selection and answers the question. It is critical to identify the level of the question and the source of the answer. When students learn to classify questions and locate answers, they learn to recognize that comprehension is influenced by both the reader and the text. Eventually, students are ready to formulate original questions in response to text. To see students in action, let's visit Khan Pham's fifth-grade art class.

The interaction between the reader and the text is known as Reader Response Theory.

Spotlight on Instruction: QAR in Fifth-Grade Art

When his fifth-graders enter the room, Mr. Pham's students are amazed. Their classroom has been transformed into an art gallery with ten posters of famous works of art displayed around the room. The center of the room has been left empty and Mr. Pham gathers his class together on the floor.

"Good morning, class. Since we're going to be visiting the art museum next week, let's begin to explore a group of artists known as the impressionists. We'll start with a gallery walk."

The students are familiar with this term, and have taken gallery walks before. Mr. Pham explains that today each student will walk with a partner. They are to read all the information accompanying each painting. The partners can use the blank chart paper next to each poster to jot down their impressions—how the painting makes them feel, what it reminds them of, or any ideas that come to them as they look at it.

Each reproduction has been labeled with the artist's name, the title of the painting and the year it was painted. Works by Degas, Monet, and Renoir are displayed. In addition, each painting has a piece of informational text about the artist and the work. For the next 30 minutes, students view the art works and discuss their impressions with their partners. When Mr. Pham calls time, he brings a Monet reproduction of *Haystacks at Chailly at Sunrise, 1865; Wheatstacks (End of Summer)* painted in 1891; and the accompanying language charts back to the circle on the floor. He displays the informational passage on an overhead projector so that all the students can view it. After a discussion of the written reactions to the paintings, he directs their attention to the text on the overhead projector.

"This is one of the paintings we'll see next week at the San Diego Museum of Art," says Mr. Pham, pointing to the earlier painting. I'd like us to use QAR to think about the types of questions we can ask ourselves as we view works of art and read about them," explains Mr. Pham.

"We're going to read this first paragraph about Monet together and then I need someone from the class to ask me a question about what we read. It needs to be a Right There question. That means I can go back to what I've read and find the answer right there. I'll read the first paragraph aloud and you follow along."

Mr. Pham begins to read from the overhead. "Claude Monet was born in Paris, France in 1840. He is an important contributor to a style of painting known as Impressionism, which was popularized in the 1870s. Impressionist artists try to capture light and color with their painting and use short brushstrokes. This style of painting was very different from what was accepted at the time. When you look at Monet's paintings, it's as if he is painting what his mind's eye is seeing. It is kind of blurry, as if you can just catch a quick glance before the scene might change."

"Okay, I need someone to ask me a question—one I can find the answer to right in the text if I need to, " Mr. Pham asks the class.

Chris offers, "When was Monet born?"

"Great example of a Right There question," says Mr. Pham. He underlines the phrase *born in Paris, France in 1840* on the transparency.

"Those are pretty straightforward," says Mr. Pham. "What about a Think and Search question? Remember, those are the ones that are in the text but in more than one sentence."

After a bit of discussion, the class agrees that the question "How is Monet's style recognized?" is a Think and Search question. At the class's direction, Mr. Pham underlines the phrases *short brushstrokes, blurry,* and *a scene that might change.*

"I'm glad you noticed that. Monet painted outdoor light a lot, and that changes all the time. Like this one of the haystacks at sunrise. A sunrise is something that lasts for only a few minutes," adds Mr. Pham.

"It must have taken him a long time to paint that, if he only got a few minutes a day," muses Anayeli.

"I think you're right," agrees Mr. Pham. "In fact, that sounds like the basis for an On Your Own question. Can you turn your comment into a question, Anayeli?"

Furrowing her brow, Anayeli contemplates this question. Her partner, Marcella, whispers in her ear and Anayeli's face brightens.

"Do you think Monet painted fast or slow?" suggests Anayeli.

"That's a great On Your Own question," says Mr. Pham. "Let's thicken it a bit. Let's add 'why?' as a follow-up question."

After adding this question to the language chart, Mr. Pham says, "All right, one more. We need an Author and You question, and I'm going to help you with this one." Mr. Pham spends the next few minutes explaining that these two paintings were done 26 years apart. He points out that the *Haystacks at Chailly at Sunrise, 1865* predated the Impressionist movement of the 1870s, and that Monet was a young man of 25 when he painted it.

"When you look at these two paintings, you can see that Monet's work changed over his lifetime. In this early painting, he doesn't use those short brushstrokes that the text talks about. You can see that he spends lots of time painting the light, but it doesn't look blurry, does it?" continues Mr. Pham. "So how about it—is there an Author and You question in there?"

In short order, Mr. Pham and the class have crafted a question that reads, "How did Monet's painting change over time?"

"You've done a nice job with this. When we go to the museum next week, I want you to be thinking about the questions that the paintings, the docent, and the written information spark in you," says Mr. Pham. "Going to a museum is more that just looking at the art. It's really about questioning what you see."

The Importance of Inquiry in Learning

Young children use questions to seek and clarify information, figure out how to solve a problem, and satisfy their seemingly limitless sense of curiosity about the world around them (Education Department of New

Zealand, 1996). This natural sense of inquiry needs to be fostered for students to apply it effectively to learn new content. One way to refine inquiry is to teach the vocabulary of questioning through experiences with questioning words.

Strategies at Work

Generating Questions in Kindergarten Social Studies

"Questions, questions, questions! So many questions!" declares kindergarten teacher Dani Cole. "I hope you can help me today with these questions."

"Mmmm, Ms. Cole, what's a question?" asks Francisco.

"Oh, Francisco, you're so clever. Think of what you just asked me. Does that give you a hint?" Francisco thinks for a bit and asks the same question again. Ms. Cole replies, "That's it exactly! When you ask someone for information, you are asking a question."

"A question is asked when you want to know about something," continues the teacher. "Think about how many times a day you want to know something. For example, 'What is for lunch? When do we go home? How do you spell this word?' Every time you want to know something, you ask a question."

Her class has been studying their school and neighborhood community in social studies. One text they have continued to return to is *Home* (Baker, 2004). This wordless picture book features a view outside a window in a home located in an urban area. The view changes as time passes and the neighborhood revitalizes itself. Details in each collage offer clues about the occupant, a girl who grows from infancy to eventually become a mother herself. The children have poured over the book to locate new information in the illustrations. Ms. Cole has chosen this familiar book to highlight the vocabulary of questioning.

To introduce different question words, Ms. Cole created sets of cards with a question word and a related picture clue on it. Children are paired and given a set of cards with the words and pictures for *who, what, where,* and *when* (see Figure 6.4). After reviewing the cards with her students, Ms. Cole explains that she will ask questions during the shared reading. Their goal is to decide what kind of question is being asked and then to hold up the appropriate card.

She begins by asking, "What is the title of this book?" Many students responded *"Home!"*

"That's right! Now listen to my question again and think about the question word at the beginning."

Figure 6.4   Ms. Cole's questioning cards.

She slowly repeats her question and directs them to look at the cards together. Students discuss the choices and most hold up the "what" questioning card. As they read the story, Ms. Cole asks *who, what, where,* and *when* questions while students respond with both their cards and verbal answers.

To further their understanding of questioning and the use of question words in their everyday reading and writing, Ms. Cole uses one question word all week long during interactive writing lessons and in journal writing. She shares examples of questions and talks with her students about the kinds of questions they can write in their journals. To encourage oral rehearsal of questions and answers, they talk with a partner before writing independently.

For example, students constructed questions that began with the word *where* to focus on places in the school community.

Where is the playground? (Monday)

Where is the office? (Tuesday)

Where is Room 10? (Wednesday)

Where are your crayons? (Thursday)

Where do you live? (Friday)

Each question was accompanied by a simple map to teach about map and location skills. Ms. Cole and her students also used these maps to generate answers for the language charts being developed by the class.

ReQuest

ReQuest (Manzo, 1969) is a useful questioning technique designed to help students formulate questions and answers based on a text passage. This procedure also builds background knowledge and vocabulary through discussions, and helps readers develop predictions about the reading. Through modeling and feedback, students are given an example and then have an opportunity to apply the strategy.

The ReQuest process is simple to implement in the elementary class-room. The teacher chooses a passage of text and designates short segments within the passage. When ReQuest is introduced, it is advisable to conduct the first round so that the teacher is the one to answer questions generated by the students. The teacher/respondent keeps the book closed during the questioning, and students may be asked to rephrase questions if necessary. Manzo advises that the teacher must answer to the best of his or her ability (1969). The students/questioners have their books open and check the teacher's answers against the text.

Once this phase is complete, the roles are reversed. After reading the next segment of text, the teacher becomes the questioner, and the students answer. As before, those who are answering the questions can ask to have the question restated or clarified. This cycle is repeated two or three times until students have the background knowledge and vocabulary to make predictions about the remainder of the reading. Once students are famil-iar with ReQuest, the sequence can be used in small groups to support their understanding of the text. Task cards for a student-led, small-group ReQuest procedure appear in Figure 6.5.

ReQuest in First-Grade Social Studies

ReQuest can be tailored to suit the specific needs of students. For instance, Ramon Espinal uses visual images as well as the written text from the so-cial studies textbook to model the ReQuest questioning technique with his first-grade students. "Boys and girls, let's look at the photographs of the people on page 23. They are from all over the world. Look at them and think about where they might live." After giving them a few minutes to study the photographs, Mr. Espinal asks for their attention.

Although they are eager to talk about their observations, Mr. Espinal asks them to wait. "When I read, I think about questions and answers. It helps me understand what I'm reading. I'd like for you to work with your partner to write two questions and answers you could ask me about these photographs. I'm going to close my book and I'll do my best to answer your questions. It's like a game show, and you get to be the host!"

Designed first for one-to-one instruction, ReQuest has been used as a group activity as well.

A text segment can range from one sentence to an entire paragraph, based on the needs of the students.

Figure 6.5 ReQuest cards for elementary classrooms.

? ? ?	**Questioner Task Card**	**? ? ?**

1. Read quietly.

2. Think of questions to ask.

3. Write your questions and answers.

4. Ask your partner your questions.

5. Take turns.

? ? ?   **? ? ?**

Answer Task Card

1. Read quietly.

2. Think of questions to ask.

3. Write your questions and answers.

4. Answer your partner's questions.

5. Take turns.

These first-graders are delighted at the prospect of "stumping the teacher" and quickly get to work writing questions and answers. Mr. Espinal reminds his students that they must be able to write an answer as well as a question. Ten minutes later, these children are eager to test Mr. Espinal's understanding of the photos in the textbook.

"I've closed my book and now I'm ready for your questions. Who will ask the first question?" inquires the teacher.

Omar and Melissa are ready to begin. "Who lives in a cold place?"

"Well," replies Mr. Espinal, "I need to think about the photographs and what the people were wearing. There was a picture of a boy wearing a fur jacket with a hood—I'll pick him."

"That's right, *Maestro!*" Omar and Melissa enjoy praising their teacher.

After several student teams take turns asking Mr. Espinal questions, he announces that they will change roles. "I'd like to ask you questions now. This time, you close your books and I will ask you questions."

When Mr. Espinal asks about the people who live in warm climates, Omar's eyes light up. "We wrote that question, too!"

"Fantastic! That's what good readers do—they think about questions as they read. You were really paying attention when you looked at those pictures," says Mr. Espinal.

Today's lesson has been an effective introduction into generating and answering questions, as well as an opportunity for students to use academic language. In subsequent lessons over the next few weeks, these first-graders will begin using ReQuest task cards as partners, reading written text together.

> Remember that English language learners need multiple opportunities to practice their speaking and listening skills.

Building Academic Background Knowledge Through Questioning

Academic background knowledge is the information a person already knows about a topic or subject. Marzano (2004) points out that background knowledge must be considered within the context that it is used. For example, an urban child's extensive background knowledge of which streets are safe to walk on is very useful for getting back and forth to school, but less useful for learning school subjects like mathematics (Marzano, 2004). Lack of experiences to build academic background knowledge is associated with lower academic achievement (Tobias, 1994).

One way to build academic background knowledge is through multiple meaningful experiences with the vocabulary of the content. In particular, this means that students have an opportunity to engage in "activities that add to their knowledge of vocabulary terms" (Marzano, 2004, p. 98).

Questioning is central to these activities because it cultivates the learners' use of the vocabulary to answer and generate questions. Skillful questioning techniques by the teacher result in a balance between literal and interpretive questions for students to consider. Literal questions check for understanding, and most teachers are good at asking these. However, asking interpretative questions is more challenging, especially when teaching younger children. However, these interpretive questions are ideal for encouraging students to use academic vocabulary while extending their powers of reasoning. Socratic questioning offers a range of interpretive types of questions that encourage students to think more deeply about what they know and what they still need to know. The six types of Socratic questions are:

1. *Questions for clarification:* What do you mean by that? Why do you say that?

2. *Questions that probe assumptions:* Why do you think that?

3. *Questions that probe reasons and evidence:* Can you give us an example?

4. *Questions about viewpoint:* How are these similar or different? What would someone else say?

5. *Questions that probe implications and consequences:* What would happen if . . . ?

6. *Questions about the question:* Why did I ask that question? (Paul, 1995).

Used in conjunction with literal questions, these Socratic inquiries serve to build background knowledge and deepen students' understanding of academic vocabulary. Perhaps most importantly, it communicates to children that knowledge is not fixed, but rather is fluid and is constructed by the learner.

Socratic Questioning in Second-Grade Mathematics

Pam Pham-Barron is using students' background knowledge to extend their understanding of plane and solid geometric figures. She uses a Socratic questioning technique to encourage their use of academic vocabulary and to facilitate their mathematical thinking.

"What is the difference between a solid figure and a plane shape?" begins Ms. Pham-Barron. (*question about viewpoints*)

"Solid means the opposite of liquid and gas," answers Bryan.

"Why do you think that?" asks Ms. Pham-Barron. (*question that probes assumptions*)

"We learned it in science. Remember?" remarks Bryan.

"Yes, solid does mean that when we talk about the states of matter in science. But what does solid figure mean in mathematics?" (*literal question*)

"It means we can hold it in our hands. And when we draw a shape on paper we can't hold it in our hands," Vanessa offers.

"We can hold the paper," Ruben objects.

"Vanessa, tell us what you mean by that," the teacher inquires. (*question for clarification*)

"Well," answers Vanessa, "you could make a square on a paper but you can't make it stand up."

"Ruben, you said you could hold the paper, and you're right about that. What would happen if we tried to stack paper squares?" (*question that probes implications and consequences*)

Ruben laughs. "You can't do that!"

"I think Vanessa means that we can't hold the shapes we drew on the piece of paper. That is a good way of explaining the difference between a solid figure and a plane shape. You can also say that plane figures can lay flat and solids can't. Solids are three dimensional."

Ms. Pham-Barron's class has been working on identifying solid figures like spheres, pyramids, cubes, and cylinders and their attributes. Today's lesson was designed by Ms. Pham-Barron to encourage connections between plane shapes and solid figures. To help students achieve this objective, the students would be constructing solid figures from plane shapes.

"Is this a plane shape or a solid figure?" inquires their teacher, holding up a cutout shape. (*literal question*)

"A plane shape because it is flat," reply several students.

"You are right. Now look carefully. What do you see inside this shape?" (*literal question*)

"There are dotted lines so you can fold them," says Edward.

"I wonder what will happened if I fold these lines?" ponders their teacher. (*question that probes implications and consequences*)

"You would get a cube," Paola responds.

"How did you figure that out so quickly?" (*question about assumptions*)

"I know that a cube is made up of six squares and I counted there are six squares inside there," explains Paola.

"Can you tell me what I would need to do to change this from a plane shape to a solid figure?" Ms. Pham-Barron asks Vanessa. (*question that probes reason and evidence*)

"You have to fold it," Vanessa gestures with her hands, "put it together like it says."

"What says?" (*question that probes reason and evidence*)

"The . . ." Vanessa scrunches up her face as she looks for the right word. "The folded lines. They say what to do."

"You're right, Vanessa. The dotted lines tell us where to fold." Ms. Pham-Barron folds the plane shape into a cube, just as Vanessa had predicted.

"Everyone tell your partner what shape I made," says the teacher. A chorus of "Cube!" resonates through the classroom.

Ms. Pham-Barron explains that the class will work in groups of four to make predictions. The students were to investigate what solid figure their shape was before actually folding it up.

"It's not a cylinder," Thy says.

"How do you know it's not a cylinder?" challenges Lani. (*question about assumptions*)

"A cylinder has two circles. This one only has one," answers Thy.

Their teacher joins the conversation. "If there is only one circle, what solid do you know that has only one circle?" (*question for clarification*)

"It has to be a cone because a cone has a circle for the base and no edges," answers Edward.

"How do you know there are no edges just by looking at it?" asks Bryan. (*question for reason and evidence*)

"There are no lines on this shape for us to fold it up," Edward replies, showing his classmate.

"Is that always the case?" asks Ms. Pham-Barron. "How can we prove your reasoning?" *(question about the question)*

Recognizing that Edward has made an important discovery, Ms. Pham-Barron calls the class back together. She asks if anyone has noticed that when the dotted lines are folded, those lines become the edges of the figure. Most had not noticed so she asks Edward to explain what he has suggested. After several groups fold their plane shape, they all agree that is true.

Ms. Pham-Barron later noted that the use of Socratic questions was useful for two reasons. First, it made students active participants in their learning because she didn't just feed them the correct answers. "What I am most happy about is how the children are using these questions in their own discussions. I can't be involved in every small group, so it's great to have so many little Socratic thinkers doing the work for me!"

Using Questioning for Study (SQ3R, SQ4R, and SQRQCQ)

Effective questioning is essential when reading for information as well as for class discussions. The ultimate purpose of teacher questioning is to teach students to formulate their own questions as they read; this tool will support their comprehension of text. It is also at the heart of three popular study strategies, SQ3R (survey, question, read, recite, review), SQ4R (survey, question, read, reflect, recite, review), and a customized framework for mathematics called SQRQCQ (survey, question, read, question, compute, question).

SQ3R is a systematic way of studying text to support the student's reading by previewing, skimming, and setting purpose questions before actually reading. This study system, originated by Robinson (1946), includes a series of steps that are offshoots of teacher-modeled reading lessons. While students read to learn, they use the following steps of SQ3R:

S	Survey	Skim text for headings and charts
Q	Question	Turn headings into questions
R	Read	Read to answer questions
R	Recite	Answer questions and make notes
R	Review	Reread for details and unanswered questions

- *Survey* the text to acquire its essence from headings, charts, and bold-print terms.
- *Question* the material. Turn each section heading into a question or set of questions.
- *Read* with the purpose of answering the questions.

- *Recite* the answers to the questions after reading and without looking back in the text, then making notes on learned concepts.
- *Review* what has been read and try to answer, from the text, all the self-questions to evaluate responses and summarize important information.

> By understanding what effective readers do, we can teach more uncertain readers some of the skills needed to improve comprehension.

The sequence used in SQ3R is intended to echo the behavior of effective readers. As students survey the material before reading, they predict what the material will be about, what prior knowledge will be relevant, and which strategies will be useful in approaching the new text. They formulate questions in anticipation of the content they are about to encounter. The students' prior knowledge and use of reading strategies assist them in constructing meaning of the content-area text. However, their comprehension does not necessarily lead to learning that is meaningful and useful. Learning takes place when the new information becomes an interactive part of existing knowledge. Therefore, they recite answers to their own questions and make notes for later use. They then review the text, rereading for details and to clarify questions that remain unanswered (Armbruster et al., 1991).

> Remember that metacognition is the ability to think about one's thinking.

The metacognitive sequence used in SQ3R is a clear model of the reading behaviors of effective readers, yet it seems to be underused in many classrooms. Vacca and Vacca (1999) suggest that this may be due to the way SQ3R is taught. Because there is a prescribed set of steps to be followed, there is a temptation to teach the strategy through rote memorization only, with little time spent on the purpose for each step. When students perceive strategies like these to be an instructional exercise with no real purpose beyond the lesson, they are unlikely to generalize them to other settings. Even more importantly, they will not adopt the approach into their metacognitive repertoire, thus defeating the purpose of teaching the strategy in the first place. Although it will take longer, we strongly urge teachers to invite students to discover why the steps are useful.

SQ3R has inspired several adaptations for guiding students to study and learn from text. These include SQ4R (survey, question, read, reflect, recite, review), and like its predecessor it is implemented across the content areas. SQ4R (Thomas & Robinson, 1972) adds a reflective step after the initial reading to make connections to what is already known. In addition to these learning strategies, there is the SQRQCQ (survey, question, read, question, compute, question), which helps mathematics learners interpret and use the needed textual information in solving word problems (Fay, 1965).

SQRQCQ is an effective framework for solving mathematical word problems because its steps form a systematic approach to determining both the information provided in the question and the mathematical operations necessary to arrive at the correct answer. Like SQ3R, it has a series of steps to be followed:

S	Survey	Skim to get the main idea of the problem
Q	Question	Ask the question that is stated in the problem
R	Reread	Identify the information and details provided
Q	Question	Ask what operation needs to be performed
C	Compute	Solve the problem
Q	Question	Ask whether the answer makes sense

- *Survey* the question to get the essence of the problem. This first reading is for general understanding.

- *Question* what the problem is asking. Restate the question using your own words, being careful not to lose the technical terminology in the problem.

- *Reread* the problem to locate details and eliminate unnecessary information, if applicable.

- *Question* the problem again. What operations are necessary to solve the problem?

- *Compute* the answer.

- *Question* again. Does the answer make sense? Does it answer the question posed in the problem?

It is not uncommon for students to be intimidated by word problems. Frameworks like SQRQCQ can increase student confidence because they learn a systematic approach to solving problems. It also encourages elimination of extraneous information meant to distract the student.

Roberta Dawson implements skillful questioning techniques like SQRQCQ to meet the diverse needs of the English language learners in her mathematics class. She adapts questions that require knowledge of facts and mathematical processes before introducing higher-level questions related to concepts and principles. Her students use the series of questions to reach a correct answer.

SQRQCQ in Third-Grade Mathematics

Mrs. Dawson's third-graders were having trouble with word problems, so she helped her class learn how to ask questions to help them solve the problems.

Mrs. Dawson posted the following problem on the board:

Each section of a canoe can fit 2 people. There are 3 sections in each canoe. If 4 full canoes are taken down river, how many people can fit altogether?

> Like many instructional approaches, these strategies change depending on the needs of students and the text. What they all have in common is attention to questioning as a means for learning.

Figure 6.6 SQRQCQ classroom poster.

S ⌐⌐	Survey	Skim the word problem.
Q ?	Question	What question is the problem asking?
R 📖	Reread	Look for the details.
Q ?	Question	What operation?
C ✍	Compute	Solve the problem.
Q ?	Question	Does the answer make sense?

Since Mrs. Dawson has many English language learners in her class at varying stages of English acquisition, she first shows a picture of a canoe, and the class briefly discusses riding in and paddling a canoe with oars. She reads the problem to the students again, then asks the children to solve the problem in 2 minutes. After setting the timer, she walks around the room to see what the students are doing to solve the problem. Many add $2 + 3 + 4$ to equal 9 people altogether. Students saw the word, "altogether" and took it as a signal to add all the numbers they saw. Some students said there were 8 people (2×4). After the timer rang, Mrs. Dawson recorded answers: some said 8, some 9, three students said 24 (a few students giggled at that answer), and a few students had no answer.

"Ladies and gentlemen, we have a problem! These answers can't all be correct. I think we need a better system for figuring out word problems. The good news is that I've got a great way to help you find the answer that makes sense," says Mrs. Dawson.

Mrs. Dawson introduces the SQRQCQ chart (see Figure 6.6) and explains that this is a method for solving word problems. "It's like a road map," she clarifies. "It tells you where to go next."

She places a transparency of the chart on the overhead projector and models how the process is used to solve the problem. First, she and the students survey the problem. "This is when you read the problem for the first time. You read it all the way to the end—don't stop when you run into numbers!" she tells them.

After reading it, she consults the SQRQCQ chart. "It says to figure out what the question is. Hmm, it's here in the last line. The question this problem is asking is how many people can fit in the four canoes?" As she says this, she underlines the phrase *how many people can fit altogether*.

Mathematics teachers recognize the importance of teaching flexible problem-solving approaches, not just memorization of algorithms.

Question

"Now that I know the question, I can reread to make sure I know all the details." As she rereads the problem, she circles *2 people*, *3 sections*, and *4 canoes*. "It's not just the numbers that are important, it's also what the numbers represent."

Reread

She continues to think aloud as she solves the problem. "Can I draw a picture from what I know? Let's see, yes. What should I draw first? I'll draw the canoe first so that I can then draw the sections and the people. Do I have to draw in detail? No, because this is just to help me see what the problem is telling me and to solve the problem. How many canoes were there?" Mrs. Dawson draws four ovals to represent the canoes.

Question

"How many sections did each canoe have?" she asks herself. She draws two lines in each oval to divide it into three sections. "How many people were in each section?" She adds two dots in each section to represent the people in the four canoes.

"Now I can really see what the problem is about. How many people can travel in four canoes?" she asks.

Once again she refers to the SQRQCQ chart. "Next I have to ask myself a new question. What operation do I need to use?" She continues her think-aloud. I know I have to add—two people in a section, and there are three sections. But wait, I need to multiply, too, because there are four canoes."

Compute

Some of the students now see where this is leading. "I'm going to look at the chart again. It says compute, and I know that means to solve the problem." Mrs. Dawson asks them to write the number sentence to solve the problem. "Work with your partner now to solve the problem," she instructs her students.

Immediately the chatter rises in the classroom as students discuss how to set up the problem. Before long, many of them are looking up at Mrs. Dawson, eager to answer.

"Wait, we're not done yet! The last step on the chart says to ask myself another question. Does the answer make sense?" Once again, the students talk with their partners about their answer.

Question

"Now we're ready. My answer is 24, and it makes sense to me because I figured out that six people can sit in each canoe. With four canoes, that means 24 people can go down the river!" she says. "I guess it wasn't such a silly answer after all!" she winks at the three students who originally arrived at the correct answer. The difference is that this time, everyone was able to solve the word problem correctly.

Questioning the Author (QtA)

Questioning the Author (QtA) is a text-based strategy that invites the reader to interact with the information and build meaning from the content by analyzing the author's purpose (Beck, McKeown, Hamilton, & Kucan, 1997). These questions, referred to as queries by Beck et al., are meant to serve as discussion prompts that invite students to develop ideas rather than restate information directly from the text. Queries require the students

Figure 6.7 Questioning the author prompts.

GOAL	QUERY
Initiate discussion	What is the author trying to say? What is the author's message? What is the author talking about?
Focus on author's message	That's what the author says, but what does it mean?
Linking information	How does that connect with what the author already told us? What information has the author added here that fits in with _____?
Identify difficulties with the way the author has presented information or ideas	Does that make sense? Is that said in a clear way? Did the author explain it clearly? Why or why not? What do we need to figure out or find out?
Encourage students to refer to text because they may have misinterpreted, or help them recognize they have made an inference	Did the author tell us that? Did the author give us an answer for that?

Source: Beck, I. L., McKeown, M. G., Sandora, C., Kucan, L., & Worthy, J. (1996). Questioning the author: A yearlong classroom implementation to engage students with text. *Elementary School Journal, 96,* 385–414. Used with permission of University of Chicago Press.

to take responsibility for thinking and for constructing understanding. As students wrestle with ideas and concepts while reading, their inquiry moves into deeper levels of meaning in narrative and expository texts by moving beyond the stated facts and becoming involved with issues. The students realize that the author is challenging them to build their ideas and concepts. As a result, collaborative discussion follows the open-ended and author-oriented queries. Figure 6.7 contains a table of QtA queries designed by these researchers.

Some teachers record the questions developed during QtA for later use.

The goals of QtA are always the same: to construct the meaning of the text, to help the student go beyond the words on the page, and to relate outside experiences from other texts. The way to achieve these goals is through discussion enriched by the student's world and personal history. QtA involves the teacher as well as the whole class as they collaboratively build understanding during the reading. During this process, the teacher participates in the discussion as a facilitator, guide, initiator, and responder. The role of the teacher is not to dominate the conversation, but to lead the students into dialogue with open-ended questions. The teacher strives to elicit the readers' thinking while keeping them focused in their discussion (McKeown & Beck, 1999). The students' answers are not evaluated in this procedure because QtA is designed to engage the readers with the text, not to rate the accuracy of their responses.

QtA is another way to integrate speaking and listening into the classroom.

We've used innovations of QtA to foster discussion of other visual and media literacies. For example, Questioning the Artist can be used to analyze and evaluate a work of art, while Questioning the Composer can be used to a similar end with a musical composition. In the following lesson, Colleen Crandall adapts the principles of QtA to analyze a scientific photograph.

QtA in Fourth-Grade Science

Colleen Crandall is teaching a fourth-grade science unit on the influence of wind, water, ice, and volcanic activity on landforms. The purpose of her lesson today is to encourage scientific observation through questioning, prediction, and investigation. Using a series of photographs from web sites, Mrs. Crandall will lead a discussion about the formation of the Fisher Towers in Moab, Utah.

She first explains that scientists use scientific observation to develop questions for further study. "Today we're going to think like scientists. We've recently discovered a set of photographs of an unusual land formation. As scientific thinkers, I want you to question the photographer to develop some hypotheses about how this strange place was formed."

She projects the first photograph of the large red rock towers, photographed from below.

"Hey, it's the Grand Canyon!" exclaim several students.

"No, it's not, although I can see why you might think that. Let's look carefully at this picture and think about what you might want to ask the photographer," says Mrs. Crandall. "I'll get you started—what does the photographer want you to understand about this place?"

"He wants us to know that it's a really big place," offers Marta.

"It could be a she," counters Kim.

"That's true," says Mrs. Crandall. "Marta, what did the photographer do to tell you that?"

"He took the picture from the bottom of this place and pointed the camera up. It makes these . . . what are these things?" asks Marta.

"They're towers, and you're right, the photographer chose an angle to make sure that we understood how tall the towers are. Let me show you another picture." With that, she displays a new image, this time of a tower with a large boulder balanced improbably on the top.

"That looks like a snake!" Jesus calls out.

Mrs. Crandall laughs. "Good observation! It's called the Cobra because it looks like a snake that's ready to strike. Now I want you to think about the photographer again. How does this picture connect with the one we just looked at?"

Stephanie is ready for this question. "This picture doesn't look like the last one. Can you show it to us again?" Mrs. Crandall clicks back to the previous picture, then returns to the Cobra. "Yeah, look, this one isn't even in the last picture. I think the photographer is telling us that these weird things are in a really large place."

Subsequent photographs include a view of the snowcapped mountains in the background of the Fisher Towers, and another with a stream in the foreground and the towers in the distance. However, the image that gets the most reaction is the corkscrew summit of a tower called Ancient Art. Even more impressive, a man stands at the peak of the corkscrew, his arms spread wide.

"Whoa, that dude better be careful!" says Jamal.

"How does this new information connect with what we already know?" asks Mrs. Crandall. "Let's think about what we know."

"OK, we know that this place is really big, and there's snow around," says Marta.

"And water," Binh adds.

"And it's a place where people climb," Jamal chimes in.

"Excellent, you're really starting to put the pieces together. This place is called Fisher Towers and it's in Moab, Utah, about 300 miles from the Grand Canyon. The Colorado River is about five miles away. It's one of the most popular places in the western United States for people to do rock climbing, and these towers are considered to be some of the most difficult climbs in the country. Now I want you to work with a partner to read these photographs like a scientist. The photographer is telling you a scientific story about the formation of these towers. I want you to make some observations about how they were formed based on what the photographer is telling you."

As students worked in pairs, Mrs. Crandall listened in on conversations and asked questions. After calling them back together, they noted that water probably had something to do with the land's formation since there were pictures of streams and snow in some of the photos. A sandstorm in the corner of one image caught the eye of two students, who suggested that maybe wind could have something to do with it as well. Mrs. Crandall pointed out that one of the photographs featured a stream of red-tinged water, similar to the red rock of the towers. She explained that every time it rains the towers get a little smaller.

"Could they disappear?" asked Robert.

"They're disappearing now," explained Mrs. Crandall. "They've been disappearing for millions of years. That's what erosion does—it is constantly changing the shape of the earth."

Although Mrs. Crandall could have simply taught about the effects of erosion on the land, she knew that inquiry and images could be used to lead students to these understandings. "Now erosion isn't just another science vocabulary word," says Mrs. Crandall. "Now they have a whole set of questions and pictures in their mind to represent that concept."

Directed Reading–Thinking Activity

The complex processes of reading require strategies to be practiced before, during, and after reading. The awareness of the necessity of these strategies and the ability to conscientiously activate them is referred to as metacognition. Struggling readers seldom make effective use of metacognitive strategies (Haller, Child, & Walberg, 1988). Even among more fluent readers, metacognitive knowledge in expository reading often lags behind narrative (McGee, 1982).

The Directed Reading-Thinking Activity (DR-TA) is an excellent instructional tool for modeling these reading processes using either expository or narrative text. DR-TA allows the readers to increase their metacognitive skills so they become aware of their own thinking processes and develop the ability to regulate, evaluate, and monitor them. These strategies can be learned if they are explicitly explained and modeled, and regularly included in literacy instruction (Helfeldt & Henk, 1990). This is accomplished through a cycle of questioning that helps readers become aware of the strategies they can activate to support their comprehension.

Stauffer (1969) describes DR-TA in three basic steps: predicting, reading, and proving. Students are instructed to continually ask themselves three questions:

- What do I think about this?
- Why do I think so?
- How I can prove it?

At each segment of the text, the readers predict aloud, read to confirm, stop, and engage in the self-questioning. The DR-TA helps students recognize that the text is split into sections that build upon each other (Richardson & Morgan, 1994). Because the text is divided into smaller portions, students can focus on the process of responding to higher-order questions. Students make predictions about specific sections of the text and then read the next segment to confirm or alter their predictions.

> It is important that students make and revise their predictions as they read.

The segmentation of the text is a critical part of teacher preparation for a DR-TA. This chunking of text information is a distinctive element of critical-thinking instruction because it allows the reader to concentrate on both larger concepts and smaller supporting details. To prepare a content-area reading for your students, read the text closely to determine where the natural stopping points are located. These may occur at the end of a paragraph, or before a major heading. We've included a teacher preparation checklist to assist you in preparing a DR-TA lesson (Figure 6.8).

Figure 6.8 DR-TA planning guide.

Teacher: _____ Date: _____ Name of Text: _____
Lesson focus: *What will students know and be able to do?*
Introducing the text: *How will I establish the purpose of the reading?*
Vocabulary: *What is the relevant vocabulary?* *How will I teach it?*
Engagement: *What is my springboard question?*
Survey the text: *What are the text features I will emphasize?*
Reading the text: *Where will I chunk the text?* **Cycle of questioning:** *What do you think? Why do you think that?* *How can you prove it?*
Check for Understanding: *What questions will I ask?*
Extension: *What will students do next with the text?*

Source: Fisher, D., & Frey, N. (2004). *Improving adolescent literacy: Strategies at work.* Upper Saddle River, NJ: Merrill Prentice Hall. Reprinted with permission.

A typical sequence of instruction for a DR-TA looks like this:

1. *Activate background knowledge.* The teacher elicits purposeful predictions to explore the students' prior knowledge relative to the reading assignment by asking questions about the title, headings, and any charts or pictures featured in the reading. Prediction or speculation aids students in setting a purpose for reading and increases their attention to text objectives and their motivation to read (Nichols, 1983). These prereading questions also serve to activate and build background knowledge (Nessel, 1988). The new text is discussed with regard to previous assignments so the students can make relevant connections. Students may be invited to write their predictions, which are reviewed and shared after the reading.

2. *Develop vocabulary.* It is essential that vocabulary be introduced prior to reading. Students need multiple opportunities to read and use new words so they can learn how they relate conceptually to one another. By introducing vocabulary at the beginning of a DR-TA, you are indicating to readers the importance of the words to the piece of text being examined (see Chapter 4 for more information on vocabulary).

3. *Identify significant patterns of text organization.* Some patterns are cause and effect, description, problem/solution, temporal sequence, and compare/contrast. Students can scan text quickly to determine what general text structures they should anticipate.

> Information on text structures was presented in Chapter 1.

4. *Ask springboard questions.* Ask questions that align with the purpose for reading and that focus the students' thinking before reading. Prepare questions that target some of the main ideas of the reading, and use their predictive questions as well. Craft questions that are not readily answered in a few words, but rather are higher-level in nature. Students will revisit these questions as they read, supporting their search for possible answers. We have found it helpful to post these springboard questions on the board so students can refer to them during the reading.

5. *Read the selection.* Identify the stopping points in the passage for students to use during the DR-TA. Remind them that they will read the text and monitor their own comprehension using the three central DR-TA questions: What do I think about this? Why do I think so? How I can prove it? These questions scaffold students' self-regulation of metacognitive strategies while reading. While the students are reading, circulate and assist students in making notes that answer these questions.

6. *Review, reinforce, and evaluate.* After the reading is completed, have students move into small discussion groups and share their predictions. In particular, they should focus on the revisions they

made to their predictions, and the parts of the reading that led them to those revisions. Lead the whole class in a discussion of the springboard questions and ask students to support their responses using the text. Additional questions are likely to evolve and should be connected to further reading or projects related to the content.

DR-TA in Fifth-Grade Social Studies

Aida Allen's fifth-grade social studies class is hard at work. Sitting in triads, the students are wrestling with a tough question. Tino reads it aloud for his group.

"Have you ever felt so strongly about something that you spoke out, even though you might be alone?"

Corina speaks first. "Hey, you guys. Think about all the people we've read about this year. People like the Little Rock Nine. I've never done anything like them—I'm just a kid. I mean, I tell my mom when I think something's not fair, but it's just me and her."

Mariah turns toward her classmate. "You told the teacher when you thought it was unfair for her to give us a test after the winter break."

"Well, that's true, " answers Corina. "But I think the question is asking if we've stood up for someone else, not just ourselves."

Source: Book cover from *Dear Benjamin Banneker* by Andrea Davis Pinkney. Illustrations copyright © 1994 by Brian Pinkney, reproduced by permission of Harcourt, Inc.

Ms. Allen calls her class back to their seats. In preparation for reading the historical biography *Dear Benjamin Banneker* (Pinkney, 1998), students discussed this springboard question.

Corina raises her hand. "Ms. Allen, are you talking about sticking up for ourselves or for someone else?"

"Sticking up and speaking out for someone else—not just yourself. I asked you to think about this question because our reading today is going to be about a man who did just that," explains Ms. Allen. "We're going to read about a man named Benjamin Banneker."

After distributing the reading and placing another copy of the text on the overhead, Ms. Allen asks her students to take a close look at the drawing on the first page. It is a portrait of a distinguished African-American man in period dress. They briefly discuss what they might ascertain from the illustration while Ms. Allen records their ideas on a language chart.

"That's terrific—you're already thinking about what to expect as you read this. Before we get into the reading, I want to introduce a few vocabulary words you'll need to know." Ms. Allen distributes a vocabulary self-awareness chart with the words *astronomer, hypocrite, eclipse, almanac,* and *surveyor* featured. She reminds the students that they

Figure 6.9 Vocabulary self-awareness chart.

VOCABULARY WORD	I KNOW IT AND CAN USE IT IN A SENTENCE	I HAVE SEEN IT OR HEARD IT	NO CLUE!
astronomer			
hypocrite			
eclipse			
almanac			
surveyor			

Adapted from Fisher, D., & Frey, N. (2004). *Improving adolescent literacy: Strategies at work.* Upper Saddle River, NJ: Merrill Prentice Hall. Used with permission.

need to consider how they might know these words. The class is familiar with this activity and within a few minutes they have written what they know about the words. The chart she used is in Figure 6.9. You can read more about using vocabulary self-awareness charts in Chapter 4.

After spending time discussing the vocabulary words and clarifying meaning, Ms. Allen gets to the heart of the DR-TA lesson. She explains that good readers ask themselves questions throughout the reading, not just at the end. She reminds them that they will be reading about a man who was not afraid to stand up for the rights of others, even though he might be alone.

For the next 20 minutes, Ms. Allen conducts a shared reading of a long passage from *Dear Benjamin Banneker*. She segmented the text before the lesson by drawing a line after every few paragraphs and writing the words "stop and discuss" in the margin. For the first few paragraphs, she models the cycle of questions:

- What do you think?
- Why do you think that?
- How can you prove it?

With each question, Ms. Allen is inviting her students to make predictions, analyze information, and monitor their understanding. After discussing three segments of the reading, she releases responsibility to her students. Now working in triads again, Tino, Corina, and Mariah use the DR-TA questioning cycle to discuss the remainder of the reading. Ms. Allen listens in on the groups as they learn about Banneker's accomplishments. As an African-American freeman in 1791, he wrote a letter to the then Secretary of State Thomas Jefferson, questioning the practice of slavery in a country founded on the principle that "all men are created equal." His letter, and Jefferson's response, were widely published and read throughout the country as citizens wrestled with the hypocrisy Banneker exposed.

After the class has finished reading the text, Ms. Allen engages her students in a dialogue. Students are asked to challenge their thinking and look to answer their own questions. She guides the discussion to focus on Banneker's contributions and accomplishments as a scientist, inventor, and intellectual and leads students to a greater understanding of how one person can impact history.

Later, Ms. Allen remarks that she finds DR-TA to be "an ideal way to model ongoing analysis of a text. I'm amazed at how often they end up using these same questions in their writing and discussions."

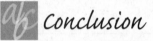 Conclusion

The range of questioning strategies discussed in this chapter provides teachers and learners with ways to monitor and guide their construction and examination of meaning in reading, writing, talking, listening, and reflecting. These strategies serve as methods for modeling guiding questions, clarifying questions, expanding questions, and revising questions. By maintaining a balance between asking and answering questions, the teacher returns responsibility for critical thinking to the students. The use of effective questioning also directs and focuses students' reading, thereby energizing the reading by inviting students to make connections to both personal experience and prior knowledge.

References

Allington, R. L. (1983). The reading instruction provided readers of differing abilities. *The Elementary School Journal, 83,* 548–559.

Armbruster, B., Anderson, T., Armstrong, J., Wise, M., Janisch, C., & Meyer, L. (1991). Reading and questioning in content areas. *Journal of Reading Behavior, 23,* 35–59.

Beck, I. L., McKeown, M. G., Hamilton, R. L., & Kucan, L. (1997). *Questioning the author: An approach for enhancing student engagement with text.* Newark, DE: International Reading Association.

Block, S. (2001). Ask me a question: How teachers use inquiry in a classroom. *American School Board Journal, 188*(5), 43–45.

Bloom, B. S. (1956). *Taxonomy of educational objectives: The classification of educational goals: Handbook I, cognitive domain.* New York: Longmans.

Brophy, J., & Good, T. (1986). Teacher behavior and student achievement. In M. Wittrock (Ed.), *The handbook of research on teaching* (3rd ed.) (pp. 328–375). New York: Macmillan.

Busching, B. A., & Slesinger, B. A. (1995). Authentic questions: What do they look like? Where do they lead? *Language Arts, 72,* 341–351.

Cazden, C. B. (1986). Classroom discourse. In M. Wittrock (Ed.), *Handbook of research on teaching* (3rd ed.) (pp. 432–462). New York: Macmillan.

Cazden, C. B. (1988). *Classroom discourse: The language of teaching and learning.* Portsmouth, NH: Heinemann.

Dillon, J. T. (1988). *Questioning and teaching: A manual of practice.* New York: Teachers College Press.

Durkin, D. (1978–1979). What classroom observations reveal about reading comprehension. *Reading Research Quarterly, 14,* 481–533.

Education Department of New Zealand. (1996). *Oral language resource book.* Melbourne, AUS: Longman Australia.

Fay, L. (1965). Reading study skills: Math and science. In J. A. Figurel (Ed.), *Reading and inquiry* (pp. 92–94). Newark, DE: International Reading Association.

Gambrell, L. (1983). The occurrence of think-time during reading comprehension instruction. *Journal of Educational Research, 77*(2), 77–80.

Guszak, F. J. (1967). Teacher questioning and reading. *The Reading Teacher, 21,* 227–234.

Haller, E. P., Child, D. A., & Walberg, H. J. (1988). Can comprehension be taught? A quantitative synthesis of "metacognitive" studies. *Educational Researcher, 17*(9), 5–8.

Helfeldt, J. P., & Henk, W. A. (1990). Reciprocal question-answer relationships: An instructional technique for at-risk readers. *Journal of Reading, 33,* 509–514.

Keene, E. O., & Zimmermann, S. (1997). *Mosaic of thought: Teaching comprehension in a reader's workshop.* Portsmouth, NH: Heinemann.

Leu, D. J., & Kinzer, C. K. (1995). *Effective reading instruction K–8*

(3rd ed.). Upper Saddle River, NJ: Merrill/Prentice Hall.

Manzo, A. V. (1969). ReQuest procedure. *Journal of Reading, 13,* 123–126.

Marzano, R. J. (2004). *Building background knowledge for academic achievement: Research on what works in schools.* Alexandria, VA: Association for Supervision and Curriculum Development.

Marzano, R. J., Pickering, D. J., & Pollock, J. E. (2001). *Classroom instruction that works: Research-based strategies for increasing student achievement.* Alexandria, VA: Association of Supervision and Curriculum Development.

McGee, L. (1982). Awareness of text structure: Effects on children's recall of expository text. *Reading Research Quarterly, 17,* 581–589.

McIntosh, M. E., & Draper, R. J. (1996). Using the question-answer relationship strategy to improve students' reading of mathematics texts. *Clearing House, 69,* 154–162.

McKeown, M. G., & Beck I. L. (1999). Getting the discussion started. *Educational Leadership, 57*(3), 25–28.

Mehan, H. (1979). *Learning lessons.* Cambridge, MA: Harvard University Press.

Nessel, D. (1988). Channeling knowledge for reading expository text. *Journal of Reading, 32,* 225–228.

Nichols, J. N. (1983). Using prediction to increase content area interest and understanding. *Journal of Reading, 27,* 225–228.

Paris, S. G., Wasik, B. A., & Turner, J. C. (1991). The development of strategic readers. In R. Barr, M. L. Kamil, P. Mosenthal, & P. D. Pearson (Eds.), *Handbook of reading research* (Vol. II, pp. 609–640). Mahwah, NJ: Erlbaum.

Paul, R. W. (1995). *Critical thinking: How to prepare students for a rapidly changing world.* Dillon Beach, CA: Center for Critical Thinking.

Pearson, P. D., & Johnson, D. D. (1978). *Teaching reading comprehension*. New York: Holt, Rinehart, and Winston.

Pithers, R. T., & Soden, R. (2000). Critical thinking in education: A review. *Educational Research, 42,* 237–250.

Raphael, T. E. (1982). Teaching children question-answering strategies. *The Reading Teacher, 36,* 186–191.

Raphael, T. E. (1984). Teaching learners about sources of information for answering questions. *Journal of Reading, 27,* 303–311.

Raphael, T. E. (1986). Teaching children question-answering relationships, revisited. *The Reading Teacher, 39,* 516–522.

Richardson, J. S., & Morgan, R. F. (1994). *Reading to learn in the content areas*. Belmont, WA: Wadsworth.

Robinson, F. P. (1946). *Effective study*. New York: Harper & Brothers.

Roehler, L. R., & Duffy, G. G. (1991). Teachers' instructional actions. In R. Barr, M. L. Kamil, P. Mosenthal, & P. D. Pearson (Eds.), *Handbook of reading research* (Vol. II). (pp. 861–883). Mahwah, NJ: Lawrence Erlbaum.

Routman, R. (2000). Teacher talk. *Education Leadership, 59*(6), 32–35.

Stanovich, K. E. (1986). Matthew effects in reading: Some consequences of individual differences in the acquisition of literacy. *Reading Research Quarterly, 21,* 360–407.

Stauffer, R. G. (1969). *Teaching reading as a thinking process*. New York: HarperCollins.

Tobias, S. (1994). Interest, prior knowledge and learning. *Review of Educational Research, 64*(1), 37–54.

Thomas, E., & Robinson, H. (1972). *Improving reading in every class: A sourcebook for teachers*. Boston: Allyn & Bacon.

Vacca, R. T., & Vacca, J. L. (1999). *Content area reading: Literacy and learning across the curriculum* (6th ed.). New York: Longman.

Wimer, J. W., Ridenour, C. S., & Thomas, K. (2001). Higher order teacher questioning of boys and girls in elementary mathematics classrooms. *The Journal of Educational Research, 95*(2), 84–92.

Children's Literature Cited

Baker, J. (2004). *Home*. New York: Greenwillow.

Pinkney, A. D. (1998). *Dear Benjamin Banneker*. New York: Voyager.

Theodorou, R. (1997). *Bat and bird: Discover the difference*. Portsmouth, NH: Heinemann.

Nancy Frey

Douglas Fisher

Elizabeth Soriano

Chapter 7

Picture This:
Graphic Organizers in the Classroom

*W*ith their resources spread out on their desks, the students in Ms. Feistel's fifth-grade class work in teams to organize the information they've gathered on Native Americans. They've read biographies, listened to stories and legends, and studied maps. Their teacher has asked them to compare and contrast several Native American tribes and has worked with the whole class to create a Venn diagram to record facts and ideas that are known to be common among several tribes. Now students are working to organize the additional information they've learned and present it to the class in teams.

The students have been told that they need to present their findings to the class in a way that makes sense and allows them to easily make comparisons about Native Americans. They've researched the Hopi, Iroquois, and Sioux tribes and the assignment rubric included a section on organization and presentation. Ms. Feistel had introduced the idea of an attribute chart to the class in a previous science unit, and she is interested to see if any of the teams will use one in their presentation.

"We can't use a Venn diagram," remarks Ivan. "There's too much stuff. It won't all fit into two or three categories. We need a way to show all the information at once so everyone can see it."

"Yeah, how are we going to show all the different ideas? Like what they wore, and ate, and the form of government for each tribe?" wonders Jaime.

"I think a poster would work. We could make one of those charts like we did on nutrition, remember?" asks Daisy. "The one with the pluses and minuses to show if the food contained protein or fat. Maybe one like that."

"But we'll need to change it to work for Indians. We can't just use pluses and minuses. The teacher said we need to give specific information on what we learned," adds Cory.

The students continue to deliberate and agree to try to make a poster report. Other teams are working, too. One group has decided to make a concept map to show how the different tribes' ideas about government and community life are related, while still another decides to try a "triple" Venn diagram to see if it will fit their purpose.

"Using three circles will work," says Lorena. "We can label one 'government and community,' another one can be for their houses and the last one will be for the different celebrations."

"But, what about everything else? Where would we put that? The dwellings and what the tribal name means?" asks Vi. "And besides, it will be messy and hard to read. I think we need to find another way to organize our work."

Circulating around the room, Ms. Feistel listens to the students' ideas and offers suggestions. She reminds them that all the information needs to be on one page and must be useful as a study guide. The group abandons the idea of a triple Venn diagram and decides to use a web instead.

"Let's make lots of small webs," suggests Carlos. "Otherwise we'll never get it all on one page and it will be harder to study. We need one for how the Native Americans got food, like whether they were hunters, gatherers, or farmers. And another one for where they lived, and one for the tools."

The teams continue to work at organizing their findings. Ms. Feistel has used many graphic organizers with her class during the year and one of the goals is for her fifth-graders to understand that the organization of information influences learning. She also wants them to be able to see relationships between the various tribes and understand the commonalities and differences.

"It's all about the tools," says Ms. Feistel. "I want them to appreciate that graphic organizers are tools for understanding, not just a worksheet to *fill out. By exposing them to lots of graphic organizers, I hope to give them tools for supporting their own learning."*

Graphic organizers are a popular tool for promoting and extending student understanding of concepts and the relationships among them. These visual displays of information, often arranged in bubbles or squares with connecting lines between them to portray conceptual relationships, are commonly found in many secondary classrooms. Howe, Grierson, and Richmond (1997) surveyed teachers to find out what content-area reading strategies they perceived as being most useful. Although 82% recommended that graphic organizers, like concept maps, should be used frequently, only 59% said that they used them often. This disparity may be due to the perceived difficulty of preparing them in advance.

> Books like Wood, K. D., Lapp, D., & Flood, J. (1992), <u>Guiding readers through text: A review of study guides,</u> Newark, DE: International Reading Association, have a variety of graphic organizers for teacher use.

In the opening scenario, the fifth-graders in Ms. Feistel's class used graphic organizers to engage in several complex learning processes. The teams created a visual representation of the concepts they had learned while using oral language, reading, and writing to arrive at a format for their oral presentations. Graphic organizers have been shown to be a valuable tool for allowing students to make nonlinear visual representations of the concepts being studied in their content-area classes (e.g., McMackin & Witherell, 2005). While using teacher-created graphic organizers is beneficial for ordering information and making connections, the goal is always to move students to the development of their own graphic organizers.

Teaching and Learning with Graphic Organizers

Why Use Graphic Organizers?

Robinson (1998) traces the origins of graphic organizers to the advance organizer work of Ausubel (1960). Advance organizers are brief textual statements that summarize the main points of the upcoming reading, as well as offer explicit connections to larger concepts that may or may not be discussed in the text. They are used as a prereading strategy to assist students in organizing the information through schema building. Advance organizers became a popular instructional strategy immediately, and interest soon turned to finding novel ways to use them. Barron (1969) arranged advance organizers in a nontraditional manner to display vocabulary in ways that represented connections between words, arguably one of the first graphic organizers. While advance organizers are always used as a prereading strategy, subsequent studies demonstrated that graphic organizers were more effective during and after the reading (Shanahan, 1982).

Graphic Organizers Facilitate Comprehension. Comprehension is the ability to derive meaning from text and requires students to mobilize strategies when they do not understand. However, it is more than just understanding—it is being aware of what needs to be done to support one's own learning, then planning and executing the strategies, and finally reflecting on their effectiveness. The opportunities presented through graphic organizers activate these comprehension strategies and metacognitive skills. Alvermann (1988) found that graphic organizers prompted students to reread text passages to clarify understanding. Another study found that students became more active readers when they had a graphic organizer to aid them (Alvermann & Boothby, 1982).

> Metacognition is the ability to think about one's thinking.

Graphic Organizers Support Students Who Struggle with Literacy. Graphic organizers have been shown to be of great assistance to students with learning disabilities. These tools can scaffold information to assist students in constructing written products (James, Abbott, & Greenwood, 2001). They are also effective in promoting recall of information (Dye, 2000). The efficacy of graphic organizers appears to extend to students with learning difficulties as well. Results from a series of studies by the University of Oregon's Behavioral Research and Teaching Project suggest that the use of graphic organizers is beneficial to students with learning disabilities, in part, because the teacher overtly identifies concepts and their relationships, resulting in more effective instruction (McCoy & Ketterlin-Geller, 2004). In other words, the practice of creating graphic organizers for students results in better teaching.

> Modifications should be based on the student's Individualized Education Plan or IEP.

When Can I Use a Graphic Organizer?

The strength of any instructional strategy is not only in its use, but in its timing. The science of teaching may be in knowing what to do; the art of teaching lies in knowing when to do it. The same is true for graphic organizers. These visual displays allow students to construct their understanding of a subject in ways that are less linear and therefore better suited for representing complex relationships. Depending on when they are used, they can activate prior knowledge, encourage brainstorming, record events in detail, or serve as a review of the topic. In all cases, they are a means of building comprehension.

Instruction in text comprehension is often spoken of in three categories: before, during, and after reading. Likewise, graphic organizers can support comprehension instruction at each of these key junctures. Take prereading strategies, for instance. Graphic organizers can alert students to important ideas they will encounter during an upcoming reading. Wood, Lapp, and Flood (1992) suggest using a Pattern Guide (Herber, 1970) as an anticipatory activity for informational text passages. Key concepts are selected in advance and written on note cards, the edges of

> Like most strategies, graphic organizers can be used at different times. We placed them in the "during reading" section to reinforce the idea that students can use specific tools as they read for information.

> Review Chapter 3 for more information about anticipatory activities.

which may be cut to resemble a puzzle piece. The page number where the information appears is logged on the back. Students then reassemble the statements and record them in their notes. In this way, students use prior knowledge, as well as their understanding of how information is organized, to predict what they will soon read in their textbook. An example of a pattern guide on cell division appears in Figure 7.1. The goal of this activity is not to predict the correct jigsaw—after all, even a very young child could accurately assemble the cards using the shapes or the page numbers written on the back. The purpose of a Pattern Guide is to "help them develop a cluster of knowledge" (Wood, Lapp, & Flood, 1992, p. 49) before reading the technical information in the text.

Graphic organizers are not confined to prereading experiences. They can also be used during reading, especially when reading for information. When used in this manner, the graphic organizer resembles a note-making tool. The teacher may partially construct a graphic organizer based on previously taught information. However, blanks are strategically used to represent the likely location of a key piece of new vocabulary or concepts. An example of this type of graphic organizer can be seen in Figure 7.2. As students read and encounter new information, they add it to the graphic organizer. The advantage of this method over traditional note making lies in the portion of the graphic organizer created by the teacher; it continually draws the student's eye back to material learned prior to the reading. In this way the graphic organizer serves as a kind of structured note-making system for the student.

In addition to their use before and during reading, graphic organizers can be used after reading for information. The goal of using a graphic organizer after the reading is to increase comprehension. Vacca and Vacca (1998) point out that strategic readers seek out the structure of the text,

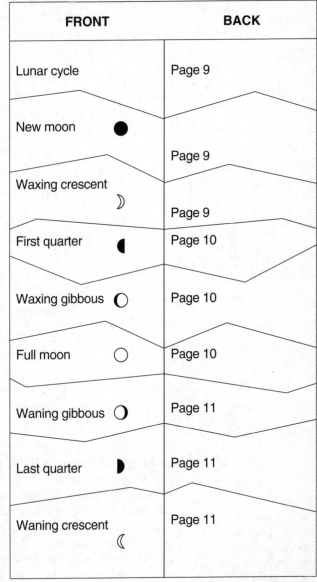

Figure 7.1 Prereading pattern guide.

FRONT	BACK
Lunar cycle	Page 9
New moon ●	Page 9
Waxing crescent ☽	Page 9
First quarter ◗	Page 10
Waxing gibbous ◖	Page 10
Full moon ○	Page 10
Waning gibbous ◖	Page 11
Last quarter ◗	Page 11
Waning crescent ☾	Page 11

See Chapter 8 for a discussion of note making.

Figure 7.2 Graphic organizer for use during reading.

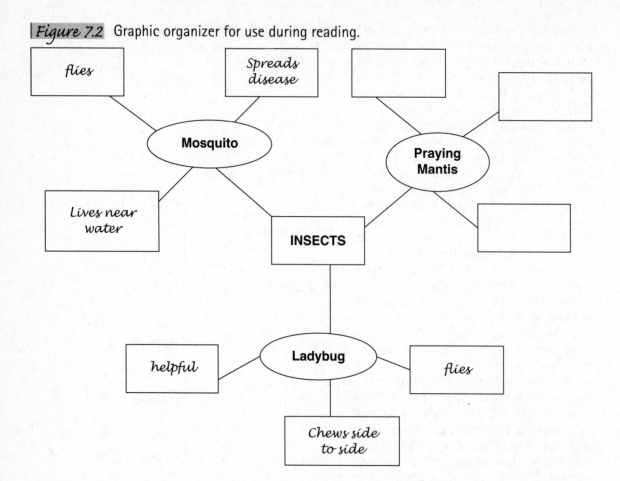

looking for the organizational patterns that will give them a framework for ordering new information. When matched carefully with text, graphic organizers can help students clarify the connections and relationships they are finding during and after the reading.

Consider the example of a Venn diagram. This is an excellent example of a graphic organizer used both during and after reading. This ubiquitous chart features two overlapping, though not congruent, circles. The portions of the circle that do not overlap are used for contrasting two ideas, phenomena, or events, and the overlapping portion in the center is reserved for similarities. Since many textbooks contain compare/contrast passages, the Venn diagram is an ideal graphic representation of such readings. Keep in mind that the success of a particular graphic organizer in boosting comprehension lies in matching it carefully with the text. It may be this difficulty that prevents so many teachers, like those in the study by Howe, Grierson, and Richmond (1997), from using graphic organizers more frequently.

You've probably determined the structure of this text—opening vignette, research base, and strategies at work—and could create a graphic organizer for each chapter.

What Are the Types of Graphic Organizers? Graphic organizers are a component of a larger category of instructional aids called adjunct displays (Robinson, 1998). Advance organizers and outlines are two other forms of adjunct displays, because they serve as complementary devices for representing the information contained in a text. Hyerle (1996) reminds us that these devices are important because they allow us to "stor[e] information outside the body . . . [because] human beings are the only form of life that can store, organize, and retrieve data in locations other than our bodies" (p. x). However, graphic organizers have been shown to be more effective for this function than outlines (Kiewra, Kauffman, Robinson, DuBois, & Staley, 1999), perhaps because they allow for nonlinear representations of relationships across concepts.

So let's define a graphic organizer. They come in a variety of forms and go by a number of names, including semantic webs, concept maps, flowcharts, and diagrams. Although there are myriad versions, they all have a few things in common. Each of them portrays a process or structure in a way that relies on relative position and juxtaposition of words or phrases that are bound by a shape or line. Frequently, they also feature lines that depict associations between and among ideas. Robinson (1998) categorizes graphic organizers into four groups: concept maps, flow diagrams, tree diagrams, and matrices.

Concept Maps. Concept maps are what most people visualize first when they think about graphic organizers. They are shape-bound words or phrases radiating from a central figure that represents the main idea or concept. Lines connect the shapes and may contain words to further explain the relationship. A concept map on the relationship between the reader and the text might look like the one shown in Figure 7.3.

Concept maps are favored by many educators because they lend themselves to quick and efficient illustrations of complicated ideas. Hyerle (1996) reminds us that concept maps should not be used as fill-in-the-blank worksheets to copy a diagram that has already been created by the teacher, because the power of the concept map lies in the learner's opportunity to "negotiate meaning" (p. 32). Instead, he advises that students be allowed the freedom to construct their own concept maps, even though they may vary from the teacher's schema.

Flow Diagrams. A second type of graphic organizer is the flow diagram. These visual displays are ideal for processes, event sequences, and timelines. Flow diagrams are derived from flowcharts, but they differ in the ways they are constructed. Flowcharts use a standardized vocabulary of shapes to describe an operation or procedure. For instance, oval shapes signal the beginning and end of the procedure, and a diamond shape contains questions. Flow diagrams do not adhere to these rules, although they do contain shape-bound text. Arrows show the direction or sequence

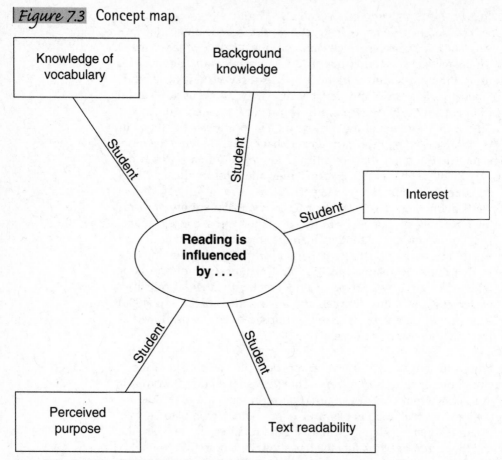

Figure 7.3 Concept map.

Source: Fisher, D., & Frey, N. (2004). *Improving adolescent literacy: Strategies at work,* 1st edition, © 2004, pp. 72, 73, 109, 110, 125, 156, 170. Adapted by permission of Pearson Education, Inc., Upper Saddle River, NJ.

of the topic illustrated. A flow diagram of a Directed Reading-Thinking Activity (Stauffer, 1969) could look like the one in Figure 7.4. A DR-TA is a format for making, and confirming or disconfirming predictions to gain detailed information from a text passage. Again, as with concept maps, students should be encouraged to create their own flow diagrams, rather than fill in a predetermined number of boxes.

DR-TAs were also discussed in Chapter 6.

Tree Diagrams. Tree diagrams are another type of graphic organizer. Like the others, they are suitable for specific purposes. Tree diagrams are most frequently used to categorize and classify information. They are commonly used in mathematics, particularly to represent probability, such as in repeated tosses of a coin. A tree diagram of the elements of language is found in Figure 7.5.

Tree diagrams can be constructed on the horizontal, as shown in Figure 7.5 or on the vertical. They typically radiate from a general concept

Figure 7.4 Flow diagram.

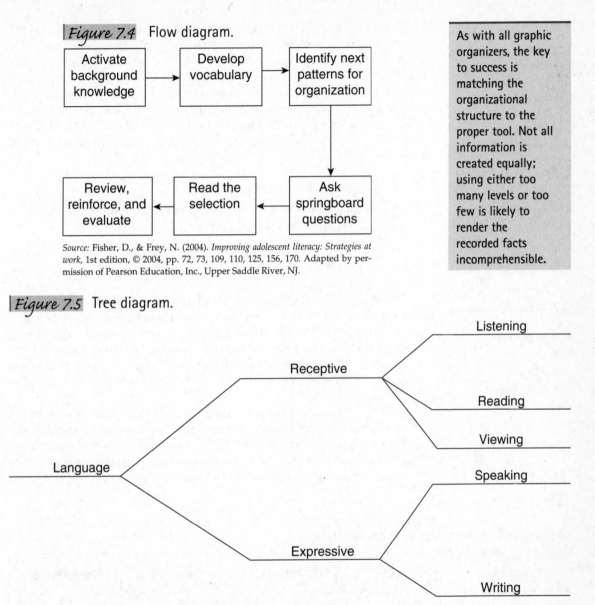

Source: Fisher, D., & Frey, N. (2004). *Improving adolescent literacy: Strategies at work*, 1st edition, © 2004, pp. 72, 73, 109, 110, 125, 156, 170. Adapted by permission of Pearson Education, Inc., Upper Saddle River, NJ.

Figure 7.5 Tree diagram.

> As with all graphic organizers, the key to success is matching the organizational structure to the proper tool. Not all information is created equally; using either too many levels or too few is likely to render the recorded facts incomprehensible.

Source: Fisher, D., & Frey, N. (2004). *Improving adolescent literacy: Strategies at work,* 1st edition, © 2004, pp. 72, 73, 109, 110, 125, 156, 170. Adapted by permission of Pearson Education, Inc., Upper Saddle River, NJ.

("language") to a primary level of classification ("receptive" and "expressive"). Supporting categories branch off the primary level of information ("listening," etc.). With each additional level, a greater degree of detail is introduced.

Matrices. A final commonly used adjunct display is the matrix. A matrix is an arrangement of words or phrases in a table format to be read both horizontally and vertically. Like many graphic organizers, matrix designs show relationships, either by comparing and contrasting concepts, or by classifying attributes. Another type of matrix display is a synectic chart (Gordon, 1961). This organizer is meant to foster creative thinking by requiring the learner to link disparate ideas. This type of creative thinking exercise demands that students look for analogies to explain relationships. It begins with a term to be defined and discussed. Students may look up the definition and record it. Then they brainstorm a list of related words that

- are similar to the focus word
- describe what the word feels like (a stretch for many students)
- are opposite of the focus word
- are similar to the focus word, but not the same as those listed before
- redefine the focus word

> The semantic feature analysis discussed in Chapter 4 on vocabulary is one example of a matrix graphic organizer.

This exercise is best done in small groups, where students can discuss each attribute to construct the matrix. Dictionaries and a good thesaurus are helpful tools in completing this type of graphic organizer. If generating words and phrases is too difficult, the teacher can supply a list of words that have been cut apart into small slips of paper to create a word sort. A synectic matrix on language might look like the one found in Figure 7.6.

After constructing the matrix, students can use their brainstormed ideas to formulate an inquiry. For instance, the teachers who made the matrix in Figure 7.6 might investigate the similarities and differences between prose and poetry, the association of language and intelligence, or the use of language in animals and humans.

> Examples of other word sorts are in Chapter 4 on vocabulary development.

Figure 7.6 Synectics matrix on language.

SIMILAR	FEELS LIKE	OPPOSITE	SIMILAR	REDEFINE
Talking	Recognition	Silent	Tongue	It separates and unites
Communicate	My identity	Quiet	Poetry	It is art
Speech	Intelligence	Still	Prose	Makes me human

How Can I Teach the Use of Graphic Organizers?

Like all good teaching strategies, graphic organizers must be introduced carefully to students. On the surface, they are such a simple tool that there is a temptation to merely distribute them and ask students to fill them in. Unfortunately, without proper scaffolding, graphic organizers can be reduced to the level of a fancy worksheet, completed only to satisfy the teacher. Organizers are visual illustrations—tools to help students understand, summarize, and synthesize the information from texts or other sources. As students create graphic representations, they manipulate and construct organizational patterns for the informational or narrative text. The students become actively involved in concrete processing of abstract ideas in print form. Here are some considerations to move from teacher-centered to learner-centered instruction for creating and interpreting graphic organizers:

- Introduce a specific type of graphic organizer by showing how it represents the structure of a text or concept.
- Model how to use the graphic organizer with a familiar text that the students have read. Emphasize that there is no one "right way" to use a graphic organizer, although there are wise practices (legibility, striking a balance between too little and too much information) that make them more helpful over time.
- Show the class examples of graphic organizers you have created for yourself so that they can see the usefulness of the tool.
- Give students questions to guide them to the important information they should seek in the text.
- When students become more practiced, choose a new text and have them apply the same graphic organizer. Create guiding questions with the students, then pair them to complete the process.
- Give students many opportunities to practice using the graphic organizer in pairs, moving toward independent use.
- As students add to their repertoire of graphic organizers, be sure to provide lots of blank copies that are readily accessible. Many teachers keep an open file in the room containing labeled folders of graphic organizers.

With practice and reflection on the process and its benefits, students may begin to alter or design their own graphic organizers. When this happens, celebrate! It's a sign that you've done a great job of teaching an important tool for learning.

How Can Graphic Organizers Be Used for Assessment?

Although we have emphasized the practicality of graphic organizers to represent learning as it is being constructed, we don't want to overlook their usefulness as an assessment tool. The goal of assessment, after all, is

Formative assessment is used throughout the unit to inform instruction. Summative assessments are administered at the end of a unit to measure cumulative student learning.

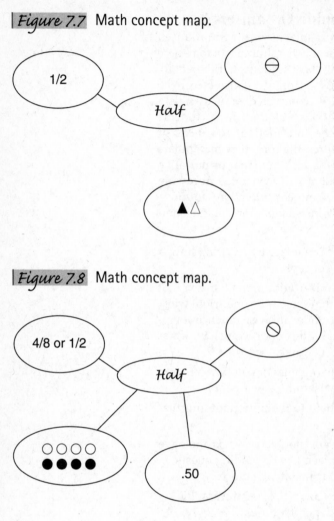

Figure 7.7 Math concept map.

Figure 7.8 Math concept map.

to provide students with an opportunity to demonstrate what they know. While this is traditionally done with tests that limit students to selecting a correct answer (multiple choice, true/false, and matching tasks), the true measure of understanding is the ability of the learner to construct an answer (Why do you think essay tests are so hard?). Extended essays can be time-consuming to grade, particularly if it is a formative (mid-unit) assessment.

Graphic organizers offer an opportunity for students to construct an answer while allowing the teacher to quickly assess their understanding (Lewin & Shoemaker, 1998). We saw this for ourselves when a fourth-grade mathematics teacher assigned students to work in small groups to create a concept map representing ways in which half could be represented. Several groups created a map that looked like the one in Figure 7.7. While all of these manifestations had been discussed during previous classes and dutifully recorded in math journals, a few other groups created concept maps that looked like the one found in Figure 7.8. As the teacher walked around the classroom, she was able to quickly assess who understood the recently taught information about decimals and who did not.

We've reviewed types of graphic organizers and their uses, including construction of understanding, promotion of creative thinking processes, and assessment. These visual displays foster nonlinear thinking and reveal the relationship of parts to whole. Let's look at how teachers use graphic organizers in their content-area classrooms.

Strategies at Work

Graphic Organizers in Kindergarten Art

Ms. Cole's class has been reading books for a week that are illustrated by 2004 Caldecott Honor Award winner Steve Jenkins. As they read each book, they also look closely at his illustrations. His bold colors and lively pictures are quite engaging for the class to examine.

After reading the first book, *What Do You Do with a Tale Like This?* (Page & Jenkins, 2003) to the class, she asks her students how they think the artist creates his illustrations. "He paints the pictures" and "he draws them" are some of the answers she hears. "Those are great ideas," begins Ms. Cole, "Steve Jenkins has a unique way of illustrating his books." She then explains the process he goes through of painting paper, cutting it into the shapes he wants, and then making a collage with all the cut paper shapes.

"We're going to read several Steve Jenkins books so we can learn about his style of illustration and writing. Then we'll make a class illustration like Steve Jenkins does."

As part of the focus on the illustrator, Ms. Cole introduces a graphic organizer for the students to use as they read and reread for information.

"Let's talk about what Steve Jenkins uses when he makes his illustrations," Ms. Cole begins. She distributes a graphic organizer to each student that they will fill in together. The circle in the middle has Steve Jenkins's name along with the names of the four books the class has read. "How many rectangles do you see on your papers?" asks Miss Cole. "Four," responds the students. "That's right. And in those four boxes we're going to write down the four things Steve Jenkins uses when he makes his illustrations. This will help us remember all the things we will need to make our illustrations."

"Who can tell me one thing Steve Jenkins uses? Let's look at his books." "Paint," says Adnan. "Yes, and what kind of colors does he use?" "Red, blue, green . . .," began Cesar. "That's right," Ms. Cole agrees, "but I want to know if the colors he uses are dull, dark, light, bright, or soft." "Bright!" the students yell. And so the first box on the graphic organizer is filled in. Using responses from the students, the rest of the boxes are filled in with the other three things Steve Jenkins uses in his illustrations: paper, glue, and scissors.

The words in the four rectangles are reviewed, and the students add a visual representation of the words they have written. In the box labeled "paper," the students glue a piece of construction paper, and a dab of glue is added to the next rectangle on the graphic organizer. A few brush strokes of brightly colored paint represents the medium used by the artist, and a precut scissors made of paper is attached to the final box.

"This is how each of you will remember to use all the tools Steve Jenkins uses to make his book illustrations," explains Ms. Cole. I want you to put this on the corner of your desk. These will be your notes for the art project."

An excellent resource for an illustrator study can be found in Developing Arts–Loving Readers (Fisher & McDonald, 2002).

Figure 7.9 Graphic organizer for Steve Jenkins art.

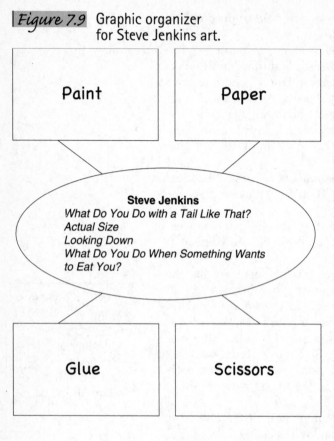

Students spend the next hour painting construction paper with brightly colored paint. They employ a number of techniques, including sponge painting, marbling with wadded newspaper, stippling with a feather, and splattering with a small brush. The following day, students look at their dried papers and use stencils to create representations of animals and objects. Since Jenkins's work is noted for showing only part of a subject (for example, the tails of animals), students cut away part of the picture so that only a portion remains. Together, the class assembles a mural on a large roll of paper Ms. Cole has painted for the occasion. They finish the lesson by consulting their graphic organizers to make sure they have used all the tools (see Figure 7.9).

"I know they can remember four items—that's really not the point. I do want to get them accustomed to putting things down on paper to keep themselves organized as they read for information. And most importantly, I want them to understand that we use it after we create it. It helps them see the purpose for completing a graphic organizer in the first place." An example of students at work can be seen in Figure 7.10.

Graphic Organizers in First-Grade Mathematics

As the students in Ramon Espinal's first-grade class move from learning about plane shapes to solid figures, he has noticed that some of them are having difficulty with the geometric terms and how to classify the shapes by common attributes. They have learned the four basic shapes (circle, square, rectangle, and triangle) and are currently mastering the corresponding three-dimensional figures of sphere, cube, rectangular prism, and triangular prism. He has decided to use a graphic organizer to help the students clarify their conceptual understanding of these solid figures and how they are related to the plane shapes.

Mr. Espinal begins with the cube. "Boys and girls, we are going to think about all the things we know about the cube. Let's make sure we have a good definition for this figure." With that, Mr. Espinal initiates a conversation with the class about the definition of a cube. When the students have difficulty agreeing on the definition, he suggests they draw a cube on their graphic organizers.

"Sometimes when you draw something, you can explain it better to someone else." After a few minutes, he and the class have crafted a satisfactory definition because they have been able to refer to their drawings as well. While he models on a language chart, the children add the definition to their graphic organizer (see Figure 7.11).

"Since we know what a cube is, can we decide what it is not?" asks Mr. Espinal. "Let's think about what other shapes or figures might confuse us when we think about a cube." Mr. Espinal understands that identifying a non-example is critical to building conceptual knowledge. His questioning and probes scaffold the children's understandings by getting them to pay attention to their misunderstandings. In short order, the class agrees that the most likely mistake they might make is to confuse a square with a cube.

"Excellent! Now we're almost done with our graphic organizer. Let's think about a real-life example of a cube. Talk with your neighbor about something you've seen that is a cube."

Warming to the task, the students discuss television sets, houses, and ice cubes. Mr. Espinal monitors the conversations and returns them to their original definition.

"Boys and girls, you told me a cube has six equal faces. Does a house or a TV have six equal sides? Or are they rectangular prisms?"

His students agree that these objects do not have equal sides. Suddenly, Raphael has a brainstorm. "What about our unifix cubes, Mr. Espinal?"

"That's a great example! Let's take a close look at them to see if it fits our definition. Mr. Espinal distributes unifix cubes to each student. "Check your definition. Does it make sense? If so, you may add it to your graphic organizer."

Mr. Espinal will repeat this process for all the solid figures his students will be learning. He offers primary language support as well as instruction in English to ensure that their academic vocabulary continues to grow in both languages. "As they get more comfortable with this graphic organizer, they will begin to work in small groups to complete them. They will add these to their mathematics notebooks for reference throughout this unit of study."

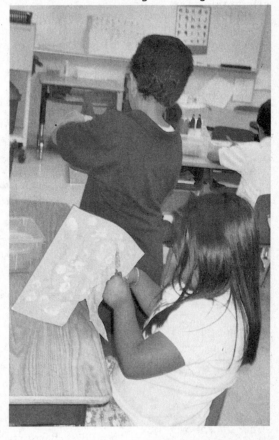

Figure 7.10 Photograph of students working on collage.

The use of realia—real objects—is an effective instructional practice for students who are English language learners.

Figure 7.11 Graphic organizer for solid figures.

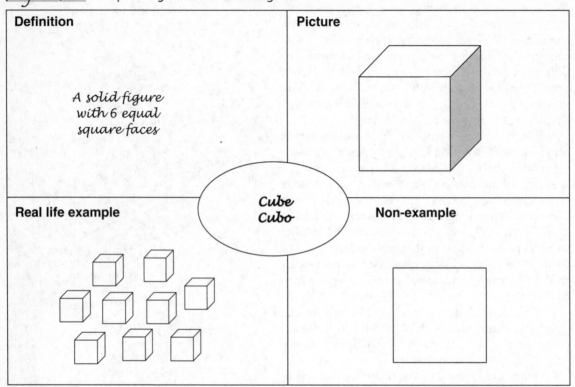

Graphic Organizers in Second–Grade Mathematics

Pam Pham-Barron draws a two-circled Venn diagram on the white board. "Who knows what this is called?" she asks. "A Venn diagram," chimed the children.

"And who can tell me what it is used for?"

Jessica responds, "To compare two stories."

"You are right. However, we can use this Venn diagram to compare any two things and not just stories. Today we are going to use this Venn diagram to compare some numbers," Ms. Pham-Barron explains.

This second-grade class has been studying multiplication concepts for the past two weeks. While the children are familiar with using this type of graphic organizer with texts, Ms. Pham-Barron wants them to appreciate the flexibility of this tool across subject areas. Her focus today is on identifying the common products of two multiples.

She begins by distributing sticky notes with one- and two-digit numbers on them to the children, then draws two large circles on the whiteboard. She writes *Multiples of 2* in the left circle and *Multiples of 4* in the right circle.

Your students will invariably ask who "Venn" was, so here's the answer. John Venn was a mathematician specializing in the study of logic. According to Dunham (1997) he was not really a very good mathematician, but he did manage to create one idea that made him really famous.

Paola is the first to speak. "Ms. Pham-Barron, aren't the circles supposed to . . . to . . . go together?"

"Overlap? I think that's the word you want." Ms. Pham-Barron goes on to explain that they are going to start out with two separate circles and then they will "squish the circles together."

"So let's get started. You've all got numbers on your stickies. Let's figure out where they belong. What is two times zero?" asks the teacher.

"Zero," answers Luis. "I've got it!" Luis goes to the board and places a sticky with the number 0 written on it onto the *Multiples of 2* circle. They repeat this for all the multiples of 2 up to 24, then do the same to organize the multiples of 4. When all the numbers have been sorted, the teacher asks if they notice anything about the two circles.

"There are numbers that are the same in both circles," says Lani.

"I'd like for you to work at your table teams to decide which numbers are the same," says Ms. Pham-Barron. "Work together to see if you can find all the repeaters."

The teams identify the common numbers and Ms. Pham-Barron invites Lani to go to the board to remove them.

"What should we do with these numbers?" questions their teacher.

"We can put them in the middle," says Jaime.

"Alright, let's make these circles overlap so we have a Venn diagram." Lani puts the numbers in the appropriate space and they continue to discuss the relationship between the multiples of two and the multiples of four.

"Oh, we're not done—I've got a challenge for all the table teams. What would you do if we added another circle to the diagram?" Ms. Pham-Barron smiles.

This class loves a challenge, and the students begin to talk excitedly. Within minutes, most of the teams have drawn a diagram like the one seen in Figure 7.12.

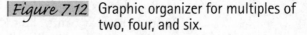

Figure 7.12 Graphic organizer for multiples of two, four, and six.

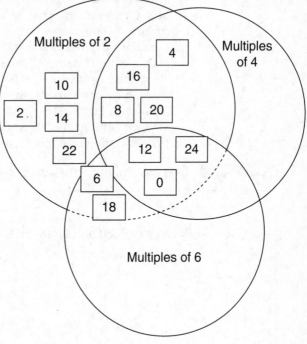

Graphic Organizers in Third-Grade Social Studies

An important theme in third-grade social studies is that all communities have a history. For the students of San Diego, one of the important local communities is the Kumeyaay, the Native American people of the region. To study the way of life of the Kumeyaay, Roberta Dawson's students read a variety of fictional and informational texts on the Kumeyaay. Previously, Mrs. Dawson read aloud *Indians of the Oaks* (Lee, 1978), a story of a young Anglo boy who comes to live with the Kumeyaay. Although historical fiction, the story offers a narrative of the culture and the way of life of the people of the time. Mrs. Dawson wants her students to obtain information about the native people of San Diego.

During the first three chapters of the read-aloud, Mrs. Dawson introduced a large chart with the following categories: sources of food and water, clothing and its sources, shelter, beliefs, recreation, language, transportation, and tools (see Figure 7.13). Students were given a graphic

Figure 7.13 Graphic organizer for Kumeyaay unit.

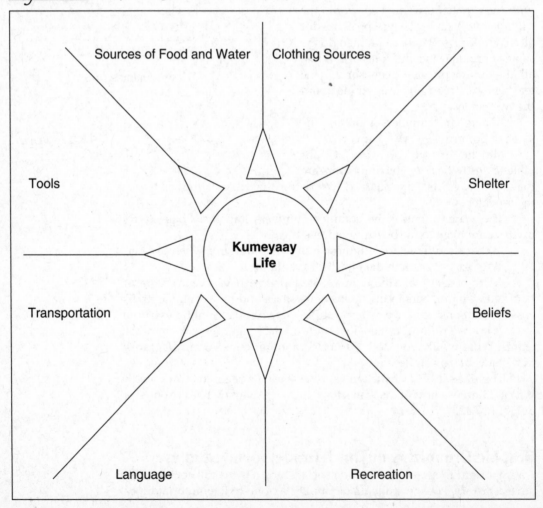

organizer with the same categories. As they read each chapter, Mrs. Dawson and the class discussed details that would be appropriate for the various categories. Mrs. Dawson modeled it on a chart, and the students added the information to their graphic organizers. Upon completion of the book, the students discovered that while the book provided some information, it did not have all the details they were seeking.

"What are other ways we can find information?" asked Mrs. Dawson, pleased that the novel piqued her students' curiosity.

Jessenia suggested that they could look for other books in the library, and Richard suggested that the people at the local historical museum, where they had been visiting, might know more.

"Those are wonderful suggestions. I'm glad you're thinking like historians. Richard, you're right that the San Diego Historical Museum will have information, and we'll be there again next week. Jessenia, I have some books and pamphlets from the Campo band of Kumeyaay Indians that will probably help us, too," said Mrs. Dawson. "We can also find information on the Internet. Let's look at this web site."

Mrs. Dawson then displayed a web site on the Kumeyaay at http://www.kn.pacbell.com/wired/kumeyaay/index.html. Designed for student use, this site features information on the lifestyle of the Native Americans of the region. "I've bookmarked this web site on our classroom computers so you can read more about them."

During the next few days, students worked in small groups to locate more information about the Kumeyaay, directed in part by the gaps in their graphic organizers. Mrs. Dawson made numerous informational print sources available, such as *Native Ways: California Indian Stories and Memories* (Margolin, 1997) and information from the Museum of Man and San Diego Historical Museum.

"I'm looking forward to expanding my collection of information with the opening of the new National Museum of the American Indian in Washington [DC]," remarked Mrs. Dawson. This graphic organizer had served as a tool for inquiry and investigation for her as well.

CALIFORNIA INDIAN STORIES AND MEMORIES
Edited by
Malcolm Margolin and Yolanda Montijo

Source: Cover of *Native Ways: California Indian Stories and Memories*, edited by Malcolm Margolin and Yolanda Montijo. Copyright © 1997 by Heyday Books. Reprinted by permission of Heyday Books.

> Many museums offer online collections. Consult your favorite museum's web site for more information.

Graphic Organizers in Fourth-Grade Social Studies

At the end of the previous school year, Colleen Crandall learned how to use a graphic organizer software program called *Inspiration* on the computer. As a result of this training, the following year she incorporated the use of this software program into her practice. To prepare students for this lesson, the school librarian, Rose Pope, collaborated with Mrs. Crandall to teach the class how to create concept webs using the *Inspiration* software. From what students produced during independent practice in the library, Mrs. Crandall determined that her students were ready to try producing a graphic organizer using this software program as part of their reading for information.

> Assessment is important for both the content and the ability to produce a graphic organizer.

"It's always important to know how to get your notes together for studying," says Mrs. Crandall, "and you know we've got a social studies test next week." While the expected groaning commences, Mrs. Crandall soldiers on.

"There are lots of ways to prepare yourself for studying, and today we're going to create webs of the chapter from the textbook using *Inspiration*." At this announcement, the mood of the class brightens considerably. Mrs. Crandall is always amused by the appeal of computers to her students.

"You've got to review before you make the web, so I want everyone to partner-read the chapter on the regions of California. It's divided into four regions, and I would like you and your partner to decide how you're going to work together." Because Mrs. Crandall's students read collaboratively nearly every day, this instruction doesn't need much elaboration.

"Before you begin, let's talk about the purpose and the structure of the graphic organizer you'll be creating with your partner. Your goal is to make an organizer that you can study from. That means you need some important details. Also, take a look at the title and the major headings in your textbook," says Mrs. Crandall. The students open their books and begin leafing through the pages of the chapter. "The title talks about the four regions of the state. That's a good hint for you that the central item should be labeled the same way. What are your major items coming off the center going to be?"

Daraiah points to the headings in her book and says, "The four regions: valley, desert . . . ."

"There you go! That's a format that will work well. You'll all get a chance to work on your graphic organizers during rotations."

After completing the partner-reading phase of the lesson, Mrs. Crandall asks the pairs to discuss details and make some decisions about what they will include. Students then worked on the classroom computers to create their graphic organizers. Zachary's version appears in Figure 7.14.

The students were so pleased about their graphic organizers that Mrs. Crandall had them give short oral presentations while projecting their assignments on the television screen. "What I'm most pleased about is that this assignment provided multiple chances for them to interact with the material. They read, discussed with a partner, created a web together and later shared it with the class. My guess is that they'll do really well on this test" said Mrs. Crandall.

Graphic Organizers in Fifth-Grade Science

"How can you describe something?" Aida Allen begins her lesson on physical properties of matter. Students volunteer a number of ideas,

> Research on collaboration and cooperative learning suggests that students make meaning when they discuss content with their peers.

Figure 7.14 Zachary's graphic organizer.

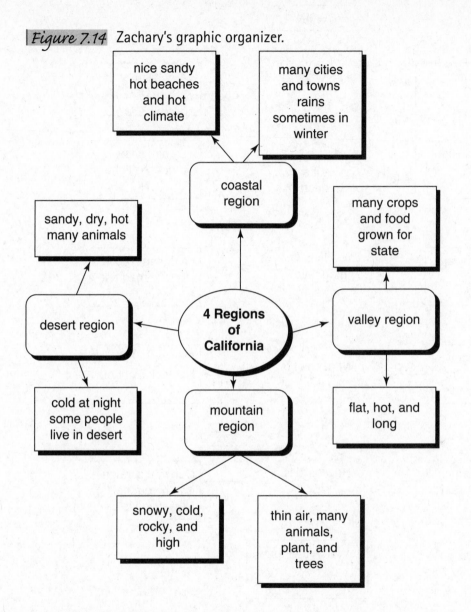

including color, shape, and size. "You're right, these are definitely ways to describe things. Here's the trouble—if I say something is purple, or round, or heavy, I could be describing a plum or Barney the dinosaur!" The class giggles at this, and Ms. Allen continues. "In order to speak scientifically, we have to be able to describe things according to their physical properties. It's a language that scientists use to communicate clearly to one another."

Figure 7.15 Flow chart for determining physical properties.

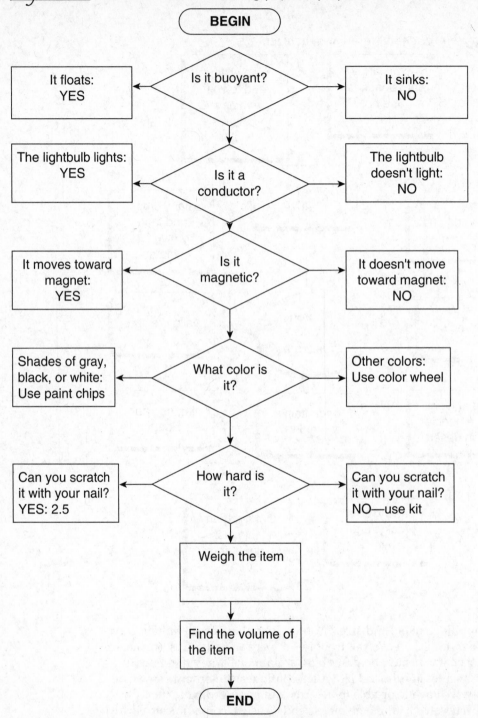

Ms. Allen introduces a graphic organizer of physical properties her students will use to describe a variety of items. Each group of five students has been given an array of items, such as a paper clip, a sponge, a rock, a block of wood, and a copper cylinder. Using the graphic organizer and a number of pieces of lab equipment, the task is to determine the physical properties of each item. This flow chart describes their science lab experiment to determine these properties using scientific terms (see Figure 7.15).

> Flowcharts have a unique vocabulary. Decisions are represented with a diamond, actions with a box, and the beginning and end of a process with an oval.

Arranged around the classroom are stations for each kind of property. A large magnet and a low-voltage conductivity indicator with a lightbulb are placed at a learning station so that students can determine magnetism and electrical conductivity. A buoyancy test station consists of a large rectangular plastic bin filled with water. The third station features a Mohs scratch plate to determine the hardness of the object, and a variety of paint chips and a color wheel serve as a device for describing the color. A fourth station has a simple balance scale to find weight and a graduated cylinder of water to determine volume. A fifth station contains a number of books about matter and the properties of matter (see Figure 7.16 on page 192). The groups are to assess their objects using these measures and then describe the physical properties of each. They use the books to locate confirming or alternative information and dip in and out of various books as they read for information.

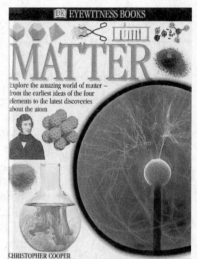

"This flow chart guides your decisions about each of the physical properties. Make sure you pick a recorder for your group. He or she will record the results of each of the tests. When you're finished, use these results to describe the physical properties in scientific language," directs Ms. Allen. She distributes the matrix for each group (see Figure 7.17 on page 193) and then spends the next hour working with the groups as they complete each station.

Cover from *Matter* by Christopher Cooper. Copyright © 1999 by Dorling Kindersley Limited, London. Published by permission of Dorling Kindersley.

"It can be kind of complicated to move students through a lot of science stations, and that's why I really like using flow charts. I can't be everywhere at once, and this works as a task sheet. I like the matrix, too, for this lab. It lets them see how these physical properties compare with one another," says Ms. Allen. In her classroom, matter is a serious matter.

Conclusion

Graphic organizers can be used throughout the curriculum to help students understand the relationships between ideas. Because they are tools for categorizing and storing information, visual displays can be useful in helping students understand complex information. In addition, they are particularly well suited for representing nonlinear information by showing the complexity of relationships between and among ideas, phrases, and words.

Figure 7.16 Books about matter and properties of matter.

Angliss, S. (2001). *Matter and materials*. Boston: Kingfisher.

Baldwin, C. (2005). *States of matter*. Chicago: Raintree Publishing.

Cooper, C. (1999). *Eyewitness: Matter*. London: DK Children.

Discovery Channel. (2002). *Matter*. Milwaukee, WI: Gareth Stevens Publishing.

Hunter, R. (2004). *The facts about solids, liquids, and gasses*. North Mankato, MN: Smart Apple Media.

Kerrod, R. (1995). *Matter and materials*. New York: Benchmark.

Oxlade, C. (2002). *States of matter*. Portsmouth, NH: Heinemann.

Graphic organizers are useful before students read, during their assigned reading, and after reading. While there is no one "ideal" time for using these visual displays, the most common application comes during the reading. However, the versatility of many graphic organizers makes them flexible across instructional events. Common graphic organizers include concept maps, flow diagrams, tree diagrams, and matrices. Other choices include Venn diagrams and compare/contrast maps. While graphic organizers are popular with students and teachers, it is important to match the tool to the text.

As with other instructional strategies, it is essential to teach students how to use and construct graphic organizers. Without instruction, they cease to be tools and become fancy worksheets to be filled out for the teacher. Each tool should be introduced and scaffolded, and the growing cadre of organizers should be on hand for students to access when needed. Most importantly, students should be encouraged to construct their own unique organizers. When students are successful in accomplishing this goal, the teacher can be assured that the learners are employing higher-order thinking skills.

Regardless of when they are used, graphic organizers aid in comprehension. They have long been recognized as metacomprehension tools, and students who successfully use graphic organizers are more likely to grasp the concepts discussed in the text. Further, graphic organizers can be used as an assessment tool providing teachers with an authentic glimpse into a student's thinking. Unlike traditional multiple-choice testing that restricts student responses, student-constructed graphic organizers can provide evidence of sophisticated levels of student knowledge.

Figure 7.17 Student recording matrix for physical properties.

Physical Properties Lab

Group names: _____

Directions: Pick a recorder for your group. As you test each item, record the properties in the matrix below.

	Buoyant (+ or Ø)	Magnetic (+ or Ø)	Conductor (+ or Ø)	Hardness (#)	Weight (#)	Volume (#)
Paper clip						
Rock						
Sponge						
Wood						
Copper						

After the lab: describe the physical properties of each item using scientific language.

Paper clip:

Rock:

Sponge:

Wood:

Copper:

References

Alvermann, D. E. (1988). Effects of spontaneous and induced lookbacks on self-perceived high and low ability comprehenders. *Journal of Educational Research, 81*(6), 325–331.

Alvermann, D. E., & Boothby, P. R. (1982, September). *A strategy for making content reading successful: Grades 4–6*. Paper presented at the annual meeting of the Plains Regional Conference of the International Reading Association, Omaha, NE. [ED221853].

Ausubel, D. P. (1960). The use of advance organizers in the learning and retention of meaningful verbal material. *Journal of Educational Psychology, 51*, 267–272.

Barron, R. F. (1969). The use of vocabulary as an advance organizer. In H. L. Herber & P. L. Sanders (Eds.), *Research in reading in the content areas: First year report* (pp. 29–39). Syracuse, NY: Syracuse University Reading and Language Arts Center.

Dunham, W. W. (1997). *The mathematical universe: An alphabetical journey through the great proofs, problems, and personalities*. New York: John Wiley and Sons.

Dye, G. A. (2000). Graphic organizers to the rescue! Helping students link—and remember—information. *Teaching Exceptional Children, 32*(3), 72–76.

Fisher, D., & McDonald, N. (2002). *Developing arts-loving readers: Top 10 questions teachers are asking about integrated arts education*. Lanham, MD: Scarecrow.

Gordon, W. J. J. (1961). *Synectics: The development of creative capacity*. New York: Harper and Row.

Herber, H. L. (1970). *Teaching reading in the content areas*. Englewood Cliffs, NJ: Prentice Hall.

Howe, M. E., Grierson, S. T., & Richmond, M. G. (1997). A comparison of teachers' knowledge and use of content area reading strategies in the primary grades. *Reading Research and Instruction, 36*, 305–324.

Hyerle, D. (1996). *Visual tools for constructing knowledge*. Alexandria, VA: Association of Supervisors of Curriculum Development.

James, L. A., Abbott, M., & Greenwood, C. R. (2001). How Adam became a writer: Winning writing strategies for low-achieving students. *Teaching Exceptional Children, 33*(3), 30–37.

Kiewra, K. A., Kauffman, D. F., Robinson, D. H., DuBois, N. F., & Staley, R. K. (1999). Supplementing floundering text with adjunct displays. *Instructional Science, 27*, 373–401.

Lewin, L., & Shoemaker, B. J. (1998). *Great performances: Creating classroom-based assessment tasks*. Alexandria, VA: Association for Supervision and Curriculum Development.

McCoy, J. D., & Ketterlin-Geller, L. R. (2004). Rethinking instructional delivery for diverse populations: Serving all learners with concept-based instruction. *Intervention in School and Clinic, 40*(2), 88–95.

McMackin, M. C., & Witherell, N. L. (2005). Different notes to the same destination: Drawing conclusions with tiered graphic organizers. *The Reading Teacher, 59*, 242–252.

Robinson, D. H. (1998). Graphic organizers as aids to text learning. *Reading Research and Instruction, 37*, 85–105.

Shanahan, T. (1982, March). *Specific learning outcomes attributable to study procedures*. Paper presented at the annual meeting of the American

Educational Research Association, New York, NY. [ED220536].

Stauffer, R. G. (1969). *Teaching reading as a thinking-process.* New York: Harper Collins.

Vacca, R. T., & Vacca, J. L. (1998). *Content area reading: Literacy and learning across the curriculum* (6th ed.). New York: Longman.

Venn, J. (1894). *Symbolic logic* (2nd ed.). London, England: Macmillan.

Wood, K. D., Lapp, D., & Flood, J. (1992). *Guiding readers through text: A review of study guides.* Newark, DE: International Reading Association.

Children's Literature Cited

Cooper, C. (1999). *Matter.* London: Dorling Kindersley.

Jenkins, S. (2001). *What do you do when something wants to eat you?* Boston: Houghton Mifflin.

Jenkins, S. (2003). *Looking down.* Boston: Houghton Mifflin.

Jenkins, S. (2004). *Actual size.* Boston: Houghton Mifflin.

Lee, M. (1978). *Indian of the oaks.* Ramona, CA: Acoma.

Margolin, M., & Montijo, Y. (1997). *Native ways: California Indian stories and memories.* Berkeley, CA: Heyday.

Page, R., & Jenkins, S. (2003). *What do you do with a tale like this?* New York: Houghton Mifflin.

Chapter 8

Douglas Fisher

Nancy Frey

Elizabeth Soriano

Getting It Down:
Teaching Students to Take and Make Notes

"*I* *think he's smart.*"
"*I think he's amazing.*"
"*I think he's a liar.*"
"*No he's not, he's famous!*"
"*Maybe he could be all of those things.*"
"*Yeah, I guess so. He doesn't tell the truth about where he was born, but he made up all kinds of tricks.*"
"*Yep. And he was famous because he could escape from anything.*"
"*Yeah, but what really happened to him?*"
This rich discussion about characterization is typical in Aida Allen's classroom. As students listen to Houdini: World's Greatest

Mystery Man and Escape King (Krull, 2005) read aloud by the teacher, they write down adjectives about Houdini on sticky notes. After the read-aloud, students place their sticky notes on a language chart. To ensure that students are familiar with Houdini's many characteristics, Ms. Allen and the students read the chart of adjectives and discuss the meaning for each word. Most importantly, she asks students to cite evidence for their describing words from the text. Later, when students return to their desks to write about Houdini in their journals, they refer to the sticky notes on the language chart. Ms. Allen likes using the sticky notes as a form of note making because she and the students can manipulate the notes and categorize student responses easily. The words generated in this note-making activity wind up in the students' original writing, and some make their way to the word wall.

Why Teach Students How to Make and Take Notes?

During a recent conversation with a group of teachers, we asked them about the strategies they use to teach students to store and retrieve information from class lectures and texts. Interestingly, note taking was a given and was considered to be something that all students should be able to do by the time they reached middle school. Yet most of the teachers we talked with admitted that they really didn't teach students any specific skills to get them ready for taking notes. One teacher said, "You know, if we want them to be successful in middle school, then we have to get them ready while they're with us." We agree with this teacher and hope that elementary educators will provide instruction in note taking because we know that this skill is critical as students read for information. However, we recognize that many educators of young children may not have a clear understanding of what skills are needed to be successful note takers. As Jim Burke (2002) noted:

> Taking notes is an essential skill, one that has many other subskills embedded within it. Taking good notes trains students not only to pay attention but what to pay attention to. It teaches them to evaluate the importance of information and the relationship between different pieces of information as they read textbooks and articles. It also teaches them to organize that information into some format that serves their purposes. (p. 21)

Preparing Students for Successful Note Taking

Preparation for successful note taking is directly related to the preparation of the lesson itself. It is instructionally sound to introduce the sequence of topics and concepts for the day's class because it prepares students for learning. This simple preview also gives students a way to organize their notes. An easy way to preview the information to be discussed is through a posted agenda like the one shown in Figure 8.1 for second-grade mathematics. Students also use these main points in their math journals to write about their lessons as the teacher instructs.

> How did you learn how to take notes? How do you use your notes to learn and remember?

Figure 8.1 Posted agenda for notes in second-grade mathematics.

Today's Math Notes

How many brothers and sisters do we have in our families?

1. What is the problem?

2. How can we solve the problem?

3. How can we graph the problem?

See Chapter 10 for further discussion of signal words.

Lecture is one way to share information with students. Lectures should be brief and focused, with opportunities for learners to apply the information through student-directed learning activities.

Once previewed, students should expect that the sequence will not be drastically altered and that the teacher will present concepts in an organized fashion. Detailed information, including technical vocabulary, names, dates, and formulas, should be presented visually as well as verbally, and well-timed pauses should be used to give students time to record this information. Signal words and phrases like "this is important" or even "be sure to write this down" will alert students to include items in their notes. Ending the class with a review enhances memory and retention and allows students to make corrections to their day's notes.

Distinguishing Note Taking from Note Making. Before we venture any further, a definition or two is in order. We use the term *note taking* to refer to students' written notes from an activity, lecture, or class discussion. We use the term *note making* to refer to the slightly different phenomenon of recording notes from printed materials—what students can do while they read for information. While many of the instructional strategies are the same, we have to remember that students cannot go back again for more information in note taking (i.e., the discussion is over) but they can in note making (by rereading the text).

Perhaps the most common way elementary students engage in note making is through the use of sticky notes. It is best to give students a purpose for writing notes; for example, collecting vocabulary or making connections, so they don't overuse the sticky notes. We model these note-making techniques on the overhead projector using colored transparencies that have been cut to the size of a sticky note. As we read a projected text, we write our notes on the colored transparency squares using a think-aloud technique (Davey, 1983). In this way, students are able to understand how readers make decisions about what they will and will not notate.

If sticky notes are in short supply, students can also use blank comment cards to make notes about their reading (see Figure 8.2). The size of a bookmark, these comment cards are handy reminders to students that reading is an active process. The blank spaces are large enough to allow for annotation, but small enough to encourage students to write only what is necessary. Elementary students seem to have a hard time writing incomplete sentences, so we model this as well. As we write on a comment card or sticky note on the overhead projector, we discuss "empty and full" words. We write our thoughts in complete sentences (which of course do not fit in the space allotted) then cross out the "empty" words until we have a phrase containing "full" words that remains meaningful. This modeled editing gives young readers the permission they need to create useful and efficient notes.

Figure 8.2 Comment card.

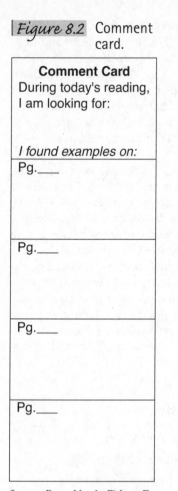

| **Comment Card** |
| During today's reading, I am looking for: |
| *I found examples on:* |
| Pg.___ |
| Pg.___ |
| Pg.___ |
| Pg.___ |

Source: Frey, N., & Fisher, D., *Language Arts Workshop: Purposeful Reading and Writing Instruction,* 1st Edition, © 2007, pp. 173, 174, 363, 401, 402, 403. Adapted by permission of Pearson Education, Inc., Upper Saddle River, NJ.

Figure 8.3 Reader's notations.

Reader's Notations Use these marks to make your notations easier to write and read!	
⟶	connection, leads to
⟵⟶	cause and effect
re	in reference to
i.e.	that is
e.g.	for example
=	equal; is
≈	approximately equal
≠	not equal; not
←pg. #	connects to another page
Def.?	unknown word to look up
W/	with
W/O	without
&	and

Source: Frey, N., & Fisher, D., *Language Arts Workshop: Purposeful Reading and Writing Instruction,* 1st Edition, © 2007, pp. 173, 174, 363, 401, 402, 403. Adapted by permission of Pearson Education, Inc., Upper Saddle River, NJ.

Abbreviations are useful in note taking and note making; however, many students are unfamiliar with their use. Figure 8.3 features a list of common abbreviations that are useful as students read for information and gather their notes. This figure can be reproduced as a classroom poster and as a bookmark for students to refer to as they read or listen to discussions. With the rise of text messaging, it is likely that older students will have a few useful abbreviations to add to the list.

The evidence on the effectiveness of note taking and note making is fairly conclusive. Better note takers generally do better in middle and high school, and specific types of note taking produce better results (e.g., Faber, Morris, & Lieberman, 2000; Kiewra, Benton, Kim, Risch, & Christensen, 1995). The reasons for this are interesting. Dating back to the seminal work of DiVesta and Gray (1972), the evidence suggests that note taking requires both a process and a product function. It seems that both of these are important to produce results—improved comprehension and retention of material.

> Students sometimes view note taking as a process function only—to scribe. When notes are used in subsequent learning activities, students see the value in quality notes.

Process and Product Functions. The process function—recording the notes—and the product function—reviewing notes later—are both needed to create useful notes (e.g., Henk & Stahl, 1985; Katayama & Crooks, 2001). Stahl, King, and Henk (1991) refer to this as the "encoding and external storage functions" (p. 614). The encoding function requires students to pay attention to the discussion or text while they write. This, in turn, allows students to transform information and deepens their understanding. The external storage function allows students to review their notes, and thus the main ideas presented, before using the information on a test, essay, or lab.

In addition to the use of graphic organizers for note taking and note making, a number of common formats have been suggested. Figure 8.4 contains "12 time-honored criteria for successful notetaking" (Stahl, King, &

Figure 8.4 General note-taking procedures.

1. Date and label notes at the top of the page.
2. Draw a margin and keep all running lecture notes to one side.
3. Use other side for organization, summarizing, and labeling.
4. Indent to show importance of ideas.
5. Skip lines to indicate change of ideas.
6. Leave space for elaboration and clarification.
7. Use numbers, letters, and marks to indicate details.
8. Be selective.
9. Abbreviate when possible.
10. Paraphrase.
11. Use underlining, circling, and different colors of ink to show importance.
12. Cover one side of notes to study.

Adapted from Stahl, N. A., King, J. R., & Henk, W. A. (1991). Enhancing students' notetaking through training and evaluation. *Journal of Reading, 34*(8), 614–622. Copyright © 1991 by the International Reading Association.

Henk, 1991, p. 615). Like all instructional strategies, these principles should be taught to students within meaningful contexts. While elementary students are not necessarily using all these elements, they serve as a sound guideline for teachers unfamiliar with the specifics of teaching note taking. In addition, these note-taking elements should be modeled by the teacher during shared and guided note taking.

These same researchers also recommend that students and teachers work as partners to evaluate the notes that are taken to provide a mechanism for giving students feedback on their current performance. We have adapted a rubric for use in the elementary classroom (see Figure 8.5). Students

Figure 8.5 Rubric for evaluation of elementary note-taking.

	3	2	1
FORMAT Notebook	*I have a notebook with my name and subject on it.*	*My notebook is not labeled.*	*I don't have a notebook.*
Handwriting	*Other people can read my notes.*	*People have trouble reading my notes.*	*People can't read my notes.*
Use of page	*I leave space to make changes.*	*I have a little bit of space for changes.*	*My notes cover the page.*
ORGANIZATION Headings	*I have headings for the main ideas.*	*I have a few headings.*	*I don't use headings.*
Abbreviations	*I use abbreviations when possible.*	*I abbreviate sometimes.*	*I don't have abbreviations or I can't remember what they mean.*
Summaries	*I write a summary of my notes.*	*I make a list for my summary.*	*I don't write a summary.*
MEANING Main ideas	*I underline or highlight the main ideas.*	*I list the main ideas.*	*I don't do anything with main ideas.*
Supporting detail	*I make arrows to show relationships between main ideas and details.*	*I list the details.*	*I have very few details.*
Examples	*I write examples.*	*I have some examples.*	*I don't have examples.*
Restatement	*I use my own words.*	*I use my own words sometimes.*	*I only copy what's on the board or overhead.*

Source: Adapted from: Stahl, N.A., King, J.R., & Henk, W.A. (1991). Enhancing students' notetaking through training and evaluation. *Journal of Reading, 34*(8), 614–622. Copyright © 1991 by the International Reading Association.

working in pairs can complete this rubric. After exchanging notebooks for review, they discuss how easy it was to read and understand the notes. They return the notebooks to one another and analyze their notes using the rubric, highlighting the descriptors they believe best fit their current note-taking strategies. This student self-assessment forms the basis for conferring individually with students about their progress in this important study skill.

 *Strategies at Work*

Interactive Note Taking in Kindergarten Social Studies

Emergent readers and writers benefit from interactive writing instruction to foster written and oral language development. Interactive writing is described as "a dynamic, collaborative literacy event in which children actively compose together, considering appropriate words, phrases, organization of text, and layout" (McCarrier, Pinnell, & Fountas, 2000, p. xv). Using interactive writing, the teacher and students jointly compose a piece of text on a language chart, often about a shared experience such as a book, field trip, or classroom event. A purpose for composing the message is established and the content of the message is negotiated between and among students. The teacher facilitates these conversations, and models, scaffolds, and coaches as students draw upon their knowledge of language, the content, writing, and reading to get the message down on paper.

Interactive writing is an ideal method for teaching principles of note taking to young students. Because the text is composed on a language chart, the children can participate in the conversations about how the printed message is arranged on the page. The teacher can model how words are selected for use in the notes, and which are omitted. Dani Cole uses interactive writing with her kindergarten students to construct notes for use in journal writing.

As part of her social studies curriculum on occupations, Ms. Cole reads the book *Jobs* (Nelson, 2004) to her class and then takes her students on a tour of their campus. She and her students visit the cafeteria, the office, the nurse, the library, and other classrooms. When they return to their classroom, Ms. Cole asks her students about the jobs of the men and women who work at the school.

"Who did we visit today?" Hands shoot up in the air.

"The person who works in the library," offers Miguel.

"The lady who gives us our food," says Angelique, while Mai chimes in, "that guy in the office."

"Wow, you remember a lot!" smiles Ms. Cole. "We better make notes so we remember all this information."

Ms. Cole reminds them that their notes should have only the most important words in them. "This is a different kind of writing," she explains. "We don't need to write

Source: Book cover used with permission of Lerner Publishing Group.

in sentences—we just need to write down our important ideas."

Ms. Cole has made a bulletin board in advance of this lesson (see Figure 8.6). The bulletin board contains large manila envelopes labeled with the community occupations they will be studying in this social studies unit.

Ms. Cole has an easel set up with 5 × 7 note cards clipped to it. "We'll use these to write our notes and then put them in the envelopes on the bulletin board." She reviews the categories and asks them again about the people they met on the tour of the school.

The children, who are sitting on the rug, decide that they will write about the cafeteria workers first. To begin the writing, Ms. Cole helps the students generate a complete sentence about the person and what he or she does. The sentence they agree upon is, "The cafeteria workers serve the food to the students." The sentence is rehearsed a few times, and the students count the number of words.

"That's too many words for our note card, isn't it? We don't really need to write all the words for notes. Let's listen for the empty words that we can get rid of."

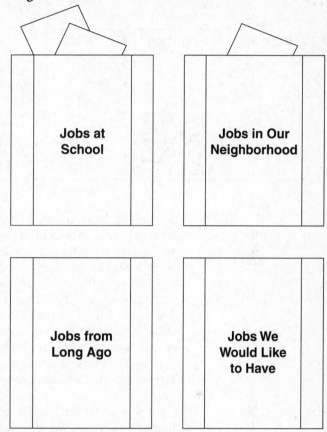

Figure 8.6 Bulletin board for interactive notes.

Jobs at School

Jobs in Our Neighborhood

Jobs from Long Ago

Jobs We Would Like to Have

The students eventually agree on the phrase, "cafeteria workers serve food" as the message for the first note card. Ms. Cole coaches them as they construct the words for the note card. Individual students are invited to the easel to write the letters. One student holds a wooden clothespin painted to look like an astronaut and dubbed, "Spaceman" to remind his classmates to put spaces between the words. When the note card is finished, Mubarek places the card inside the envelope on the bulletin board.

Over the next few weeks, more cards are added to each of the categories featured on the bulletin board. Once completed, the note cards are used to write a class book on jobs. The note cards are referenced for spelling and content as children use them in their independent writing.

Note-Making Scavenger Hunt in First-Grade Science

Mr. Espinal's first-grade students are studying the characteristics of living things in their science class. As an introduction to the informational reading

Figure 8.7 Scroll of textbook pages.

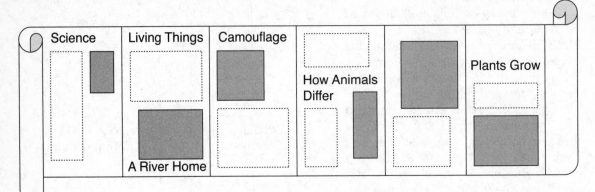

they will be doing during this unit, Mr. Espinal models how information for note making is located in the textbook. Using poster-sized photocopies of the chapter from the science textbook, Mr. Espinal teaches note making through a scavenger hunt.

"Boys and girls, we're going to be science detectives today. We are going to look for clues in our science book," he begins. "Like all good detectives, I need to make notes so I won't forget the most important ideas." With that, he unfurls the chapter they will be reading. He has taped the pages end to end to form a continuous scroll for the students to see (see Figure 8.7). "Please take out your science books and open them to page 63. You will see that you have the same pages," instructs Mr. Espinal.

For the next few minutes, he conducts a picture walk of the text so that his students will have a good idea of the information in the chapter. Together, they examine the photographs, charts, and captions so they can predict the content. This gives him a chance to teach about text features as well as the science content. After he is sure that the students have had an opportunity to preview the chapter, he distributes copies of a scavenger hunt for them to complete with a partner (see Figure 8.8).

Mr. Espinal believes that note-making skills are first taught by showing children how to extract information from the text. This also promotes skimming and scanning skills needed for rapid retrieval of information. The textbook scroll allows students to see the information they are about to read as connected text, rather than isolated pages that don't seem to relate to one another. By previewing the textbook as a scroll, and fostering scanning, he is teaching students important comprehension skills for reading informational text.

> Skimming and scanning is an important test-taking skill. See Chapter 10 for more discussion.

Note Making in Second-Grade Music

Slow, solemn music fills the second-grade classroom of Ms. Pham-Barron. As the piece ends, the sound of an orchestra swells and a choir's collective voice rises to a crescendo. As Mozart's *Requiem* fades, Ms. Pham-Barron

Figure 8.8 Scavenger hunt for science textbook chapter.

Names: _____

What is the title of the chapter? _____

What animals are in the picture on page 34?

1. _____

2. _____

3. _____

What animal is hiding in the picture on page 35? _____

What does the bird on page 37 eat? _____

Draw a picture of a plant and an animal in the book.

Plant	Animal

says, "What did you think of when that music was playing? Tell your partner how the music made you feel." The children turn to one another, but
their voices are quieter than usual, as if the mood of the music has lingered.
After a few minutes, Ms. Pham-Barron asks for some volunteers to share
what their partner said.

"My partner, Guadalupe, said the music made her sad because she remembered the time when her sister sat on her Chihuahua." Ms. Pham-Barron suppresses a smile, knowing that this can be a dramatic event in the life of a seven-year-old.

"Julian said that the music reminds him when he went shopping with his mom at the mall." Ms. Pham-Barron imagines how appropriate this funeral music might be to a small boy dragged through endless stores.

"Do you know who composed this musical piece? Who wrote this music?" asks Ms. Pham-Barron.

"I think it's Ricky Martin," says Jaime.

"No, it's B. B. King," Alizay argues.

"Who's that?" questions Ruben.

The class pauses for the teacher to continue. "Today we are going to read and learn about an Austrian composer who wrote many musical masterpieces long ago that are still popular today. His name is Wolfgang Amadeus Mozart." Ms. Pham-Barron shows the class a portrait of Mozart as a young boy and locates Austria on the map.

"He's a kid!" several students murmur.

"You're right, boys and girls. Mozart began writing music when he was only five years old. We're going to read about his life and listen to more of his music." She distributes a short reading about the composer and pre-teaches essential vocabulary including *Mozart, musician,* and *compose.* Partners receive a set of the three words on small cards and practice using the words to recall their meaning.

"These note cards help us to remember details. As we read this together, you and your partner will write notes on the blank cards. Later, you'll use those note cards to retell the reading, just like we practiced."

With that, Ms. Pham-Barron conducts a shared reading of an excerpt from *Mozart,* part of the Famous Children Series (Rachlin, 1995). She stops periodically to model note making using colored transparency overheads that have been cut to the size of her students' note cards. After reading a passage on Mozart's tour with his father at the age of six, Ms. Pham-Barron writes on the transparency note card, *played concerts when he was six* and places it to the side of the overhead projector. "These notes will help me when I retell the story," she says. The children write a similar note card for themselves.

After the shared reading, Ms. Pham-Barron plays an aria from *The Marriage of Figaro,* a decidedly more cheerful piece of music, while the students use the note cards to retell what they learned from the text (see Figure 8.9).

"It's important to model note making to my students," Ms. Pham-Barron remarks later. "I use a think-aloud strategy during shared reading so they can understand how I choose the information I write on the note

> See Chapter 4 for more information about pre-teaching or front-loading vocabulary.

> While the instructional strategies are similar, remember that note making typically focuses on gaining information from texts while note taking is for discussions.

Source: Book cover used with permission of Barrons Educational Series, Inc.

card." Later, they will use the note cards to write a summary in their home writing journals.

"Now you'll have something important to tell your family tonight," says the teacher. "You can ask them whether they know the famous composer who began to write music when he was five. And you can show them your notes!" Later in the unit, Ms. Pham-Barron's students will write an informational essay on Mozart, using information from their note cards. Thuy's essay appears in Figure 8.10.

Research Grid in Third–Grade Science

The ability to research a topic, synthesize information, and report on findings is an essential part of critical thinking in any content area. Roberta Dawson's third-graders learn about research reports through a series of lessons about this writing genre. Her students begin to understand that writing a research report will guide them to learn more about something they are interested in. Mrs. Dawson gives students the chance to choose what they want to investigate about their subject. She explains that the purpose of a research report is to collect and present information about their topics to share what they have learned. It is an opportunity to explore different sources of information including newspapers, magazines, books, encyclopedias, and the Internet. Mrs. Dawson's students also learn that they have to read for information and collection, and have to store information to complete this project well.

Research takes time, because students must find the information, then read it and take notes. It is important to keep a record of the sources they plan to use in their reports. These sources are important because they allow others to look at the information presented in the report.

The students in Mrs. Dawson's third-grade science classroom are now in the midst of a research project. Each group of students has been assigned a habitat to research and report about to the class using a poster and their notes. Mrs. Dawson has differentiated this project to meet the needs of her students by choosing print resources and providing varying levels of teacher support. One group of students is responsible for the Amazon rainforest. However, they seem to be stuck, so she confers with them to identify the problem.

How's your project going?" asks Mrs. Dawson as she settles into a chair at their worktable.

"OK, I guess. We have cards!" offers Javier. He hands Mrs. Dawson some index cards with information written on them.

As she looks through the cards, she says, "You've got some interesting facts. Did you remember to write down where you found them?"

The children look at each other sheepishly, then admit they did not.

"Let's see if I can help you organize your information." She locates a research grid from her folder and asks them to gather the books they have been using. Two students retrieve some informational books from

Figure 8.9 Note-making cards from second grade.

Mozart was a musician

He wrote and played music

Wrote music at 5

Played concerts when he was six

Was a famous musician

Figure 8.10 Thuy's essay on Mozart.

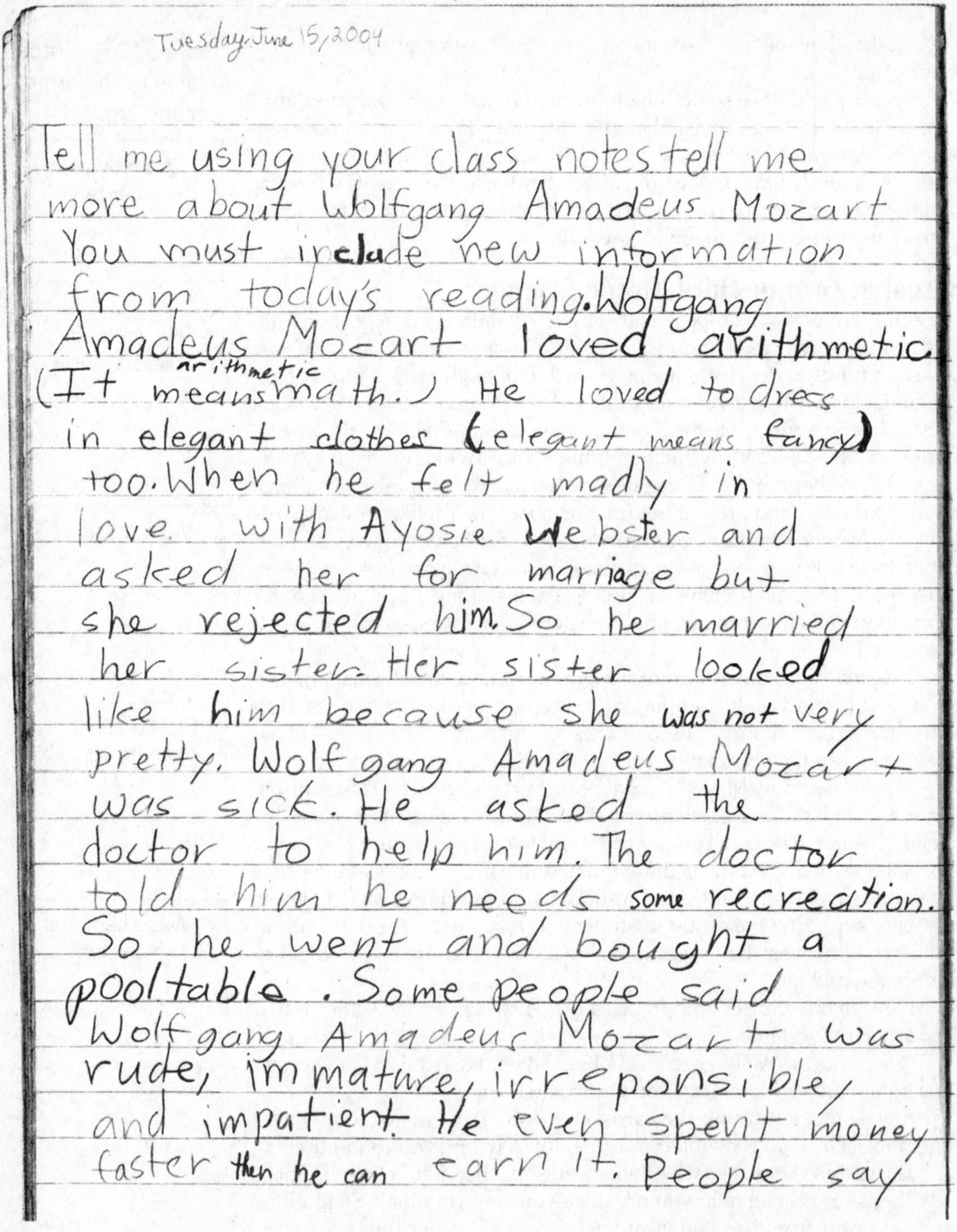

Tuesday, June 15, 2004

Tell me using your class notes. tell me
more about Wolfgang Amadeus Mozart
You must include new information
from today's reading. Wolfgang
Amadeus Mozart loved arithmetic.
(It means math.) [arithmetic] He loved to dress
in elegant clothes (elegant means fancy)
too. When he felt madly in
love. with Ayosie Webster and
asked her for marriage but
she rejected him. So he married
her sister. Her sister looked
like him because she was not very
pretty. Wolfgang Amadeus Mozart
was sick. He asked the
doctor to help him. The doctor
told him he needs some recreation.
So he went and bought a
pooltable. Some people said
Wolfgang Amadeus Mozart was
rude, immature, irreponsible,
and impatient. He even spent money
faster then he can earn it. People say

Figure 8.10   Thuy's essay on Mozart. *(continued)*

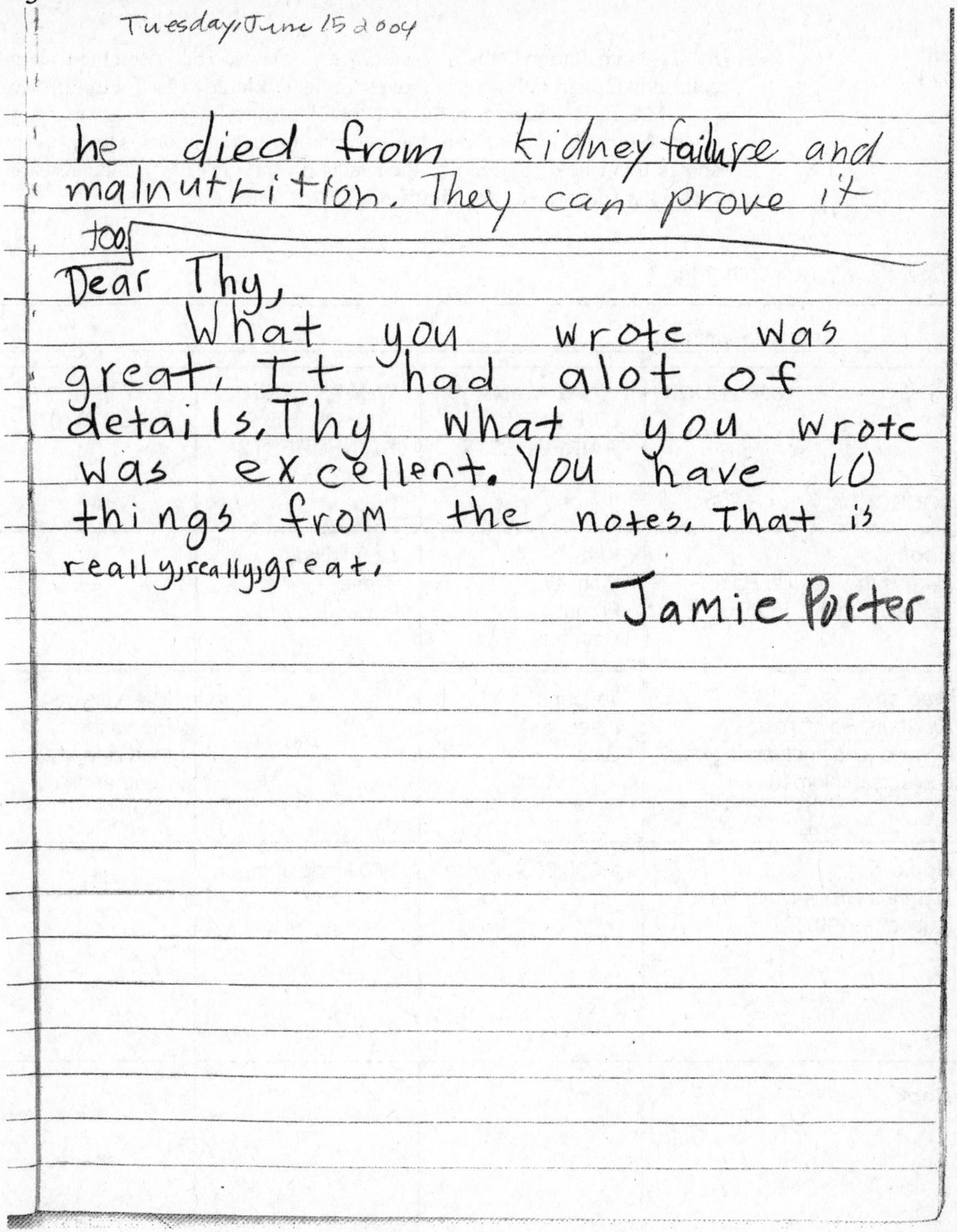

Tuesday, June 15 2004

he died from kidney failure and malnuttrition. They can prove it too.

Dear Thy,
    What you wrote was great, It had alot of details,Thy what you wrote was excellent. YOU have 10 things from the notes, That is really,really,great,

                              Jamie Porter

the Research Station in their classroom. Mrs. Dawson has assembled a large collection of materials on ecosystems for her students to use for this project.

Mrs. Dawson and her students spend the next few minutes sorting out their note cards and locating the information in the books. Mrs. Dawson shows them how to organize their facts on the grid using their research questions and sources (see Figure 8.11).

Figure 8.11 Research grid.

Our Topic: __Amazon Rainforest__

QUESTIONS / SOURCES	WHAT ANIMALS LIVE IN THE RAINFOREST?	WHAT PLANTS LIVE IN THE RAINFOREST?	WHY IS IT IMPORTANT?
Book *Here is the Tropical Rain Forest* (Dunphy, 1994)	Birds Monkeys Frogs Caimans	Bromeliads Trees	
Web site *All About Rainforests* (www.enchantedlearning.com/ subjects/rainforest)	Toucans Insects Bats		Make oxygen Plants for medicine Keep earth's air clean
Book *Nature's Green Umbrella* (Gibbons, 1997)	1,000,000 insects	300 kinds of trees	
Book			

"Mrs. Dawson, we found stuff on the computer, too," says Li.

"I'm glad you remembered that. Let's find those cards and write down the web site address." Fortunately, Mrs. Dawson has book-marked several web sites on the classroom computers and they are able to easily locate the one they used.

"Now you've got your information in one place," says Mrs. Dawson. "You'll still use your cards, but this will help you decide what else you need. What do you notice is missing on your grid?" she asks.

The children peer at the research grid un-til Javier offers, "More plants?"

Figure 8.12 Sentence strip notes for oral presentations.

Front of sentence strip – facing audience

Many desert animals only come out at night.

Back of sentence strip – facing speaker

1. They come out because it is cooler at night. 2. Bats, Gila monsters, snakes, coyotes, and mountain lions are nocturnal.

"Yes, I agree! You need to be able to tell us more about the plants in the rainforest. Let's go over to the Research Station and find a book that will tell you about rainforest plants." In a few minutes, the group has se-lected *Plants and Planteaters* (Chinery, 2000) to round out their report. They will add this title and interesting facts to the research grid Mrs. Dawson has begun with them.

Another group is ready to prepare their oral presentation but needs a bit of help. Mrs. Dawson works with each student in the group to write his/her most important facts on a sentence strip to use during the talk. On the back of the sentence strip, the student writes more de-tailed notes to recall facts. Later, when each member of the group holds a strip, the notes can be easily viewed from the back as they read aloud (see Figure 8.12).

As a final assessment, each group has to make a diorama of a habi-tat other than the one they researched, using the notes they have taken during the presentations. "This project lets them experience note taking for multiple purposes—from gathering information to preparing a presentation. I also find that when they have to take notes during presen-tations and then use them, the notes are a better quality," explains Mrs. Dawson.

The research grid is a matrix format for note taking. According to Kiewra, Benton, Kim, Risch, and Christensen (1995), a matrix format builds on the traditional outline format familiar to many secondary stu-dents. While both provide students with specific information about inter-nal connections, the matrix format emphasizes the relationships that exist across topics. As they note, "information across topics can be drawn more easily and quickly from a matrix than a linear representation" (p. 174). While not all content lends itself to the matrix format, the task Ms. Butler had in mind was perfect for this style of note taking.

Note-Taking Technology in Fourth-Grade Social Studies

Oral presentations are an important part of the fourth-grade curriculum, and Colleen Crandall requires her students to do numerous prepared and extemporaneous speeches in content classes. Many of these presentations are done in small groups to foster teamwork; however, other speeches are prepared and delivered individually. Mrs. Crandall is also conscious of the need for her students to be familiar with a variety of technologies used in and out of the classroom. For a research unit on the California missions, Mrs. Crandall models the use of PowerPoint as a means for presenting information. Students use a graphic organizer to take notes from her lectures on the Spanish missions and their impact on California Native Americans.

"What do all of you think about creating your own PowerPoint presentations for your California missions report?" asks Mrs. Crandall.

"Looks like a lot more work!" pipes up one student.

"I think it would be helpful if I showed you how to use PowerPoint," says Mrs. Crandall. "I'd like for you to take notes so you can do this on your own."

Mrs. Crandall shows students her notes from a class she has recently completed on making a PowerPoint slide show. Then she hooks up her computer to the TV screen so they can watch her read through her notes on how to create the slide show. By modeling the authentic use of her notes to create a slide show, the students can identify pertinent information to include in their notes. Right before their eyes, she creates a PowerPoint slide show.

The students are dazzled by the result—they especially like getting to choose a background for the slides—and they unanimously vote a hearty, "Yes!" to using PowerPoint in their oral presentations. She distributes a rubric for the oral presentation and discusses the expectations (see Figure 8.13). Each student will select one of 21 California missions to profile in his or her presentation, which will include a PowerPoint slide show.

Students research the missions and construct their PowerPoint presentations during the next week. Christopher's presentation on the Santa Cruz mission appears in Figure 8.14. Christopher uses his notes during every step of the project and later says, "This stuff is hard, but the notes helped me by learning what to do step by step. Now, I'm glad that I can make a PowerPoint, but I couldn't have done it without the notes."

> Rubrics can be created on the Internet at www.rubristar.com

Dictoglos in Fifth-Grade Mathematics

The students in Aida Allen's fifth-grade mathematics class have just completed a problem-based learning activity on division with remainders called "What's Fair?" Members of the group assumed the identity of shipwrecked survivors on a desert island who must distribute an uneven

Figure 8.13 Oral presentation rubric.

	1	2	3
Content	Inaccurate information	Some important details omitted (ex., location, history)	Information is accurate and complete
Mechanics	3 or more spelling or formatting errors	1–2 spelling or formatting errors	Spelling and formatting is correct
Graphics	No graphics	Some graphics are unrelated	Graphics support content
Eye Contact	No eye contact	Speaker makes eye contact occasionally with audience	Speaker makes eye contact frequently with audience
Voice	Audience must strain to hear speaker	Speaker is sometimes difficult to hear	Speaker can be heard easily

amount of resources salvaged from the sinking vessel. In particular, they had to determine what they should do with the extra supplies. Should they be thrown back into the sea? After all, that would be "fair" because no one would benefit from an unequal number of supplies. The groups needed to show mathematically how they resolved the issue. Not surprisingly, many groups came to the conclusion that throwing undistributed supplies away (the mathematical equivalent of rounding down) was unwise, while rounding up was not possible. The groups all proposed creative solutions for storage of the extra supplies, and one group even suggested rules of emergency use.

> Problem-based learning activities like this are an effective anticipatory activity to build background knowledge.

"I agree with your proposals to store the extra supplies. In mathematics, this is represented through the use of a remainder. Some problems that require division, like the one you just solved, need a remainder to show an accurate solution. Rounding up or down just doesn't make sense," says Ms. Allen.

She then begins her direct instruction on interpreting the remainder in division. After introducing technical vocabulary and explaining the algorithm, she asks her students to take out their mathematics journals. "We're going to do a dictoglos," says Ms. Allen. "These will be your first set of notes for this unit." The purpose of this listening and note-taking strategy is to give students experience in hearing and recording English spoken fluently (Wajnryb, 1990).

> Herrell (2000) identifies dictoglos as one of 50 effective instructional strategies for teaching English language learners.

Figure 8.14   Student PowerPoint presentation.

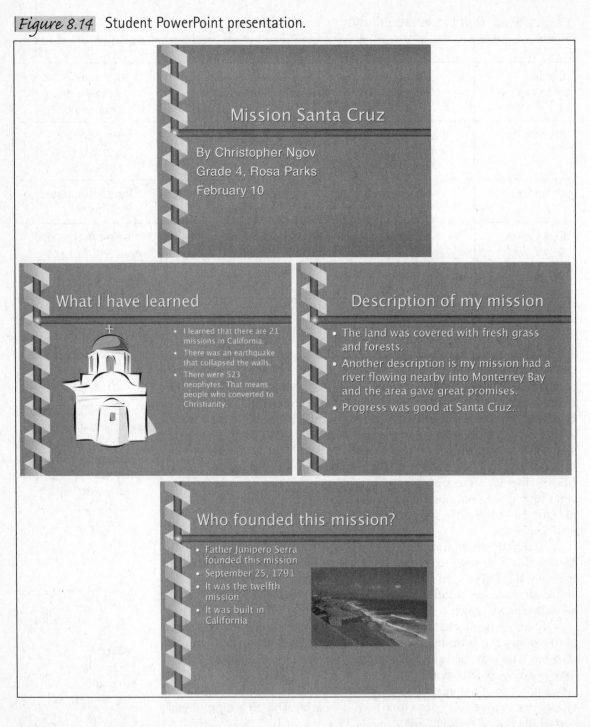

To begin the dictoglos activity, Ms. Allen asks her students to listen to a summary of her mathematics lesson. She reads aloud to them while they listen:

> Some division problems cannot be answered with a whole number. A remainder is used to show a quantity left over from the dividend. It is represented as R. Every quotient with a remainder can be converted to fractions or decimals.

After discussing the meaning, she reads the summary aloud two more times. During these next two read-alouds, the students take notes on what they hear, so that they can re-create the text as accurately as possible. She pauses for a few minutes after each reading, so they can write what they remember.

After two attempts at writing exactly what they heard, the students pair up and share what they have written, adding more details to their notes. Two pairs then join and the four students collaborate to re-create the text verbatim. By this time, students have reviewed their notes, listened to and read others' notes, and revised their own.

Ms. Allen finds that by giving her students practice in dictoglos they become better note takers and skilled listeners. She notes several benefits to teaching note taking in this way. First, when the students initially hear the text, and even during the second and third reading of the passage, they must listen carefully and maintain an intense focus for the entire reading. This practice teaches students to block out other distractions, a necessary skill for taking notes during a lecture. Most lectures are not repeated so students have only one opportunity to record information. Second, students must learn to focus on the most important phrases during their first writing attempt, selecting only the key words that carry the meaning, even if some of the details are not yet scripted. This practice is also essential to good note taking because students cannot write everything they hear. As students learn how to listen for key phrases, their notes become more valuable to them as study aids. Thus, with periodic practice of dictoglos, her fifth-grade students practice elements of good note taking—selective listening and scripting of key phrases. "Besides," offers Ms. Allen, "it's a way for me to make sure they have the right information in their math journals!"

Conclusion

In nearly every middle school classroom, students will be required to take notes from lectures and books. The reasons for this are sound—students who understand note taking and note making do better on tests and essays. These students also learn more of the content. However, most students do not have sophisticated note-taking strategies. Instead, they rely on haphazard collections of facts and details that are not systematic. This process problem is compounded as many of these same students do not organize and review their notes later. Therefore, teachers in elementary school should provide students with systematic instruction in note taking and note making to guide them to independence in this most important study skill.

References

Burke, J. (2002). Making notes, making meaning. *Voices from the Middle, 9*(4), 15–21.

Davey, B. (1983). Think-aloud: Modeling the cognitive processes of reading comprehension. *Journal of Reading, 27*(1), 44–47.

Divesta, F. J., & Gray, S. G. (1972). Listening and note taking. *Journal of Educational Psychology, 63,* 8–14.

Faber, J. E., Morris, J. D., & Lieberman, M. G. (2000). The effect of note taking on ninth grade students' comprehension. *Reading Psychology, 21,* 257–270.

Henk, W. A., & Stahl, N. A. (1985). *A meta-analysis of the effect of notetaking on learning from lecture.* Paper presented at the 34th meeting of the National Reading Conference, St. Petersburg, FL. [ED258533].

Herrell, A. L. (2000). *Fifty strategies for teaching English language learners.* Upper Saddle River, NJ: Merrill/Prentice Hall.

Katayama, A. D., & Crooks, S. M. (2001). Examining the effects of notetaking format on achievement when students construct and study computerized notes. *Learning Assistance Review, 6*(1), 5–23.

Kiewra, K. A., Benton, S. L., Kim, S., Risch, N., & Christensen, M. (1995). Effects of note-taking format and study technique on recall and relational performance. *Contemporary Educational Psychology, 20,* 172–187.

McCarrier, A., Pinnell, G. S., & Fountas, I. C. (2000). *Interactive writing: How language and literacy come together, K-2.* Portsmouth, NH: Heinemann.

Stahl, N. A., King, J. R., & Henk, W. A. (1991). Enhancing students' notetaking through training and evaluation. *Journal of Reading, 34*(8), 614–622.

Wajnryb, R. (1990). *Grammar dictation.* Oxford, England: Oxford University.

Children's Literature Cited

Chinery, M. (2000). *Plants and planteaters: Secrets of the rainforest.* New York: Crabtree.

Dunphy, M. (1994). *Here is the rain forest.* New York: Hyperion.

Gibbons, G. (1997). *Nature's green umbrella: Tropical rainforests.* New York: HarperTrophy.

Krull, K. (2005). *Houdini: World's greatest mystery man and escape king.* New York: Walker & Company.

Nelson, R. (2004). *Jobs.* Minneapolis, MN: Lerner Publications.

Rachlin, A. (1995). *Mozart: Famous children series.* Hauppauge, NY: Barron's Educational.

After Reading Activities

Part 4

Douglas Fisher

Nancy Frey

Sheryl Segal

Chapter 9

The Power in the Pen:

Writing to Learn

R amon Espinal's first-grade bilingual students are beginning a new unit on plants and flowers. He begins by showing the students index cards with words written on them, one side in Spanish and the other in English. He explains that many words, particularly in science, sound almost the same in both languages. "Our first word is plant. In Spanish the word is planta," he says. Using a diagram from the book What is a Plant? The Science of Living Things (Kalman, 2000), Mr. Espinal uses the English and Spanish vocabulary of plants to explain the major components. The finely detailed illustrations of the roots, stems, and leaves are especially helpful for his young students. Soon the activity is interactive, with students placing the vocabulary cards on the diagram, now projected onto the whiteboard.

"Now I want you to think about what you've learned today," Mr. Espinal announces. *"I am going to turn the projector off, and I would like you to draw a diagram of a plant and label the parts. After you've finished, write two sentences about what you've learned about plants." With that, his students settle into the business of stem and tallo, root and raiz, flower and flor. This writing-to-learn activity will provide Mr. Espinal with valuable insight into his teaching and his students' learning.*

Writing to Learn and Reading for Information

The reciprocal relationship between reading and writing for young readers has been well documented in the field (e.g., Clay, 1979; Gee, 1990; Holdaway, 1979). Further support for writing as an important function in reading for information can be found in Hayes's extensive review of writing and cognition in reading (2004). In particular, he notes that writing and reading support one another in at least three ways: "reading for comprehension, reading to define the writing task, and reading to revise. The quality of writers' texts often depends on their ability to read in these three ways" (Hayes, 2004, p. 1419). In her book, *When Writers Read* (2001), Hansen contends that when children are given frequent opportunities to write, they read with a new lens. In particular, they actively search for the author's voice and evaluate what they have read based on the evidence the author has offered. Further, as fellow writers, they approach text with a purpose—to determine what can be learned from this writer (Hansen, 2001). To learn how to read for information, students must write to learn.

Before we examine the research and instructional strategies used in writing to learn, a few definitions are in order. Writing to learn differs from learning to write in several important ways. Students need to "learn to write" throughout their lives. When they are in elementary school, children learn to encode words, spell, construct sentences, figure out the mechanics of paragraphs, and develop understandings of grammar. These are essential for effective writing, and teachers who focus on learning to write typically use process writing as an instructional approach (Atwell, 1998; Graves, 1983). While the processes used by each writer differ and are usually quite recursive, student writers typically go "through some variation of these steps:

1. prewriting activities (jotting down ideas, listing thoughts, brainstorming, gathering information, and so on);
2. writing a draft;
3. peer review of the draft;
4. revising;

> Try writing to learn for yourself. Take a few minutes to write about the types of knowledge you believe are necessary for academic learning. We'll discuss this further in the next section.

5. editing;

6. writing the final draft; and

7. publishing" (Jenkinson, 1988, p. 714).

Writing to learn differs from other types of writing because it is not a process-writing piece that will go through multiple refinements toward an intended final product. Instead, it is meant to be a catalyst for further learning—an opportunity for students to recall, clarify, and question what they know and what they still wonder about. Writing to learn also provides teachers an opportunity to find out what students understand about the information they are studying. This instructional activity possesses several key features:

Writing-to-learn pieces do not go through revisions.

- Brief in length—anywhere from one minute to ten minutes in duration

- Usage—to activate prior knowledge, and scaffold conceptual understanding

- Metacognitive—students notice what and how they are learning

Writing to learn "involves getting students to think about and to find the words to explain what they are learning, how they understand that learning, and what their own processes of learning involve" (Mitchell, 1996, p. 93). As Jenkinson (1988) explains, "writing should be a process in which writers discover what they know and do not know about their topics, their language, themselves, and their ability to communicate with specific audiences" (p. 714).

Prior knowledge refers to schemas a student has already created. These are influenced by experiences, topic knowledge, and cultural perspectives.

For example, after reading *How We Crossed the West: The Adventures of Lewis and Clark* (Schanzer, 1997), a fourth-grade teacher asks students to respond in writing to the question "What do you think Lewis and Clark said to one another when they first spotted the Pacific Ocean?" Responding to this prompt requires that the student consider their prior knowledge about the Pacific Ocean, what they have read about the expedition, and how to best convey this information in writing.

Applying Three Kinds of Knowledge

Therefore, writing to learn requires students to use different kinds of knowledge at different times. Cognitive scientists generally think of three kinds of knowledge—declarative, procedural, and conditional (Paris, Cross, & Lipson, 1984; Sternberg & Williams, 2002). These types of knowledge are illustrated in Figure 9.1 using questions a science teacher might use.

Declarative Knowledge. Declarative knowledge focuses on things that we "know" such as labels, names, facts, and lists. Although often considered boring, declarative knowledge is an important part of what we know as adults. It is also the easiest kind of knowledge to impart in lectures and

Figure 9.1 Types of knowledge.

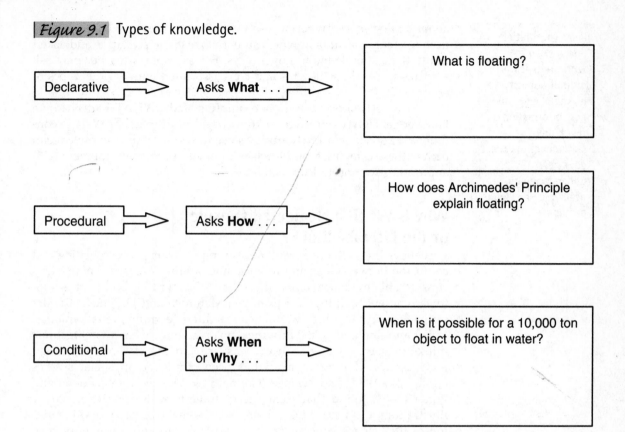

reading assignments. In school, students must have a number of experiences that develop their declarative knowledge. Some writing to learn prompts can be used to demonstrate this type of knowledge. For example, a teacher may ask students to explain the types of joints in the body.

Procedural Knowledge. In addition to declarative knowledge in which they recall specific information, students must demonstrate their understanding of procedural knowledge. This requires that students know how to do something; they must know how to apply their knowledge. This type of knowledge is more difficult to convey in a traditional lecture or reading—students need experience putting their knowledge into practice. Again, some writing to learn prompts can be used to facilitate and assess this type of knowledge. For example, a teacher may ask students to describe the steps necessary to complete a science lab or solve a mathematics problem.

Conditional Knowledge. Finally, conditional knowledge is concerned with when or why something is done—the various conditions that influence our decisions to use knowledge. Stated another way, conditional knowledge is

Read your initial response to the writing–to–learn prompt about types of knowledge. Add new information and revise any statements to reflect your new understanding of academic knowledge demands.

about strategies and when to use them. Again, writing to learn can be used to create prompts in which students are given scenarios and asked to use their knowledge in novel ways. For example, a teacher may ask students to consider the pros and cons associated with various types of energy.

In other words—and rather simply stated—WHAT is declarative knowledge, HOW is procedural knowledge, and WHEN or WHY is conditional knowledge. Clearly students need to develop their knowledge in each of these categories, and teachers can monitor this development with appropriate writing-to-learn activities.

Why Is Writing Neglected Outside of the Literacy Block?

We believe this is likely a result of overemphasis on process writing and confusion between learning to write and writing to learn. There exists considerable evidence across disciplines that writing builds and reinforces content learning. For example, McIntosh and Draper (2001) describe the ways in which writing can facilitate learning in mathematics. Miller and England (1989) provide data on an improvement in algebraic thinking when writing to learn was used in the classroom. Beyond mathematics, writing to learn has been employed in social studies (Holbrook, 1987) and science (Connolly & Vilardi, 1989). Edens and Potter (2003) found that elementary students who drew explanatory illustrations and wrote about them had a better conceptual understanding of the science concept of the law of conservation of energy than those who did not.

Effectiveness of Writing to Learn

Over the past few decades, writing to learn has grown in prominence as an instructional strategy for comprehension development. A number of researchers have advocated this approach as a tool for students to clarify their understandings (and misunderstandings) of a topic (e.g., Britton, 1970; Hayes & Flower, 1980; Langer & Applebee, 1987). In 2004, Bangert-Drowns, Hurley, and Wilkinson conducted a meta-analysis of 48 studies of the effects of writing to learn. Their results found that it had a positive effect on content learning and student achievement in elementary classrooms. Not surprisingly, they also noted that the frequency with which writing-to-learn events were used (two-to-four times per week for more than a semester) was associated with increased learning. Perhaps the most unusual finding was in relation to the length of the writing. These researchers found that brief writing events (less than 10 minutes) were more effective than longer writing prompts (Bangert-Drowns, Hurley & Wilkinson, 2004). Another surprising finding was that feedback from the teacher on the quality of the writing appeared to have no effect on achievement.

The results of this meta-analysis also highlighted what teachers have known for years about writing to learn—it is most useful to assist students in becoming more cognizant of their own learning. "This pattern suggests that the educational importance of writing [to learn] might not lie in its affinity with personally expressive speech . . . but in the scaffolding that it can provide for metacognitive and self-regulatory processes. The particular value of metacognitive prompts here is consistent with research on learning strategies and writing" (Bangert-Drowns, Hurley & Wilkerson, 2004, p. 50). The National Research Council's extensive review of learning history, science, and mathematics recommended three instructional practices: activate prior knowledge, teach for factual and conceptual knowledge, and teach for metacognition (NRC, 2005). Writing to learn provides an efficient and elegantly simple means for doing all of these as students read for information.

Using Writing Prompts

There are a number of ways that writing to learn can be implemented in content classrooms. Writing to learn is based on writing prompts that the teacher provides students. These prompts can range from very open ended—"What did you think was confusing about this topic?"—to fairly specific—"What's wrong with this equation? $4 + .3 = .7$," which allows students to explore their conceptual knowledge about rational numbers. The range of prompts can include (Andrews, 1997; Fisher, 2001; Mitchell, 1996):

> Researchers found that 51% of fifth-graders thought the equation was correct (National Research Council, 2001).

- *Admit slips* (upon entering the classroom, students write on an assigned topic such as "What did you think was the most interesting fact in yesterday's reading about volcanoes?" or "Explain the difference between jazz and rock")

- *Crystal ball* (students describe what they think class will be about, what will happen next in the book they are reading, the next step in a science lab experiment they are conducting, etc.)

- *Found poems* (students reread an assigned text and find key phrases that "speak" to them, then arrange these into a poem structure without adding any of their own words)

- *Awards* (students recommend someone or something for an award that the teacher has created such as "Artist of the Century")

- *Cinquains* (a five-line poem in which the first line is the topic (a noun), the second line is a description of the topic in two words, the third line is three *-ing* words, the fourth line is a description of the topic in four words, and the final line is a synonym of the topic word from line one)

- *Yesterday's news* (students summarize the information presented the day before)
- *"What if" scenarios* (students respond to prompts in which information is changed from what they know, and they predict outcomes. For example, students may be asked to respond to the question, "What would be different if honeybees disappeared?")
- *Take a stand* (students discuss their opinions about a controversial topic such as "What caused the dinosaurs to become extinct—an asteroid, or a volcano?")
- *Letters* (students write letters to others, including elected officials, family members, friends, people who made a difference. For example, students may respond to the prompt, "write a letter to Dr. Martin Luther King informing him of the progress we have made on racism since his death")
- *Exit slips* (used as a closure activity at the end of the day, students write on an assigned prompt such as "The three best things I learned today are . . .")

The critical element that all of these writing-to-learn events have in common is that students do not correct or rewrite their pieces. Instead, each becomes a starting point for learning.

Naturally, there are several hundred additional ways to structure writing-to-learn prompts. Students can be taught perspective writing during writing to learn by using RAFT prompts (Santa & Havens, 1995). This writing-to-learn activity is particularly useful as students read for information.

> In perspective writing, there is rarely one "right" answer. Instead, it can serve as an excellent means of prompting discussion among students who can use their written pieces to support their viewpoint.

Perspective Writing Through RAFT

RAFT stands for:

R = role (who is the writer, what is the role of the writer?)

A = audience (to whom are you writing?)

F = format (what format should the writing be in?)

T = topic (what are you writing about?)

When students are first introduced to RAFT, everyone responds to the same prompt. For example, students who have just read about the dwellings of the Inuit people of Alaska and Canada in *Houses of Snow, Skin and Bones* (Shemie, 1989) may respond to the following RAFT:

R = an Inuit father or mother

A = your child

F = directions

T = how to build a snow house

The students could then explain how the snow house is constructed by digging blocks of snow from the center of the floor, thereby making it possible for a person to stand.

Once students become familiar with the RAFT format, teachers can assign groups different components and then invite group conversations about the topic at hand. For example, in a social studies class, students might enter the room to find the following written on the board:

	Last name A–M	Last name N–Z
R	Picasso	Matisse
A	Matisse	Picasso
F	letter	letter
T	Why I am the greatest artist	Why I am the greatest artist

As you can imagine, this type of writing provides students with an opportunity to use their knowledge and skills in writing and discussion as they share their responses to the RAFT. RAFTs also provide students with a unique opportunity to transform the information they have read into original writing. We encourage students to select an informational picture book from a special bin in the classroom designated as such. Inside the front cover, students will find a RAFT. Their task is to independently read the picture book and then respond to the RAFT. A set of sample RAFTs can be found in Figure 9.2. For example, a fifth-grade student, Calvin, selected the book *From Cocoa Bean to Chocolate* (Nelson, 2003). Inside the book, he found the following RAFT:

R	Digestive System
A	Chocolate
F	Love letter
T	Why I need you

Calvin, using the content information he learned in science, responded by writing the following:

Dear Chocolate,

I like how you get into my mouth and how my teeth can bite you into little, yummy pieces. I can't resist you! I also like it when you work with my saliva and break down into even smaller, yummy pieces. When I eat too much of you, my molars hurt. My esophagus works to push you down. I can't taste you anymore when you pass into my stomach and then intestines. I really need you because you help my small

| Figure 9.2 | Sample RAFT prompts.

A PICTURE BOOK OF HARRIET TUBMAN (Adler, 1993)

R Slave catcher
A The public
F Wanted poster
T "Moses"

FROM SLAVE SHIP TO FREEDOM ROAD (Lester, 1998)

R Author
A Reader
F Position statement
T Would you risk going to jail for someone you didn't know?

THE STAR-SPANGLED BANNER (Spier, 1973)

R American soldier in charge of flag
A His family
F A letter
T Last night at Ft. McHenry

THE LIFE OF AN ASTRONAUT (Walker, 2001)

R An astronaut applicant
A NASA
F Letter of application
T Why I want to be an astronaut

SCIENCE IN ANCIENT EGYPT (Woods, 1998)

R Archeologist
A Colleague
F Letter
T The scientific contributions of the Ancient Egyptians

---

intestine by giving me the milk so my bones can grow stronger. Soon
I'll be saying good-bye to you as you leave my system. I just say, "Can
I have some more?" I can't live without you.

Sincerely,

Calvin

As you can see, Calvin had to mobilize his reading comprehension strategies to read and understand the text he selected. He also had to demonstrate

his understanding in writing, organizing his writing to ensure that readers could understand his perspective.

Strategies at Work

Writing to Learn in Kindergarten Mathematics

The students in Dani Cole's kindergarten class had been learning about graphing in mathematics. Up until now, the objects were given to them, and they created bar and line graphs to represent the data. For example, Ms. Cole would give them a plastic bag full of different shapes and each had to sort and then graph the objects on a premade graph.

Ms. Cole is interested in moving students to the next level of independence. She wants her students to be able to collect data themselves, graph it, and then interpret the graphs they make. She reads the book, *Tiger Math: Learning to Graph from a Baby Tiger* (Nagda, 2000). The students are intrigued by the true story of an orphaned tiger cub that is cared for at the Denver zoo. The book features several graphs depicting his growth and care, including bar and line graphs. As she reads, she discusses how the information is represented in both the text and the graph. They look at the picture graph of the number of tigers by species left in the world.

"When I look at this graph, I can tell that the Bengal tiger is the most common kind. When I read the graph, I can see that there are 4,000 of these left in the world," says Ms. Cole, using a think-aloud technique to model comprehension (Davey, 1983). I can also tell which are the rarest— that means there aren't very many. These two [pointing to the Sumatran and Siberian tigers] are very rare. When I use my eyes and finger to find the number of tigers, I find out there are only 500 of them," she continues. She reads the text on the page, and shows the students the sentence that contains similar information about the scarcity of the Sumatran and Siberian tigers.

After reading the book, Ms. Cole tells the class they will create a bar graph of their own. "Graphs can give us information quickly, just like the ones we read in the book. We're going to make a graph of the kinds of food people like. Since there are so many different kinds of food," Ms. Cole explains, "let's think of three choices to give people." After discussion and voting, the class decides on pizza, hamburgers, and tacos.

In groups of five, the students (led by a teacher or other adult) interview students and teachers from other classrooms about their preferred food. After collecting responses from ten people, the students come back to class and graph the results.

With their completed graph in front of them, the students' next task is to write about the information they just gathered. "Let's look at *Tiger Math* again to see how the author did this," says Ms. Cole. They reread the pages featuring the graphs and notice that the author writes about the most

Source: Book cover from *Tiger Math: Learning to Graph from a Baby Tiger* by Ann Whitehead Nagda and Cindy Bickel. Cover photograph © 2002 by the Denver Zoological Foundation Inc. Cover reprinted by permission of Henry Holt and Company, LLC.

important facts, but not all the information represented on the graph. "You still have to read the graph to know everything," Daniel wisely observes.

"How many people like pizza?" Ms. Cole asks.

"Five," responds one student.

"Good, now how can we say that in a complete sentence?"

"Five people like pizza," says another student. The students each write that sentence on their papers.

The same format is used for the two remaining foods, and the following sentences are generated and written: "Three people like tacos. Two people like hamburgers." The students then examine the graph to compare the three food preferences.

"Which food did people like the most?" asks Ms. Cole.

"Pizza!" the students exclaim.

"And how do you know that by looking at the graph?" Miss Cole continues.

"Because it is the tallest one."

"That's right," Miss Cole confirms.

"Let's write that down. How can we say it?"

"People like pizza the most," one student says.

Ms. Cole asks the students other questions based on the graph. They answer all of them verbally, but only choose to write one more sentence. Like the author of *Tiger Math*, they create a comparative statement supported by the graph: "More people like tacos than hamburgers."

Entry Slips in First–Grade Science

Ramon Espinal uses entry slips to activate prior knowledge and monitor learning. Mr. Espinal begins a science unit in life sciences by having his students stand up to play "Simon Says." By asking students to put their hands on their hips, shoulders, and kneecaps, Mr. Espinal is already learning how much prior knowledge his students have about the human body.

Mr. Espinal then asks students to return to their seats with paper in hand. Once there, students are asked to write down parts of the body with which they are familiar.

"Boys and girls, I would like for you to write sentences, if you can. If this is hard, you can write a list," he tells them. One student makes the following list:

- Han (hand)
- Lig (leg)
- Figer (finger)
- foot

Another student is able to construct the following paragraph:

My leg is nx [next] to my foot. I have 10 twos [toes] and 10 figers [fingers]. My lbows [elbows] are on my arems [arms]. My hed [head] is on my necke [neck]. And I have 2 iiys [eyes] on my hed.

Over the course of the next two weeks, Mr. Espinal introduces his students to a variety of books about the human body. The first one he chooses in *My Body/Mi Cuerpo* (Rosa-Mendoza, 2002), a bilingual book designed to expand the reader's knowledge of vocabulary in English and Spanish. The pages of the book feature colorful collage characters using their body parts, each labeled in both languages. The text at the bottom of each page also appears in English and Spanish. Each lesson begins with an entry slip. Some days he asks his students to "look into their memories" and write down what they already know about the topic. Examples of this kind of writing-to-learn activity prompt includes:

- Write or draw everything you know about your bones.
- How do you walk?
- What happens to your body after you run around the field at recess?

"Writing-to-learn activities tell me a lot about my students," explains Mr. Espinal. "I'm able to know what my students know about a topic, what questions or wonderings they have about a topic, and what they have learned." This first-grade teacher uses entry slips and other writing-to-learn activities during parent/student/teacher conferences as well to show the progress that has been made in science.

Writing to Learn in Second-Grade Science

Pam Pham-Barron's students have been studying the water cycle in their second-grade science class. She began the unit earlier in the month using a book called *The Drop in My Drink: The Story of Water on Our Planet* (Hooper, 1998) so that her students could begin to follow the path of water as it travels from ocean to clouds and then back to the earth as a raindrop. She also used the poetic *A Drop Around the World* (McKinney, 1998) with its personification of Droplet, to help her students understand the extraordinary journey that occurs around them. Now it is time for them to witness the water cycle in their own classroom. Using the water cycle section featured in *The Earth: The Geography of Our World* (Taylor, 2001), Ms. Pham-Barron and her students read and follow the directions for building a terrarium. Within days, small droplets of moisture are forming on the inside of the five-gallon water bottle containing the terrarium.

> Following written directions is an important skill for reading for information.

"We've been studying the water cycle, and now we've made a small one right here!" says Ms. Pham-Barron. She and the students discuss the finer points of what they are observing, including the difference in the size of the drops of water and the fogged sides of the bottle.

"I think you're ready to write about this. Remember when we read about Droplet, the little water drop who wanted to turn into rain? I want you to imagine you are a droplet of water inside our terrarium. Let's all write for the next eight minutes. Tell me what happens to you inside the terrarium."

These brief writing events are a frequent occurrence in Ms. Pham-Barron's classroom. While there are many opportunities to write, edit, and revise other pieces, she sees value in spontaneous writing. "There are so many times when you need to just get your ideas down on paper. Sometimes just doing so gives you an idea of what you know and what you don't know," says Ms. Pham-Barron. Almost on cue, a hand goes up.

"Ms. Pham-Barron, can you help me?" asks Maya. "I'm stuck."

With that, the teacher walks over to Maya's desk to help her clarify her understanding about the water cycle.

Exit Slips in Third-Grade Science

The students in Roberta Dawson's third-grade science class are studying the solar system. Mrs. Dawson's class began the unit with *The Universe* (Simon, 1998). The visuals in this picture book provided her students with a dazzling vision of what space travel might be like.

After this anticipatory activity to whet their interest in space, Mrs. Dawson announces that it is time to study the nine planets of our solar system.

> Questioning and prediction build interest and activate background knowledge.

"We're all going to take an imaginary trip in a special spacecraft and spacesuit and be the first people to visit the nine planets in the solar system," she says. The class predicts why no person has been to planets other than Earth. Mrs. Dawson tells the class that they will check their predictions as they visit each planet.

Using the book *The Life of an Astronaut* (Walker, 2001), her students learn how they must prepare for their space journey each day. After passing an "astronaut test" using NASA's Astronaut School web site, Mrs. Dawson presents the students with their space passports—small booklets with their school photograph and name, as well as pages for each planet. Students receive a stamp in their space passport for each successful interplanetary trip.

> NASA's Astronaut School web site can be found at http://edspace.nasa.gov/

Mrs. Dawson tells the class that they will write postcards from each of the planets they visit. She shows the class postcards she has received from family and friends visiting foreign countries. They discuss what kinds of things people write about when sending postcards, such as reports about what the traveler is doing and what the place is like.

For the next eight days, the class reads excerpts from books about the planets. One book in particular, *All About Space* (Becklake, 2002), is particularly valuable because its encyclopedia format and text features are informative and engaging. At the end of each lesson on a featured planet, Mrs. Dawson passes out 8 1/2" × 5 1/2" postcards. On one side of the postcard students write, "Greetings from (name of planet)." On the other side of the postcard, the students write to their "Earthling Friends" telling them facts about the planet in a manner that makes it sound like they are really on the planet, much like a traveler would write about the country he or she is visiting. These postcards serve as exit slips at the end of each class, and Mrs. Dawson is able to get immediate feedback about what her students have taken away from the day's lesson.

Writing to Learn in Fourth-Grade Social Studies

"Learning about the Gold Rush in California is lots of fun!" Jesus exclaims. In Colleen Crandall's fourth-grade social studies class, the challenge is not just to make the subject matter fun. It is crucial to find out if the students can synthesize the material they are learning and understand different points of view. Writing to learn is a useful strategy for teachers to understand what students have learned.

> Moss (2003) notes that "such pairings can help students develop different perspectives about a particular time, person, or phenomenon" (p. 74).

Mrs. Crandall uses a variety of texts and reading approaches to teach about the California Gold Rush. Students read several lessons from the social studies textbook on the Gold Rush period to gain a sense of the time and setting. On some days, she begins the lesson with "Yesterday's News"—a writing-to-learn prompt to summarize what they learned the previous day. Each day, she reads aloud a chapter from the historical novel *By the Great Horn Spoon!* (Fleischman, 1988). Although a work a fiction, Mrs. Crandall finds it effective to pair historical novels with informational texts to bring a time period to life. She stops periodically to ask students to "look into their crystal ball" and predict what they believe will happen next in the novel.

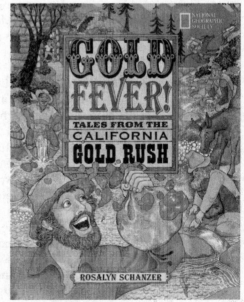

These readings serve as excellent preparation for their field trip to the local Junior Theater. During this week-long program, students learn more about life during the Gold Rush period and do some acting about how settlers came to California, diseases people may have caught on their journey, types of environments encountered along the way, and how people might have felt in their new home. Mrs. Crandall reads the picture book *Gold Fever! Tales from the California Gold Rush* (Schanzer, 1999). This informational text is especially valuable because it uses primary source documents, including excerpts from letters, newspaper articles, and government reports, to bring the era alive.

After this experiential learning, students are asked to sit down on the floor and write a letter to the folks back home using what they have just watched or personally acted out. They can use any material from the textbook reading or read-alouds, or facts they learned at the Junior Theater.

Source: Book cover reprinted with permission of National Geographic School Publishing.

The following is a letter one of her students wrote after this experience:

Dear Family,

Today, my day was no luck! I did not find any gold. My trip was a disaster because I was squished in the boat. The lunch that I ate was so good. I had a egg, sausage, and bacon. In the boat I was starving and I had thirst. I was working day and night for gold. When I went to the general store, I bought supplies that I needed. California is so cool! I was so excited about gold. I was trying my best to find gold. I was so excited when I got to California. My trip was so long I did not change my cloth. I just got to my cabin and went straight to bed. I got up early and I only got three hours to sleep. But when I did not find any gold I did not quited. I was going to do it again.

Sincerely,

Jose

By combining textbook entries, primary source documents, and historical fiction, Mrs. Crandall is able to see how her students are synthesizing information as they learn about the Gold Rush.

Writing to Learn in Fifth-Grade Mathematics

Aida Allen has noticed a new phenomenon among some of the girls in her fifth-grade mathematics class—and she's not happy about it. She has required that her students keep a math journal throughout the year, and lately some disturbing comments are cropping up in some of the journals. Maria wrote, "Factors are too hard. I don't know why I have to learn them." A few weeks earlier, Karla wrote, "Last year I wanted to be a doctor. My sister said you have to be good at math and I'm not, so now I want to be an actress on TV." Ms. Allen knows that aversion to math is not uncommon among girls as they enter middle school, and that too many students believe that only some people are good at math (Resnick, 1987).

To address this problem, Ms. Allen has decided to form a book club for the girls using the book *Math Smarts: Tips, Tricks, and Secrets for Making Math More Fun!* (Long, 2004). Each member of the Math'itude Club (so-named from a page in the book) reads and discusses each section of the book. At the end of each book club discussion (about 15 minutes in length), Ms. Allen presents a writing-to-learn prompt about the topic. Her intention is to promote a more positive attitude toward math and make them more metacognitively aware of how they best learn math. Her prompts included:

- Why does math matter? Here are ten fun things I can't do without math.
- Do I need a new math'itude? Instead of thinking _____, I can think _____.
- I found out that I learn math best when I. . . .
- Ten ways I can study for math.
- Five ways I can improve my math note taking.
- My favorite math trick is. . . .
- Word problems are a snap when I. . . .
- When I take a math test, I want to remember to. . . .

The boys are not forgotten during math book club. They have named themselves the Math detectives and are solving a series of crimes from the book *Whodunit Math Puzzles* (Wise, 2001). While the girls meet to discuss their reading from *Math Smarts*, the boys choose a case and attempt to solve it using math. Some of the 22 puzzles are more difficult than others, and Ms. Allen moves back and forth between the two book clubs to offer support. After solving the crime, they engage in a writing-to-learn activity called Name That Math. Ms. Allen was inspired by Chuck Hayden, a mathematics teacher at the high school, who developed this for use with his own students (Fisher & Frey, 2004). She wants students to make a habit of asking themselves the following questions when she asks them to Name That Math:

1. What's the key word in the problem?
2. What's the rule?
3. What's the first step?

For the first step, students read the problem and think, "What key word can I identify in the problem that tells me what I need to know?" Next, they discuss question #2, "What's the rule?" They have learned that rules are the formulas or definitions that are connected to the key word. After all, until they know what the rule is, they can't do the first step. The third question, explaining the first step to solve the problem, asks students to consider how they will set up the problem. Students begin to see that they can attempt the first step of solving the problem only after finding the key word and identifying the rule.

"I don't often do book club in math, but I really saw an attitude problem beginning to spread among the girls. I wanted to be able to interrupt that cycle before it became too deeply rooted," Ms. Allen remarked later. "At the same time, it seemed like a good time to introduce some activities that stretch their mathematical thinking. *Whodunit Math* was a good choice for that. Now I'm thinking that I am going to switch books and have the groups read the other title!"

Conclusion

Writing to learn "is a tool we can use to see how students are thinking about and understanding what they are doing and learning in the classroom" (Mitchell, 1996, p. 93). It differs from learning to write in its purpose. Process writing is used by students to refine their pieces through editing and rewriting. In contrast, writing to learn serves as a way to activate prior knowledge, recall newly learned information, make connections to other concepts, and promote reflective questioning.

This instructional strategy is useful across content areas, in part because what students write about can be easily tailored to the subject. Prompts can be constructed to access declarative, procedural, or conditional knowledge. First, it allows students to think about the content at hand and to focus on the subject. Students are invited to compose their thoughts and take stock of their beliefs and opinions before engaging in discussion. This rehearsal of language is likely to be especially useful for English language learners, who benefit from the chance to order ideas before sharing them with others. Second, writing to learn provides students with data that they can use later for essays or class assignments. Learning logs are especially useful for this because they create a record of previous learning, allowing students to see how the teacher assembled the conceptual framework of the unit. Finally, writing to learn provides teachers a glimpse inside the student's mind—a rare opportunity to assess student's understanding of the content. These brief writing events allow the teacher to witness each student's use of logic, reasoning, and information to arrive at solutions and apply concepts.

The strength of writing to learn lies in its intended audience. Process writing ultimately must find an outside audience to influence, persuade, and move, for that is "the power of the pen." Writing to learn has an audience of one—the writer. Teachers create a quiet space for students to engage in an internal dialogue that leads them on a journey of self-reflection. How often have you heard writers remark that they didn't know what they thought about something until they read what they had written? And so it is with writing to learn. When students discover that these writing events illuminate their own understanding, they discover the power *in* the pen.

References

Andrews, S. E. (1997). Writing to learn in a content area reading class. *Journal of Adolescent and Adult Literacy, 41*, 141–142.

Atwell, N. (1998). *In the middle: Writing, reading, and learning with adolescents* (2nd ed.). Upper Montclair, NJ: Boynton/Cook.

Bangert-Drowns, R. L., Hurley, M. M., & Wilkinson, B. (2004). The effects of school-based writing-to-learn interventions on academic achievement: A meta-analysis. *Review of Educational Research, 74*, 29–58.

Britton, J. R. (1970). *Language and learning*. London: Allen Lane.

Clay, M. (1979). *Preventing reading difficulties in young children*. Portsmouth, NH: Heinemann.

Connolly, P., & Vilardi, T. (1989). *Writing to learn mathematics and science*. New York: Teacher College.

Davey, B. (1983). Think-aloud: Modeling the cognitive processes of reading comprehension. *Journal of Reading, 27*, 44–47.

Edens, K. M., & Potter, M. (2003) Using descriptive drawings as a conceptual change strategy in elementary science. *School Science and Mathematics, 103*, 135–145.

Fisher, D. (2001). "We're moving on up": Creating a schoolwide literacy effort in an urban high school. *Journal of Adolescent & Adult Literacy, 45*, 92–101.

Fisher, D., & Frey, N. (2004). *Improving adolescent literacy: Strategies at work*. Upper Saddle River, NJ: Merrill Plentice Hall.

Gee, J. P. (1990). *Social linguistics and literacies: Ideology in discourses*. London: Falmer.

Graves, D. H. (1983). *Writing: Teachers and children at work*. Portsmouth, NH: Heinemann.

Hansen, J. (2001). *When writers read* (2nd ed.). Portsmouth, NH: Heinemann.

Hayes, J. R. (2004). A new framework for understanding cognition and affect in writing. In R. B. Ruddell and N. J. Unrath (Eds.), *Theoretical models and processes of reading* (5th ed.). Newark, DE: International Reading Association.

Hayes, J. R., & Flower, L. S. (1980). Identifying the organization of writing processes. In E. Gregg & E. R. Steinberg (Eds.), *Cognitive processes in writing* (pp. 3–30). Hillsdale, NJ: Lawrence Erlbaum.

Holbrook, H. T. (1987). Writing to learn in the social studies. *The Reading Teacher, 41*, 216–219.

Holdaway, D. (1979). *The foundations of literacy*. New York: Scholastic.

Jenkinson, E. B. (1988). Learning to write/writing to learn. *Phi Delta Kappan, 69*, 712–717.

Langer, J. A., & Applebee, A. N. (1987). *How writing shapes thinking*. Urbana, IL: National Council of Teachers of English.

McIntosh, M. E., & Draper, R. J. (2001). Using learning logs in mathematics: Writing to learn. *Mathematics Teacher, 94*, 554–557.

Miller, L. D., & England, D. A. (1989). Writing to learn algebra. *School science and Mathematics, 89*, 299–312.

Mitchell, D. (1996, September). Writing to learn across the curriculum and the English teacher. *English Journal, 85*, 93–97.

Moss, B. (2003). *Exploring the literature of fact: Children's nonfiction trade books in the elementary classroom*. New York: Guilford.

National Research Council. (2001). *Adding it up: Helping children learn mathematics*. Mathematics Learning

Study Committee, J. Kilpatrick, J. Swafford, & B. Findell (Eds.). Center for Education. Washington, DC: National Academy.

National Research Council. (2005). *How students learn: History, mathematics, and science in the classroom.* Committee on *How people learn: A targeted report for teachers,* M. S. Donovan and J. D. Bransford (Eds.). Division of Behavioral and Social Sciences and Education. Washington, DC: National Academy.

Paris, S. G., Cross, D. R., & Lipson, M. Y. (1984). Informed strategies for learning: A program to improve children's reading awareness and comprehension. *Journal of Educational Psychology, 76,* 1239–1252.

Resnick, L. B. (1987). *Education and learning to think.* Committee on Mathematics, Science, and Technology Education, Commission on Behavioral and Social Sciences and Education. Washington, DC: National Academy.

Santa, C., & Havens, L. (1995). *Creating independence through student-owned strategies: Project CRISS.* Dubuque, IA: Kendall-Hunt.

Sternberg, R. J., & Williams, W. M. (2002). *Educational psychology.* Boston: Allyn & Bacon.

Children's Literature Cited

Adler, D. (1993). *A picture book of Harriet Tubman.* New York: Holiday House.

Becklake, S. (2002). *Scholastic first encyclopedia: All about space.* New York: Scholastic.

Fleischman. S. (1988). *By the great horn spoon!* New York: Little, Brown.

Hooper, M. (1998). *The drop in my drink: The story of water on our planet.* New York: Viking.

Kalman, B. (2000). *What is a plant? The science of living things.* New York: Crabtree.

Lester, J. (1998). *From slave ship to freedom road.* New York: Dial.

Long, L. (2004). *Math smarts: Tips , tricks, and secrets for making math more fun!* Middleton, WI: Pleasant Co.

McKinney, B. S. (1998). *A drop around the world.* Nevada City, CA: Dawn.

Nagda, A. W. (2000). *Tiger math: Learning to graph from a baby tiger.* New York: Henry Holt.

Nelson, R. (2003). *From cocoa bean to chocolate.* Minneopolis: Lerner.

Rosa-Mendoza, G. (2002). *My body/Mi cuerpo.* Wheaton, IL: Mi+Me.

Schanzer, R. (1999). *Gold fever! Tales from the California gold rush.* Washington, DC: National Geographic Society.

Schanzer, R. (1997). *How we crossed the west: The adventures of Lewis and Clark.* Washington, DC: National Geographic Society.

Shemie, B. (1989), *Houses of snow, skin, and bones.* Plattsburgh, NY: Tundra Books.

Simon, S. (1998). *The universe.* New York: Harper Collins.

Spier, P. (1973). *The star-spangled banner.* New York: Doubleday.

Taylor, B. (2001). *The earth: The geography of our world.* New York: Kingfisher.

Walker, N. (2001). *The life of an astronaut.* New York: Crabtree

Wise, B. (2001). *Whodunit math puzzles.* New York: Sterling.

Woods, G. (1998). *Science in ancient Egypt.* New York: Franklin Watts.

Chapter 10

Assessing and Testing Reading for Information

H ow will you know if your students have learned anything? How will you know if your students can use the strategies you have taught them? Naturally, you will assess them using a variety of informal assessments, and maybe some formal ones. We are reminded that the act of assessment is what distinguishes teaching from learning, because it is the teacher's way of ascertaining whether learning has taken place.

How will you and other stakeholders know if the students in the classes you teach do well compared with other students in the state? Your students will be tested using a variety of norm-referenced and criterion-referenced instruments. These formal assessments are used for accountability purposes at the local, state, or national level.

Of course there are many types of assessments. Figure 10.1 provides an overview of the various types of informal and formal assessments that teachers and schools use. Students are assessed for a variety of reasons, including:

- diagnosing individual student needs (e.g., assessing developmental status, monitoring and communicating student progress, certifying competency, determining needs)

- informing instruction (e.g., evaluating instruction, modifying instructional strategies, identifying instructional needs)

- evaluating programs

- providing accountability information (Lapp, Fisher, Flood, & Cabello, 2001, p. 7)

In this chapter, we will discuss the roles of informal assessment and formal testing as a means for answering the questions posed earlier. These practices form the bookends for teaching students to read for information, because they serve as measures of progress and points for making instructional and programmatic decisions.

Classroom Assessment Practices

Over the years, we've come to realize that assessments are the link between teaching and learning. This concept lies at the heart of elementary teaching because our classrooms are based on learner-centered instruction. This means the teacher doesn't merely march lockstep through the content of a standards-based curriculum, but rather balances the content with the needs of the learner. These needs are identified through ongoing assessment that is linked to subsequent instruction. In this model, assessment and instruction are considered to be recursive because they repeat as students learn new content. In learner-centered classrooms, teachers first assess to establish what children know and do not know, then plan instruction based on this information. Next, they deliver the instruction they have designed and observe how learners respond. Based on these observations, educators reflect on the results and assess again to determine what needs to be taught next. A diagram representing this concept can be seen in Figure 10.2.

This model may sound as if it would take a lot of time to complete; in fact, effective teachers perform these complex tasks rapidly. In well-organized classrooms, informal assessment happens throughout the day as teachers use questioning, discussions, and assignments to measure progress. In addition, teachers administer assessments to monitor progress and formulate future instruction. The first step is selecting the correct assessments.

Figure 10.1 Guide to formal and informal assessments.

Formal Assessments		
TYPE OF TEST	**PURPOSE**	**ADMINISTRATION**
Standardized	Yields a student's academic performance ranking compared to a normed sample of students.	• Schedule determined by state and local agencies; often yearly. • Tests are usually timed and have strict protocols.
Criterion-Referenced	Measures a student's performance compared to a set of academic skills or objectives. Scores are reported as the proportion of correct answers.	• Tests may be untimed or timed. • May be administered annually or more frequently.
Informal Assessments		
TYPE	**PURPOSE**	**ADMINISTRATION**
Observation	Gathers information about a student's academic, behavioral, or social skills used in an authentic setting.	Teacher records observational data in anecdotal notes, journals, or daily logs.
Portfolio	Provides evidence of a student's academic growth through the collection of work samples.	Student and teacher select representative samples of student work for display in a binder or other organizer.
Inventory	Documents student use of specified skills during a single observation.	A commercially or teacher-produced form of observable behaviors is completed by the teacher.
Conference	Involves the student in direct feedback to the teacher in a one-to-one discussion.	Often scheduled by teacher at regular intervals to gauge progress on more complex academic behaviors such as reading comprehension.
Self-Assessment	Allows student to engage in reflective learning.	Students assess their own academic performance using an age-appropriate checklist of indicators.
Survey	Collects student feedback about their interests, prior knowledge, or motivation about a topic.	Student completes a commercially or teacher-produced survey of items.

Source: Fisher, D., & Frey, N. (2004). *Improving adolescent literacy: Strategies at work.* Upper Saddle River, NJ: Pearson Merrill Prentice Hall. Used with permission.

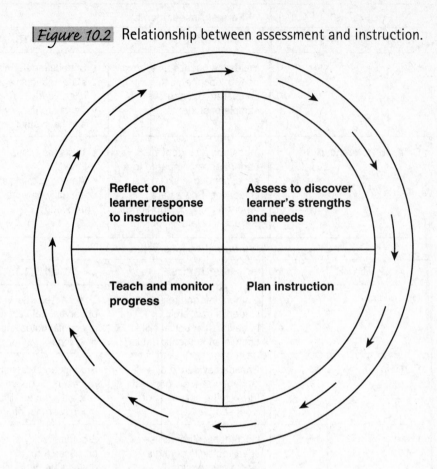

Figure 10.2 Relationship between assessment and instruction.

Reflect on learner response to instruction

Assess to discover learner's strengths and needs

Teach and monitor progress

Plan instruction

How Do I Select an Assessment?

The usefulness of every assessment is dependent on a proper fit between purpose and type of assessment used. It is important to remember that every assessment is useful and not useful *at the same time*. Any given assessment is useful in the hands of a conscientious educator who understands the limitations of the tool being used. Any given assessment is useless if it is interpreted to show something it was not intended to show. You would be very suspicious of a doctor who ordered a chest x-ray when you were seeking help for a sprained ankle. There is nothing inherently wrong with a chest x-ray; it is simply the wrong test for the task. In the same regard, the type of reading or writing assessment selected must match its intended use.

Guillaume (2004) offers these considerations for selecting an assessment. Each assessment needs to be:

- tied to your stance on learning;
- driven by learning goals;

- systematic;
- tied to instruction;
- inclusive of the learner; and
- integrated into a manageable system. (p. 131)

Tied to Your Stance on Learning. Every teacher brings a philosophy of education and a view of literacy to his or her practice. It is important to recognize how assessment choices fit into that perspective. For example, an educator who possesses a viewpoint of learning as a developmental phenomenon will be interested in assessment instruments that reflect benchmarks of developmental phases of learning. Teachers with a skills-based orientation will find skills measures to be useful.

Driven by Learning Goals. Assessments used should be consistent with state content standards for the grade level. Currently, 49 of the 50 states have content standards (Iowa is the exception), and these standards can be found on most state department of education web sites.

Systematic. Teachers select assessments that can be administered and analyzed in a systematic way at both the individual and class levels. Good assessments should possess data-recording protocols that make it easy for the teacher to interpret the information at a later date. In addition, the teacher must determine how often they will be administered. Finally, each assessment should measure what it purports to measure (valid) and yield results that are consistent across administrations and assessors (reliable).

Tied to Instruction. Although this seems apparent, it is worth stating again. Assessment should be linked directly to instruction, either to determine what should be taught next (pretesting) or to check for understanding of skills or strategies that have just been taught (posttesting). An assessment that is not connected to instruction is likely to be frustrating for students because it appears purposeless, and inadequate for teachers because it does not provide relevant information.

Inclusive of the Learner. Assessments are intended to be completed in conjunction with the needs of the learner. Most of the assessments in this chapter are not completed in isolation by students, who then return the completed tests to the teacher. Instead, these assessments are designed to capture the work of children in the act of learning. Whether through listening to a student reading text (running records and Informal Reading Inventories) or using a rubric to discuss a student's writing (holistic writing assessment), these tools are intended to involve the learner in her or his own measures of progress. A position statement issued by the International

The complete version of this position statement can be viewed at www.reading.org/ resources/issues/ position_high_stakes. html

Reading Association suggests that "children have a right to reading assessment that identifies their strengths as well as their needs and involves them in making decisions about their own learning" (IRA, 2000, p. 7).

Integrated Into a Manageable System. No teacher can devote all of his or her time to collecting and analyzing assessment data. The demands of assessment on the time available can become overwhelming and even crowd out equally valuable instructional time. Therefore, it is in the interests of the teacher to understand what each assessment does, then select the one that best fits the needs of the students, teacher, and curriculum. Having a collection of good, all-purpose assessments is preferable to administering overlapping assessments that do little to shed new light on a student's progress.

Types of Informal Assessments

There are a number of informal assessments commonly used in elementary classrooms to assess students' progress in learning to read for information. They include observations, portfolios, inventories, rubrics, conferences, self-assessments, and surveys.

Observations. Observations are perhaps the assessment tool most commonly used by teachers and are identified by them as the most useful (West, 1998). There are several advantages to the use of observation as a tool for assessment:

- It focuses on student work in authentic learning situations (Frey & Hiebert, 2003).
- It mitigates some of the problems associated with formal testing, especially learner stress, because it occurs in the daily learning environment.
- The teacher is able to obtain and analyze the information immediately, allowing for flexibility in instructional plans.

Observational notes can be difficult to collect if you don't have a system. Begin by identifying specific students you want to observe during a particular day, perhaps one to three students. If you select two or three students per day for targeted observation, you can collect notes on all of your students in ten days. Having said that, we also know that opportunities for observation sometimes arise serendipitously. The trouble arises when you make a note of something then lose the note! To handle that problem, we create a clipboard of index cards, one for each student, at the beginning of the year. Each card contains pertinent information about the student. The cards are taped individually to the clipboard in a slightly overlapping fashion so that each card can be lifted. The student's name is written at the bottom edge of the card so it can be seen at all times. Anytime we jot a note on a Post-It® about a student, we can place it on their card for later organization and filing. See Figure 10.3 for a diagram of this organizational system.

Figure 10.3 Clipboard for classroom observations.

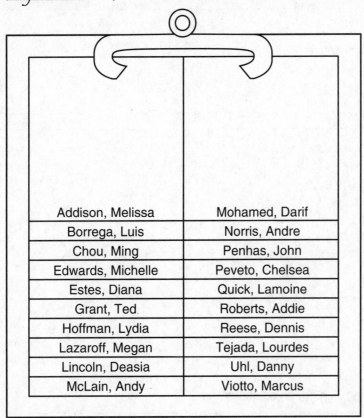

Addison, Melissa	Mohamed, Darif
Borrega, Luis	Norris, Andre
Chou, Ming	Penhas, John
Edwards, Michelle	Peveto, Chelsea
Estes, Diana	Quick, Lamoine
Grant, Ted	Roberts, Addie
Hoffman, Lydia	Reese, Dennis
Lazaroff, Megan	Tejada, Lourdes
Lincoln, Deasia	Uhl, Danny
McLain, Andy	Viotto, Marcus

Source: Frey, N., & Fisher, D. (2006). *Language arts workshop: Purposeful reading and writing instruction.* Upper Saddle River, NJ: Pearson Merril Prentice Hall. Used with permission.

Although the act of reflective teaching is defined by a recursive cycle of teaching, observing, and reflecting, it is not realistic to think that any teacher could (or even would want to) record every observation. However, a simple observation form like the one in Figure 10.4 can assist a busy teacher in documenting meaningful observation data.

Portfolios. The term portfolio is used to describe a collection of student work that represents progress made over time (Tierney, Clark, Wiser, Simpson, Herter, & Fenner, 1998). Like an artist's portfolio, they are constructed by the learner in partnership with the teacher. Students are often invited to select a range of work, not just the most exemplary pieces, to represent their learning. The assembled portfolio is then used as a

Figure 10.4 Classroom observation form.

Name: _____	Date: _____
Time: From _____ to _____	

Student observed working:
  Independently
  Collaboratively with _____
  Guided instruction with _____

Task observed:

Sequence of events observed:

Notes and reflections:

Abbreviations
S_1 = student being observed
T = teacher
$S_2 - S_5$ = other students working with observed student

Source: Frey, N., & Fisher, D. (2006). *Language arts workshop: Purposeful reading and writing instruction.* Upper Saddle River, NJ: Pearson Merrill Prentice Hall. Used with permission.

conference tool between parent, teacher, and student. Wilcox (1997) suggests that a portfolio of student work be organized around the following topics:

- *Reading artifacts* like reading journals and book reviews.
- *Thinking artifacts* that demonstrate the learner's process of understanding. Examples include notes, concept maps, and self-assessments.
- *Writing artifacts* like finished pieces and works in progress.
- *Interacting artifacts* that reflect work accomplished with peers. These might include reciprocal teaching sheets and written summaries of readings that have been collaboratively read through a jigsaw process.
- *Demonstrating artifacts* that represent public performance by the student, including oral reports, demonstrations, and lab experiments. (p. 35)

See Chapter 2.

Figure 10.5 Critical literacy checklist.

| Name: _____ | Date: _____ |
| Book: _____ | Author: _____ |

CRITICAL LITERACY SKILL	EVIDENCE
☐ **States purpose for reading this text** *Why did you choose this book?*	
☐ **Does text match reader's purpose?** *Did you learn about your topic from this book? Why or why not?*	
☐ **Considers author's source of information** *How do you think the author learned about this topic?*	
☐ **Identifies what might be missing from the text** *What should the author add to the book?*	
☐ **Identifies other possible sources of information** *What other ways can you learn more about this topic?*	
☐ **Expresses opinion of text and supports opinions** *Did you like this book? Why or why not?*	

Inventories. An inventory of a store lists the items contained within the store. Likewise, skills inventories are lists of observable behaviors that can be easily identified and recorded by the teacher. These inventories most often come in the form of a checklist for easy transcription. An inventory can be commercially prepared, or may be constructed by the teacher. A checklist of observable behaviors is especially useful when meeting with parents to discuss their child's progress. An example of a critical literacy inventory for young readers can be found in Figure 10.5.

Rubrics. Students often have difficulty predicting precisely what the teacher wants to see in an assignment or project. This is due in part to the

Figure 10.6 Basic rubric.

What makes a good cheeseburger?
The basics: Bun, patty, cheese
Enhancements: lettuce, tomatoes, bacon, ketchup, mustard, pickles — you name it!
Appearance: smooth bun, stacked up in an even column, no ingredients hanging out
Mistakes to avoid: don't overcook or undercook; don't drop on floor

Now let's develop a cheeseburger rubric for _____

	WHAT DOES IT LOOK LIKE?	EVIDENCE
The basics		
Enhancements		
Appearance		
Mistakes to avoid		

Source: Frey, N., & Fisher, D. (2006). *Language arts workshop: Purposeful reading and writing instruction.* Upper Saddle River, NJ: Pearson Merrill Prentice Hall. Used with permission.

A helpful web site for developing and storing your rubrics can be found at rubistar.4teachers.org

difficulty teachers sometimes have in defining what they want. Rubrics are designed to clear up such confusions. These scoring guides are distributed and discussed in advance so that students are clear about what is expected. Rubrics are usually designed by the teacher, although many choose to develop rubrics with the class to prompt discussion about the characteristics of a good performance. An all-purpose rubric suitable for development with students appears in Figure 10.6.

Conferences. Effective teachers routinely meet individually with students during the independent phase of instruction to discuss learning. These conferences are valuable because they are an opportunity to collect informal assessment information about a student. The information gathered during a conference on a child's learning provides authentic assessment data for use in planning future instruction.

Self-Assessments. As we have discussed on several occasions throughout this book, the ability to self-assess is an essential skill for developing metacognitive awareness. You will recall that metacognitive awareness is the ability of a learner to describe how he or she best learns. In addition, it refers to a learner's ability to develop a plan for learning, then monitor and evaluate that plan (Kujawa & Huske, 1995). For example, a student of ours wrote, "I just wanted to let you know some of the skills I would like to work on. One of them is 'inference' or 'reading between the lines.' For

Figure 10.7 Self-assessment of group work.

Name: _____		Date: _____		
Project: _____		Members of my group:		

Please rank yourself based on your contributions to the group. Circle the one that best describes your work.

5 = always   4 = almost always   3 = sometimes   2 = once or twice   1 = never

	5	4	3	2	1
I completed my tasks on time.	5	4	3	2	1
I contributed ideas to the group.	5	4	3	2	1
I listened respectfully to the ideas of others.	5	4	3	2	1
I used other people's ideas in my work for the project.	5	4	3	2	1
When I was stuck, I sought help from my group.	5	4	3	2	1

Additional comments:

Source: Frey, N., & Fisher, D. (2006). *Language arts workshop: Purposeful reading and writing instruction.* Upper Saddle River, NJ: Pearson Merrill Prentice Hall. Used with permission.

example, I am very bad at answering questions in someone else's shoes such as 'What would this author say. . . .', or 'Why was this piece written'." One of the ways students develop metacognitive awareness is through the use of self-assessments. An example of a self-assessment for students working in groups appears in Figure 10.7.

Surveys. Assessment tools such as surveys can be an efficient way for a teacher to collect information about a large number of students in a short period of time. Surveys can be constructed on any topic and can measure student background knowledge or interest. Information collected from surveys can then be compiled to make instructional decisions. A reading survey for the beginning of the school year can be found in Figure 10.8.

An effective teacher uses a variety of assessments, including observations, portfolios of student work, inventories, rubrics, conferences, and self-assessments, to monitor the progress of students and plan future instruction. Using a variety of assessment instruments, both formal and informal, provides the student with opportunities to more fully demonstrate his or her strengths in reading for information and reveal areas of

Figure 10.8 Reading-for-information survey.

Name: _____ Date: _____

Please circle the answer that is best for you.

Reading for Information Survey

When I am interested in a topic, I look for a book on the subject.

Always   *Sometimes*   *Never*

I know how to find a book on the subject I am interested in.

Always   *Sometimes*   *Never*

These are the things I like in an informational book. (circle as many as you like)

Photographs   *Colorful illustrations*   *Lots of interesting facts*

Directions for making things   *Short chapters*   *Sidebars*

These are the kinds of things I read. (check off all the ones you like)

Chapter books _____   Books with pictures _____
Web sites _____   Newspapers _____
Magazines _____   Textbook _____
Encyclopedia _____   Biographies _____

These are the things I am most interested in reading about. (check off all the things you like)

Science Topics   Social Studies Topics
___ Animals   ___ People from other countries
___ Dinosaurs   ___ Explorers and pioneers
___ Insects   ___ Government
___ Weather   ___ Life long ago
___ Space   ___ Life today
___ Human body   ___ United States history
___ Other   ___ Our state
                                    ___ Other

Mathematics Topics
___ Numbers   The Arts
___ Using math in everyday life   ___ Dance
___ Building things   ___ Painting and drawing
___ Math puzzles   ___ Athletics
                                    ___ Sculpture
                                    ___ Music
                                    ___ Performance
                                    ___ The lives of artists and musicians

continued need. When paired with informal assessments, the formal testing necessary for accountability purposes becomes more useful. It is not, however, without controversy.

Reading for Information and Its Role in Formal Testing

As stated earlier, the reasons for testing and accountability fall into four categories: diagnosing individual student needs, informing instruction, evaluating programs, and providing accountability information (Lapp, Fisher, Flood, & Cabello, 2001).

How Did We Get Here? Legislative Support for Testing

Educational reform over the past decade has focused on this fourth point—standards, assessments, and accountability. In 1994, the standards and assessment movement received significant and tangible support through the Goals 2000: Educate America Act. This federal act provided fiscal resources and other incentives for the development of standards and assessments across the nation.

Another Goals 2000 expectation has received increased attention. The development of assessments or tests that are aligned to the approved state standards will soon be in place across the nation. These assessments are supposed to help educators, parents, and community members understand student performance and hold schools accountable for this performance. To ensure that schools are moving in the desired direction, "valid, nondiscriminatory and reliable state assessments that are aligned to State standards, involve multiple measure of student performance and include all students, must be developed" [Goals 2000 Sec. 306 (c) (1) (B)].

> Accountability is a term used to refer to a broad range of goals and measures of those goals.

Once standards were aligned with assessments, the third element of educational reform—accountability—could take place. Accountability measures are commonly seen as standardized testing results, but may also include school satisfaction measures, graduation and grade retention rates, and attendance. In January 2002, another federal act, No Child Left Behind, was signed into law. Seen as one of the most sweeping reforms of K–12 education in decades, the act proposed stronger accountability for student performance results. Districts and schools that fail to make adequate achievements in student performance will be subject to sanctions, corrective actions, and restructuring measures. Schools that meet or exceed their goals will be eligible for awards and financial incentives. Thus, teachers today must not only use strategies that help their students understand the content, they must also provide students with information about testing and assessment systems.

> Financial rewards and sanctions are often described as the "carrot and stick" approach to school reform.

Concerns About Testing

This approach to school reform through high-stakes accountability is not without its critics. Numerous educators have expressed dismay at the efficacy of achieving higher levels of student achievement through these means (Meier, Kozol, & Cohen, 2000; Ohanian, 1999). Alfie Kohn, a psychologist long involved with issues of education, has criticized the emphasis on accountability measures as a method that is ineffective for promoting reform and harmful to students and teachers whose anxiety about test results may actually impede performance (Kohn, 2000). These controversies are likely to remain throughout the next decade, and, as educators, we believe it is important to consider opposing viewpoints on matters of such importance. But we are also cognizant of the present realities faced by today's teachers. Students will be tested; teachers and schools will be evaluated according to student performance on these tests. Therefore, the remainder of this chapter will provide guidance for ensuring that students perform well on these accountability measures.

Characteristics of Formal Assessments

Formal assessments have been developed to be administered to students using a prescribed format concerning time, directions, and level of assistance. Most often, these assessments are given under conditions that do not reflect the ways in which students learned the tested skills. Most formal assessments include a lengthy testing protocol and student test booklets for collecting data. Protocols are the detailed directions for administering the text. Examples of formal assessments include the National Assessment of Educational Progress (NAEP), given in all fifty states, as well as achievement tests like the Stanford Achievement Test (SAT-9) and Terra Nova (CAT/6). These assessments are *norm-referenced* using thousands of students in order to compare each individual's achievement with other students. Other standardized assessments are *criterion-referenced,* meaning that they measure a student's achievement against those skills expected at a particular age or grade level. Examples of criterion-referenced formal assessments include the Stanford Diagnostic Reading Test (SDRT) and the Gates-MacGinitie Reading Test (GMRT).

Most formal assessments scoring is completed by the test publisher, and the results are then reported back to the school and district, often several months later. Many of these formal assessments are used to measure school and district progress toward various state and national accountability targets.

Addressing High–Stakes Tests

At this point in time, standardized tests, with significant rewards or consequences attached to them, are a part of the educational landscape. With the arrival of these high-stakes tests, teachers and schools are called upon to immediately improve student performance. To address the newly arriving expectations, several steps can be taken both in the short- and long-term. First and foremost, students must be motivated to do well on assessments. They must understand that the assessments they participate in matter. Consider the following classroom discussion:

Ms. Allen:	Remember, in a few weeks, we're going to have some test days. Why do we have to take those tests?
Miriam:	So that the government knows we learned something?
Ms. Allen:	Yes, that's one important reason. Why else?
Tino:	So we know what we still need to learn?
Ms. Allen:	Another excellent reason. Do your parents and I think you have to get all of the questions right?
Joe:	No way—they make the test hard. You told us to just keep trying.
Ms. Allen:	Yes, they make the test really hard but we're going to show them how much we've learned, right?
Class:	Yeah, classroom 302 will rock the test!

As this scenario illustrates, the student's own perception, attitude, and positive disposition toward the test is essential. If students are to succeed on these assessments, they must view them as worthwhile, important, and achievable. To bring such a positive outlook about, it is essential that all school community members, especially the faculty, see the test as worthwhile, important, and achievable. Should the teachers discount, disparage, or exhibit significant anxiety over the tests, the impact upon student performance will be quite negative. Such teachers have, in effect, told students that these tests are not important or that success with such tests is not possible. Given such an outlook by the teacher, students are not likely to put forward any significant effort into test taking, and will instead assume failure before beginning.

To create a positive and successful testing climate, the entire school should engage in a long-term campaign that addresses three major areas:

1. test format practice,
2. reading strategies instruction, and
3. student engagement in reading (Guthrie, 2002).

As we look more closely at each of these areas, we must be careful not to allow the test practice to become the curriculum (Santman, 2002). In other words, we are not advocating that schools "teach to the test." Rather, we believe in teaching to the standards that are tested. When students are well versed in standards-based content, they are more likely to do well on the test. School is still about creating citizens who can participate in the democracy.

For more information on motivating students, see Harry K. Wong's (1992) The First Days of School.

Don't forget to include testing information in parent involvement activities. Family Nights, open house, and newsletters can be used to increase awareness of high-stakes testing and its ramifications.

Additionally, we believe that students should be "test-wise." Consider the times in your adult life when you have been in a situation where the outcome could greatly affect your future. Perhaps it was giving testimony in a court case, or meeting with an Internal Revenue Service agent for an audit of your taxes. None of us would ever consider walking into such a high stakes event without doing our best to prepare ourselves for the task. You've come by this wisdom from years of life experience. We believe that our students should also be wise about important events like standardized testing. The first step to being test-wise is to understand the format of the test. Like any genre, knowing the characteristics of the test assists the learner in understanding it.

Area #1: Test Format Practice

The worthiness of test format preparation depends upon how well it is infused into the curriculum, how connected it is to good general learning, and how it connects with effective literacy strategies (e.g., Duke & Ritchart, 1997). It is not enough, and may even be harmful to learning, if teachers simply find test items for their students to practice. Popham (2001) calls this type of practice "item-teaching" and believes that while it may improve student's scores, teachers cannot "infer that students can satisfactorily do other problems of that ilk" (p. 17). In other words, when teachers practice "item-teaching" they are preparing students only for specific test questions; little hope is provided that the learner has any fundamental understanding or can apply the concept to other areas.

Popham suggests that teachers instead be involved in "curriculum-teaching," whereby they focus upon specific content or skills that will later be tested, or as he states, "test-represented." According to Popham, curriculum-teaching "will elevate students' scores on high stakes tests and, more importantly, will elevate students' mastery of the knowledge or skills on which the test items are based" (2001, p. 17).

Langer (2001) makes a similar point in her study of characteristics of literacy instruction in "beating the odds" schools. Langer identifies two quite different approaches to test preparation commonly practiced by teachers: separated or integrated. Test preparation can be either treated as a separate approach involving test practice and test hints or it can be directly integrated into the regular curriculum.

Schools that outperform their demographic counterparts often use integrated test preparation. In an integrated approach, teachers spend time "carefully analyzing test demands and reformulating curriculum as necessary to be sure that students would, over time, develop the knowledge and skills necessary for accomplished performance" (p. 860). This stands in contrast to Popham's item-teaching approach that is predicated on how well the teacher matches his or her direct teaching to the test questions featured on this year's exam.

> Have you ever crammed for a test? How much did you remember six months later?

In high-performing schools, teachers see tests as an opportunity to "revise and reformulate their literacy curriculum" (Langer, 2001, p. 860). Such teachers provide their students enriched course work by using the tests to go deeper into an understanding of literacy skills, strategies, and content. In the process, test preparation is not seen as an additional activity, but one of many that ensures overall literacy learning (Langer, 2001).

To ensure that test format practice is integrated into the curriculum, we suggest that teachers focus on attitude, general test-wise skills, direction words, multiple-choice questions, and skills for reading passages.

Figure 10.9 Classroom poster.

You too could become the next high SCORER!
S – Schedule your time while taking the test.
C – Use clue words to help answer questions.
O – Omit difficult questions at first.
R – Read questions carefully.
E – Eliminate unreasonable choices.
R – Review your responses.

Fostering a Test-Wise Attitude. As we have noted, students' attitudes toward the test may be one of the most important factors for success. We have all seen students use the answer sheet to make designs, clearly not paying attention to the test questions. Students sometimes refer to this as "Christmas treeing" the score sheet because the arrangement of bubbles on the scantron can be easily transformed into this holiday symbol. One school-wide strategy is to use a mnemonic that the students can learn. The "High Scorer" posters remind students that the test is important and provides them with general information about test taking (see Figure 10.9). These posters should be reviewed on a regular basis. Additionally, students should be asked to think about the following:

> A mnemonic is a strategy for remembering a string of information, based on the first letter of each word. For example, a mnemonic device for remembering the Great Lakes is HOMES: Huron, Ontario, Michigan, Erie, and Superior.

1. *Be prepared.* Get a good night's sleep the night before test days. Eat a good breakfast on the mornings of test days.
2. *Relax.* It's normal to feel a little nervous. Some questions will be easy, others hard. Very few people get all of the answers right. Don't worry about information you don't know, just do your best.
3. *Think positively.* Tell yourself, "I'm going to do the best I can." Then do it.
4. *Practice your skills.* They really will help you do your best work.

Regarding the aforementioned answer sheet transformations that become works of art for some students: as the test sheets are collected and secured at the end of each test day, those with designs are noted. These budding Picassos are invited to meet with the principal to discuss the importance of test performance for the student.

General Test-Wise Skills. The following items comprise an overall approach from the start of testing when directions are read and questions can be

Some students have difficulty with test stamina—the ability to focus in a testing situation for prolonged periods of time.

asked, to the last few minutes of testing—when stray marks can be erased. The points suggest that the test taker begin the test with confidence and curiosity, tackle the questions systematically, and finish the test with diligence and attention to detail. Again, many of these are things that students have not been taught. These skills should be reinforced in each class, especially when students complete teacher-created tests throughout the year.

1. Listen and read along with the teacher as he or she reads the directions to the test. Ask questions if you do not understand.

2. At the start of the test, quickly scan the pages and notice the types and number of questions—what's easy and what's hard. This will help you to make the best use of your time.

3. Budget your time, making sure you allow enough time to answer all of the questions. Pace yourself. Watch the time. If you don't know the answer to a question, move on and come back to it later.

4. Answer the questions you know first. You will have time to read the others more closely the second time you go over the test. When you skip a question, mark your answer sheet so you won't use that space to answer another question. Keep an eye on the answer sheet to be sure you're marking the right space.

5. When you skip a question, be alert for answers or clues in other questions. Answers often pop up in other questions. In addition, as you take the test your background knowledge about the subject will become more active and make it more likely you will be able to figure out the harder questions later.

6. When you get to the end of the test, start over with the first question you skipped. Be sure to erase stray marks when you go back over the test. Complete the answer sheet correctly by filling in the bubbles completely and erasing any other pencil marks.

7. Do not change an answer unless you can prove your first answer is wrong. Your first instinct is usually correct.

8. During the last two minutes of the test, go back and fill in all blank answers with the same letter. If you leave an answer blank, you're guaranteed to get it wrong!

Direction Words. An important skill in reading for information is the ability to correctly interpret direction words. Success on each test item is dependent upon the clear understanding of exactly what the question is asking. If students do not take time to consider or do not know what the words mean in the question stem, there is little chance of success. Like the signal words associated with specific text structures, these direction words signal the test taker to the task at hand. Extensive practice with these stems as part of the classroom's general pattern of instruction is essential. Teachers must teach students to read the questions carefully and look for important direction words such as:

first step is	best answer is	the same as	refers to
most important	except for	most likely to	a fact
opinion	the purpose of	infer from	

Practicing with questions using these stems will allow students to arrive at, and become familiar with, the type of answer each stem is likely to require.

Additionally, there are common terms used on tests that students should understand. The following terms comprise a good start at understanding direction words:

You'll remember from Chapter 1 that teaching about text structures provides students with an important comprehension strategy.

These terms can be incorporated into your vocabulary instruction.

- *Analyze*. Break the subject into parts and discuss the parts.
- *Approximate, estimate*. Make a reasonable guess.
- *Characterize, identify, explain, describe*. Name the characteristics that make something special.
- *Choose the best answer*. Select the answer that is most correct.
- *Examine*. Look carefully at similar answers as one will be a better choice.
- *Chronological order*. Time order.
- *Comment*. Give your opinion and support it with facts and examples.
- *Compare*. Tell how two or more things are similar and how they are different.
- *Contrast*. Tell how two or more things are different.
- *Discuss*. Tell all you can about the topic in the time available.
- *Evaluate*. Give evidence on each side of an issue, draw a conclusion from the evidence, and make a judgment about the topic.
- *Fill in the blank; Complete the sentence*. If a list of possible answers is given, use the best word from the list. If not, use the word you know that best fits the meaning of the sentence.
- *Interpret*. Explain the meaning.
- *Justify*. Furnish evidence to support your answer.
- *Name, list, mention*. List the information that is asked for.
- *Put in your own words*. Rewrite complicated language in everyday English.
- *Rank*. List the information that is asked for in some special order, such as order of occurrence or chronological order.

- *Skim.* Glance through passage quickly, looking for answers to specific questions.
- *State.* Give a short, simple answer. No discussion is necessary.
- *Summarize.* Briefly restate the passage, being sure to include the main points. Leave out small details. Your answer should be shorter than the original passage.
- *Trace.* Give major points in chronological order.

Multiple-Choice Questions. In addition to specific vocabulary suggestions for the words in the test directions, teachers should also address effective test-wise skills for multiple-choice questions themselves. The following considerations examine the choices the test taker must make among a variety of potential answers to discover which is the correct answer. Making choices between the correct answer and the attractive "distracters" is a matter of both knowledge about the question and knowledge about test taking. Figure 10.10 contains a checklist for creating assessment items, including multiple-choice items. This checklist can be used as a guide to creating assessment items that ensure students have test format practice.

> Distracter items are constructed to fool test takers. They often use words and phrases that appear in the text passage but also contain a phrase that makes the response incorrect.

1. Read all of the choices carefully. The people who write tests know that many people will not read carefully. Even if you are sure you see the right answer, read them all to be sure there is no surprise hiding at the end.

2. Don't get fooled by answers that seem to contain the exact words that appeared in the passage. Read those carefully to see if the context is correct.

3. Most of the time, there will be one or two obviously wrong choices. Ignore these and concentrate on the ones that might be right.

4. If you are sure that two of the answer choices are correct, the correct answer is usually "all of the above." Do not choose this answer unless you are sure that at least two of the choices are correct.

5. Watch for negative words in the instructions such as no or not. Watch out for trick questions! Some tests use the word "not" to fool you; stop and ask yourself what the question is really asking.

6. Absolute words, such as none, all, never, or always usually indicate an incorrect choice. Very few things are absolute. Statements with words like generally, some, often, usually, or most often are more likely to be correct. Please note: Statements must be completely true to count as true. Statements with absolute words are often false.

Figure 10.10 Checklist for creating assessments.

All Items

Is this the most appropriate type of item to use for the intended learning outcomes?

Does each item or task require students to demonstrate the performance described in the specific learning outcome it measures (relevance)?

Does each item present a clear and definite task to be performed (clarity)?

Is each item or task presented in simple, readable language and free from excessive verbiage (conciseness)?

Does each item provide an appropriate challenge (ideal difficulty)?

Does each item have an answer that would be agreed upon by experts (correctness)?

Is there a clear basis for awarding partial credit on items or tasks with multiple points (scoring rubric)?

Is each item or task free from technical errors and irrelevant clues (technical soundness)?

Is each test time free from cultural bias?

Have the items been set aside for a time before reviewing them (or reviewed by a colleague)?

Short-Answer Items

Can the items be answered with a number, symbol, word, or brief phrase?

Has textbook language been avoided?

Have the items been stated so that only one response is correct?

Are the answer blanks equal in length (for fill-in responses)?

Are the answer blanks (preferably one per item) at the end of the items, preferably after a question?

Are the items free of clues (such as *a* or *an*)?

Has the degree of precision been indicated for numerical answers?

Have the units been indicated when numerical answers are expressed in units?

Binary (True-False) and Multiple-Binary Items

Can each statement be clearly judged true or false with only one concept per statement?

Have specific determiners (e.g., usually, always) been avoided?

Have trivial statements been avoided?

Have negative statements (especially double negatives) been avoided?

Does a superficial analysis suggest a wrong answer?

Are opinion statements attributed to some source?

Are the true and false items approximately equal in length?

Is there approximately an equal number of true and false items?

Has a detectable pattern of answers (e.g., T, F, T, F) been avoided?

Matching Items

Is the material for the two lists homogeneous?

Is the list of responses longer or shorter than the list of premises?

Are the responses brief and on the right-hand side?

Have the responses been placed in alphabetical or numerical order?

Do the directions indicate the basis for matching?

Do the directions indicate how many times each response may be used?

Are all of the matching items on the same page?

(continued)

Figure 10.10 Checklist for creating assessments. (*continued*)

Multiple-Choice Items

Does each item stem present a meaningful problem?

Is there too much information in the stem?

Are the item stems free of irrelevant material?

Are the item stems stated in positive terms (if possible)?

If used, has negative wording been given special emphasis (e.g., capitalized)?

Are the distractors brief and free of unnecessary words?

Are the distractors similar in length and form to the answer?

Is there only one correct or clearly best answer?

Are the distractors based on specific misconceptions?

Are the items free of clues that point to the answer?

Are the distractors and answer presented in sensible (e.g., alphabetical, numerical) order?

Have *all of the above been* avoided and *none of the above* used judiciously?

If a stimulus is used, is it necessary for answering the item?

If a stimulus is used, does it require use of skills sought to be assessed?

Essay Items

Are the questions designed to measure higher-level learning outcomes?

Does each question clearly indicate the response expected (including extensiveness)?

Are students aware of the basis on which their answers will be evaluated?

Are appropriate time limits provided for responding to the questions?

Are students aware of the time limits and/or point values for each question?

Are all students required to respond to the same question?

Performance Items

Does the item focus on learning outcomes that require complex cognitive skills and
  student performances?

Does the task represent both the content and skills that are central to learning outcomes?

Does the item minimize dependence on skills that are irrelevant to the intended purpose
  of the assessment task?

Does the task provide the necessary scaffolding for students to be able to understand the
  task and achieve the task?

Do the directions clearly describe the task?

Are students aware of the basis (expectations) on which their performances will be
  evaluated in terms of scoring rubrics?

For the Assessment as a Whole

Are the items of the same type grouped together on the test (or within sections; sets)?

Are the items arranged from easy to more difficult with sections or the test as a whole?

Are items numbered in sequence, indicating if the test continues on subsequent
  pages?

Are all answer spaces clearly indicated and is each answer space related to its
  corresponding item?

Are the correct answers distributed in such a way that there is no detectable pattern?

Is the test material well spaced, legible, and free of typos?

Are there directions for each section of the test and the test as a whole?

Are the directions clear and concise?

Source: Adapted from Linn, R. L., & Gronlund, N. E. (2000). *Measurement and assessment in teaching* (8th ed.). Upper Saddle River, NJ: Merrill Prentice Hall. Used with permission.

Test-Wise Skills for Reading Passages. Just as the heart of a successful education is literacy instruction, the heart of successful test performance is reading comprehension. Strategies for reading for information have been the focus of this book. When testing is the issue, nothing can substitute for proven and engaging literacy instruction if students are to demonstrate test achievement. However, like the general test-wise skills discussed previously, we advocate for teachers to instruct students to do the following:

1. If the questions are based on a reading passage, read the questions first. Then you will know what to look for as you read. Don't read the choices yet; they will distract you.

2. After you have read the passage, read each question and answer the question in your head before you read the choices. If you know what kind of answer you are looking for, it will be easier to choose the right one.

Remember that these suggestions were not intended to be used six weeks before the test is given. The likelihood of successfully boosting achievement scores is diminished because without multiple opportunities to practice these techniques, students must rely on a confusing list of memorized, but not internalized, tips. For example, a student may ask, "Do I read the questions and the answers before the passage, or just the questions?" Instead, these strategies should be introduced and modeled from the beginning of the school year. Students should be expected to use these strategies throughout the school year on teacher-created tests and practice events. The goal is for students to see these standardized testing events as an extension of what they have done in the classroom throughout the year. As Raphael and Au (2005) note, strategies such as Question Answer Relationships (QAR) help students succeed on tests. It is through the careful use of content literacy strategies such as those outlined in this book that students develop their comprehension skills—and it shows when they're tested.

Area #2: Reading for Information on Standardized Tests

Many of the skills for success on standardized tests are the same skills students need to be literate. Concerned educators should keep in mind that nothing can substitute for good instruction. Through direct instruction in reading strategies, teachers address the single most influential factor for improving student test performance (Feuer, Holland, Green, Bertenthal, & Hemphill, 1999). Preparing students for high-stakes tests through test-format practice can be a highly effective activity, especially for students with little experience or familiarity with such tests. However, if test format practice is conducted for extended periods of time and to the exclusion of other instruction and content, students will score poorly (Guthrie, 2002). If

| Knowing how to answer questions but not knowing the content is ultimately insufficient. |

done in isolation, test format practice provides students with few long-term gains. It is not in itself a well-rounded classroom practice.

An effective way to avoid the pitfalls of isolated test practice is to heed Langer's (2001) findings about "beating the odds schools." These high-achieving schools chose to emphasize curriculum improvement over separate and distinct test prep. Like Langer, our experience suggests that when schools adopt a set of instructional practices that work well across content areas, test scores increase (Fisher, 2001; Frey & Fisher, 2006). When teachers across the campus begin to apply common literacy strategies to boost learning in their classroom, they are also employing an integrated approach to curriculum and testing. In other words, students learn to transport a set of strategies to new and novel situations.

This position is validated by research with elementary students. A series of studies about reading comprehension assessment reveals that while background knowledge of the topic of the passage had a statistically significant influence in second and third grades, it diminished quite a bit by fourth grade. The researchers found that successful performance on tests of reading comprehension in fourth through sixth grades depended on the use of strategies to extract information from the passages—in other words, the ability to read for information (Rupley & Wilson, 1996; Wilson & Rupley, 1997).

Reviewing Types of Questions. In thinking about the test format suggestion, "Read Questions Carefully. . . ." we can conclude that a great deal of instruction and practice must occur for students to be successful with this skill. Simply reading or reviewing the test format suggestions may bring about some awareness. However, reviewing is not sufficient. Students must be provided practice, familiarity, and application of the suggestions if they are to use them on test days. Student practice with questions about their readings, identifying the type of questions and corresponding answers, and constructing their own questions, will likely improve student test performance. After all, a test is itself a compilation of questions.

| See Chapter 6 |

Accessing Prior Knowledge. Anticipatory activities can help students make use of their prior knowledge during test taking. Students adept at the processes readers use to enter a reading can gather information about the text and quickly identify features that stand out, such as charts, pictures, and subtitles. Regular classroom use of the KWL process (Ogle, 1986) is particularly helpful because it creates some habits of mind useful for approaching unfamiliar text. We are not advocating that students construct a KWL chart to answer test questions. We are suggesting that frequent use of anticipatory activities models—the practice of assessing what one knows and what one wants to know—is especially useful for answering timed test questions. Anticipatory activities also keep students focused on the content so that their performance later is enhanced.

See Chapter 3

Building Knowledge and Fluency. The chapter on read-alouds and shared reading may not seem connected to test taking at first glance, but consider the teaching that takes place during one of these events. During read-alouds or shared readings, a teacher can model the fluent expression signaled by the content and the punctuation. Read-alouds and shared reading can also build background knowledge and provide students with explicit instruction in the self-monitoring that goes on in the mind of a reader. Faced with an unfamiliar piece of text on a standardized test, a student exposed to these teaching events can apply the same strategies to better answer the questions associated with the passage.

See Chapter 5

Focusing Thinking and Recall. The note-taking and note-making chapter can help teachers provide their students with skills to glean and prioritize main ideas quickly from the text. Note taking enhances students' thinking by developing thought processes that eliminate extraneous details and instead focuses upon essential points. Note-making skills are also helpful when taking standardized tests because students learn to glean information quickly from long text passages.

See Chapter 8

Representing Knowledge. Teaching students various ways to categorize information using graphic organizers can help them understand the graphs and charts that are frequently found on science and social studies tests. Through the use of graphic organizers, students become familiar with different types of text structures. Using graphic organizers will help students complete the test on time.

See Chapter 7

Understanding the Words on the Test. Comprehensive vocabulary instruction allows teachers to enrich their students' vocabulary, an essential and directly tested component of many standardized tests. Strategies for successful vocabulary instruction include transportable vocabulary skills such as prefixes and suffixes, semantic features of words, and multiple-meaning words. Each of these areas of focus, as well as many others in the chapter, will pay dividends on accountability tests.

See Chapter 4

Assessing Content Knowledge. Writing to learn provides teachers with a way to check for student understanding of content. In addition, writing to learn helps students think about what they learned, how they learn, why the content is important, and what they still don't know. Regular writing-to-learn activities also provide students practice in analyzing the tests and the questions on the test for their underlying query.

See Chapter 9

Comprehension Strategy Practice. Finally, reciprocal teaching and other collaborative reading experiences help students perform better on tests because they have learned to read texts critically. Reciprocal teaching provides students with experience in comprehension skills as they discuss the parts of the text they know about, make predictions about the text, and ask questions of the text. In other words, reciprocal teaching provides students with the skills to tackle reading passages in confidence and with effectiveness.

In sum, the use of a set of strategies for teaching reading for information can serve the dual functions of good instruction and effective preparation for standardized tests. The ways of thinking inherent in these comprehension strategies are necessary to perform well on the test. Further, when students have multiple opportunities to apply these strategies across content areas and throughout the day, they become a part of their learning repertoire. Once internalized, they are able to use these strategies in testing situations.

Area #3: Student Engagement in Reading for Information

If students are to become better test takers, they must read more (Guthrie, Wigfield, Metsala, & Cox, 1999). Reading for knowledge, information, and pleasure are the essential endeavors of successful and contributing members of a literate society. To ensure that students do become fluent readers, teachers must encourage reading in every subject matter and classroom, as well as outside the classroom.

Engaging students in reading and addressing the challenges of high-stakes standardized tests is, for the school, a team effort. Test format awareness and employment of literacy strategies are good first steps. But the work does not stop here. The use and enjoyment of reading as a part of life-long learning does not stop at the classroom door. The successful dissemination and use of effective literacy strategies is an ongoing endeavor for both students and their teachers.

Student enjoyment of reading can be fostered through a Silent Sustained Reading program (Pilgreen, 2000). In such a program, the school schedules a period of time each day that is devoted to reading. Everyone in the school, from the principal to the clerical staff to the kindergarten students, are provided time to read from books or other texts of their own choosing. As students watch their teacher model reading, they learn directly of the activity's pleasure and importance. When students are allowed to choose their own reading, the inherent interest in the material itself fosters better reading habits and ability. With students spending more time reading, they become better readers and better readers become better test takers. Of course, the genres of books available to students should include informational selections that provide students with further opportunities to explore their interests.

See Chapter 2

Consider your reading habits. How much time do you spend reading for information?

Using the Results of Informal and Formal Assessments

Conclusions can be drawn about a school's successes or failures by examining the assessment and test results and reviewing the wide variety of demographic and other data that accompany the results. These data-based decisions allow the school to directly confront the issues that matter (e.g., Chen, Salahuddin, Horsch, & Wagner, 2000). If low scores point to a weakness in specific content or a need for a change in instruction, steps can be taken to provide training in that area. If certain groups of students consistently score poorly, then steps can be taken to provide them with additional intervention and support. Without an awareness of what the tests indicate, the school will not likely address the needs of its faculty or students (Schmoker, 1996, 2001). For example, a group of faculty may meet to discuss test results. Their analysis may lead to an understanding that vocabulary was the most depressed area on the test. Upon further analysis, they may learn that multiple-meaning words were the lowest score within the vocabulary domain. This finding could lead to changes in the curriculum across the school. The results from the next assessment could be used to determine if the curriculum change was effective.

> The recursive process of collecting data by the teacher to improve instructional practice is referred to as "action research."

A criticism of standardized tests is that by the time the results are posted six months later, the students have advanced to the next grade level and are no longer on the administering teacher's roster. This is true; standardized tests are likely to be a poor source for obtaining meaningful information for designing next Monday's lesson. These curriculum decisions should be informed by the ongoing informal assessment data gathered by the teacher. However, standardized test results can be viewed as a snapshot of the entire student body. A photograph of all the students in the school is unlikely to be useful in pinpointing the attributes of a single student, but it can create a group portrait of the school at large. Similarly, close analysis of the results can illuminate areas of concern and strength.

A forum for discussing such concerns can diffuse defensive responses while assisting schools in getting down to the business of curriculum improvement. One such structure is a Total Quality Review committee, based on the Total Quality Management work of Edward Deming (2001). A TQR committee usually serves in an advisory capacity to the school's governance and is charged with analyzing data and making recommendations based on these results. The committee is typically comprised of representatives of all stakeholders, including noninstructional staff, parents, students, and community members, as well as teachers and administrators. By establishing such work groups, schools can make data-driven decisions without engaging in the "blame games" that sink many school reform efforts (Detert, Louis, & Schroeder, 2001).

> This is often a subcommittee of the school's site governance team.

See <u>Understanding by Design</u> by McTighe and Wiggins (2000) for more information on backward planning.

A coordinated series of discussions to align curriculum to tested standards might also take place. The goal of such curriculum discussions would be to better prepare students for high-stakes tests and to allow teachers a reflective process to discern success. Learning about the content of tests will help to ensure that it is covered in core subject matters. Reading across the curriculum is encouraged when test-relevant reading content is shared with teachers from different subjects. In such a process, effective strategies can be linked to important reading content, appropriate test format practice can be provided, and essential test vocabulary can be disseminated. A Curriculum Discussion Cycle might take the following steps:

1. **Standards Review:** course content alignment to test.
2. **Curriculum Construction:** activities and tasks, scaffolding, materials and assessment events development, rubrics, integration of test questions, vocabulary and strategies suggestions.
3. **Curriculum Delivery:** timelines for delivery, dates for key pieces (trigger events), schedules for test practice, development of common deliveries and common student work submissions.
4. **Examination of Student Work and Test Scores:** reflective conversations regarding student work and tests results, group discussions of expected student performance, review of curriculum delivery.

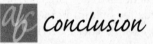 *Conclusion*

In this chapter, we have discussed the importance of informal and formal assessments for measuring progress in students' ability to read for information. Informal assessment should be ongoing and can include observations, portfolios, inventories, rubrics, conferences, self-assessments, and surveys. The choice of instruments should be driven by learning goals, linked to classroom instruction, and systematic in administration and analysis.

Formal assessments, particularly standardized tests, have become increasingly important in this decade. We advocate an emphasis on test wisdom, where students receive integrated practice throughout the school year. Of particular value is test-format practice, especially for students who are not familiar with the standardized test genre. Students must also be taught to be strategic readers of information. Through implementation of effective literacy strategies, students are able to use the techniques of life-long learners (e.g., Calkins, Montgomery, Santman, & Falk, 1998).

Equally important are the ways in which the entire school can increase student engagement in reading for information. If students are to read more, the school must find innovative ways to present students with informational texts. Providing important and relevant reading content might take place through a sustained silent reading program that allows for student self-selection.

Finally, ongoing faculty dialogue around literacy and literacy strategies is essential if text is to be found important. Such faculty conversation can take many forms including staff development discussions, teacher literacy demonstrations, collegial coaching activities, and curriculum discussion cycles.

References

Calkins, L., Montgomery, K., Santman, D., & Falk, B. (1998). *A teacher's guide to standardized reading tests: Knowledge is power*. Portsmouth, NH: Heinemann.

Chen, J., Salahuddin, R., Horsch, P., & Wagner, S. L. (2000). Turning standardized test scores into a tool for improving teaching and learning: An assessment-based approach. *Urban Education, 5*, 356–384.

Deming, W. E. (2001). *Out of the crisis*. Boston: MIT Press.

Detert, J. R., Louis, K. S., & Schroeder, R. G. (2001). A culture framework for education: Defining quality values and their impact in U.S. high schools. *School Effectiveness and School Improvement, 12*, 183–212.

Duke, N. K., & Ritchart, R. (1997). No pain, high gain standardized test preparation. *Instructor, 107*(3), 89–92, 119.

Feuer, M. J., Holland, P. W., Green, B. F., Bertenthal, M. W., & Hemphill, F. C. (1999). *Uncommon measures: Equivalence and language among educational tests*. Washington, DC: National Academy Press.

Fisher, D. (2001). "We're moving on up:" Creating a schoolwide literacy effort in an urban high school. *Journal of Adolescent & Adult Literacy, 45*, 92–101.

Frey, N., & Fisher, D. (2006). *The language arts workshop: Purposeful reading and writing instruction*. Upper Saddle River, NJ: Pearson Merrill Prentice Hall.

Frey, N., & Hiebert, E. H. (2003). Teacher-based assessment of literacy learning. In J. Flood, D. Lapp, J. R. Squire, & J. M. Jensen (Eds.), *Handbook of research on teaching the English language arts* (2nd ed., pp. 608–618). Mahwah, NJ: Erlbaum.

Goals 2000: *Educate America Act*. (1994). Washington DC: United States Congress Act.

Guillaume, A. M. (2004). *K–12 classroom teaching: A primer for new professionals* (2nd ed.). Upper Saddle River, NJ: Merrill Prentice Hall.

Guthrie, J. T. (2002). Preparing students for high stakes test taking in reading. In A. E. Farstrup & S. J. Samuels (Eds.), *What research has to say about reading instruction* (pp. 370–391). Newark, DE: International Reading Association.

Guthrie, J. T., Wigfield, A., Metsala, J. L., & Cox, K. E. (1999). Motivational and cognitive predictors of text comprehension and reading amount. *Scientific Studies of Reading, 3*, 231–256.

International Reading Association. (2000). *Making a difference means making it different: Honoring children's rights to excellent reading instruction*. Newark, DE: Author.

Kohn, A. (2000). *The case against standardized testing: Raising the scores, ruining the schools*. Portsmouth, NH: Heinemann.

Kujawa, S., & Huske, L. (1995). *The strategic teaching and reading project guidebook* (Rev. Ed.). Oakbrook, IL: North Central Regional Education Laboratory.

Langer, J. A. (2001). Beating the odds: Teaching middle and high school students to read and write well. *American Educational Research Journal, 38*, 837–880.

Lapp, D., Fisher, D., Flood, J., & Cabello, A. (2001). An integrated approach to the teaching and assessment of language arts. In S. R. Hurley & J. V. Tinajero (Eds.), *Literacy assessment of second language learners* (pp. 1–26). Boston: Allyn & Bacon.

McTighe, J., & Wiggins, G. P. (2000). *Understanding by design*. Upper Saddle River, NJ: Prentice Hall.

Meier, D., Kozol, J., & Cohen, J. (2000). *Can standards save public education?* Boston: Beacon.

No Child Left Behind Act of 2001. (2002). Washington DC: United States Congress Act.

Ogle, D. M. (1986). K-W-L: A teaching model that develops active reading of expository text. *The Reading Teacher, 39*, 564–570.

Ohanian, S. (1999). *One size fits few: The folly of educational standards*. Portsmouth, NH: Heinemann.

Pilgreen, J. (2000). *The SSR handbook: How to organize and manage a silent sustained reading program*. Portsmouth, NH: Boynton/Cook.

Popham, W. J. (2001) Teaching to the test? *Educational Leadership, 58*(6), 16–20.

Raphael, T. E., & Au, K. H. (2005). QAR: Enhancing comprehension and test taking across grades and content areas. *The Reading Teacher, 59*, 206–221.

Rupley, W. H., & Wilson, V. L. (1996). Context, domain, and word knowledge: Relationship to comprehension of narrative and expository text. *Reading and Writing, 8*, 419–432.

Santman, D. (2002). Teaching to the test? Test preparation in the reading workshop. *Language Arts, 79*, 203–211.

Schmoker, M. (1996). *Results: The key to continuous school improvement*. Alexandria, VA: Association for Supervision and Curriculum Development.

Schmoker, M. (2001). *The results handbook: Practical strategies from dramatically improved schools*. Alexandria, VA: Association for Supervision and Curriculum Development.

Tierney, R. J., Clark, C., Wiser, B., Simpson, C. S., Herter, R. J., & Fenner, L. (1998). Portfolios: Assumptions, tensions, and possibilities. *Reading Research Quarterly, 33*, 474–486.

West, K. R. (1998). Noticing and responding to learners: Literacy evaluation and instruction in the primary grades. *The Reading Teacher, 51*, 550–559.

Wilcox, B. (1997). Writing portfolios: Active vs. passive. *English Journal, 86*(6), 34–35.

Wilson, V. L., & Rupley, W. H. (1997). A structural equation model for reading comprehension based on background, phonemic, and strategy knowledge. *Scientific Studies of Reading* (1), 45–63.

Wong, H. K. (1992). *The first days of school*. Mountain View, CA: Harry K. Wong Publications.

Index

References are to pages. Pages followed by "f" indicate figures; "t," tables.